WILL GAYS
GO TO
HEAVEN?

www.willgaysgotoheaven.com

WILL GAYS
GO TO
HEAVEN?

www.willgaysgotoheaven.com

WHICH AND WHOSE SINS DID JESUS' SHED BLOOD NOT FORGIVE?

By Tim Finley
Messenger Of The Good News

"IN FACT, ACCORDING TO THE LAW OF MOSES, NEARLY EVERYTHING WAS PURIFIED WITH BLOOD. FOR WITHOUT THE SHEDDING OF BLOOD, THERE IS NO FORGIVENESS."
Hebrews 9:22 (NLT)

GIFT PAGE

"For this is how God loved the world: He gave his one and only Son, so that everyone who believes in him will not perish but have eternal life. God sent his Son into the world not to judge the world, but to save the world through him.

There is no judgment against anyone who believes in him. But anyone who does not believe in him has already been judged for not believing in God's one and only Son."
John 3:16-18, Jesus' words

Date _____

To _____

From _____

I know for certain that I am going to Heaven and I want all my loved ones and friends to spend eternity there, too. You are one of them.

My eternal life in Heaven will not be the result of anything I have done, but what Jesus Christ did for me.

If you have not accepted Jesus Christ as your Savior, please read this book. If you are already a Christian, then this book will help you to become more knowledgeable, making you a more resourceful disciple of Jesus.

Dedication

This book is dedicated to those nice folks who have been downcast by Christian churches and church people. Until age 34, I rejected Jesus because of unkind, self-righteous Christians who misrepresented him. Do not allow this to happen! I love this story about Gandhi.

> Mahatma Gandhi is one of the most respected leaders of modern history. Although a Hindu, Gandhi admired Jesus and often quoted from the **Sermon on the Mount**. Once when the missionary E. Stanley Jones met with Gandhi he asked, "Mr. Gandhi, though you quote the words of Christ often, why is it that you appear to so adamantly reject becoming his follower?"
>
> Gandhi replied, "Oh, I don't reject your Christ. I love your Christ. It's just that so many of you Christians are so unlike your Christ."
>
> Apparently, Gandhi's rejection of Christianity grew out of an incident that happened when he was a young man practicing law in South Africa. He had become attracted to the Christian faith, had studied the Bible and the teachings of Jesus, and was seriously exploring becoming a Christian. He decided to attend a church service, but as he went up the steps of the large church, a white South African elder barred his way at the door. "Where do you think you're going, **kaffir** (a disparaging term for a black person)?" the man asked Gandhi in a challenging manner.
>
> Gandhi replied, "I'd like to attend worship here."
>
> The church elder barked at him, "There's no room for **kaffirs** in this church. Leave here or I'll have my assistants throw you down the steps."
>
> From that moment, Gandhi said he decided to adopt what good he found in Christianity, but would never again consider becoming a Christian if it meant being part of a church.

Jesus would not have turned Gandhi away because Jesus accepts all who sincerely seek him.

God came to Earth in the form of this man, named Jesus, to endure humiliation and the excruciating pain of crucifixion, initiated by "religious" people, so he could pay for the sins of all mankind — for all time. He loves those who others reject, and he doesn't reject those who do not deserve his friendship.

Jesus will love you when others don't. He died a painful death so you may live.

> *"For God loved the world so much that he gave his one and only Son, so that everyone who believes in him will not perish but have eternal life. God sent his Son into the world not to judge the world, but to save the world through him.*
>
> *There is no judgment against anyone who believes in him. But anyone who does not believe in him has already been judged for not believing in God's one and only Son."* John 3:16-18, Jesus' words

Jesus offers you a free gift. Accept it.

> *God saved you by his grace when you believed. And you can't take credit for this; it is a gift from God. Salvation is not a reward for the good things we have done, so none of us can boast about it.* Ephesians 2:8-9

Acknowledgments

TOM. When I began writing this book, I was unaware my 45-year-old son, Thomas Hunter Finley (1968-2013), wouldn't be alive to read it. Tom went to Heaven suddenly and unexpectedly on October 4, 2013. Our entire family and his many friends were, and still are, devastated. Tom was one of the kindest people I have had the pleasure of knowing. I am not saying that because he was my son — he really was kind.

Although devastated by Tom being called home at such a young age, we have the peace of knowing he is in Heaven, and that all who have accepted Jesus as Savior will be with him again. When Tom was nine-years-old, he accepted Jesus' free gift of eternal life in Heaven.

> *God saved you by his grace when you believed. And you can't take credit for this; it is a gift from God. Salvation is not a reward for the good things we have done, so none of us can boast about it.* Ephesians 2:8-9

Tom's death has motivated me to strike my computer keyboard more passionately than when I began this book because I want to spread the Good News of Jesus Christ's finished work on the Cross so more families can be assured their loved ones are, or will be, in the glory that awaits Christians in the next life.

I love you, Tom, more than words can describe, and I am devastated that you left this Earth before me, but I know we will be together again someday. Thank you, Jesus!

LOVEDA KNORE FINLEY. My loving and devoted wife for 37 years, and my best friend. Thank you for being so patient with my lack of knowledge regarding the intricacies of the computer. Just as you don't understand the mechanics of an automobile, I don't understand the mechanics of this complex computer. I take care of the cars and you take care of the computer.

Without you, this book would never have been completed. Your excellence in proofing was a major contribution to its completion. Our teamwork accomplished the Lord's calling.

I apologize for my temper outbursts, mood swings, and complaining that were caused only by my frustrations trying to be an effective author and evangelist. Thanks for sticking around. I am the sparkle, but you are the glue. I love you.

PATRICK GAMBLE. Words cannot express my appreciation for the hundreds of hours of creative thought and technical contribution you devoted to our website design, which included tutoring Loveda so she could make necessary adjustments and maintain what we pray will be a venue that leads thousands of folks to the Lord Jesus. You have been a great friend and supporter through the entire process.

JOSEPH. In the middle of a conversation you stated that a person could not commit multiple murders and then on his deathbed accept Jesus as his Savior and be welcomed into Heaven. I disagreed stating that Jesus paid for all sins.

I pray that by now you grasp the magnitude of Jesus' death on the Cross. It is only when a person realizes Jesus' magnificent grace that Christianity ascends above those world religions that require works for salvation.

Joseph, keep in mind that the very instant a person is born again, the Holy Spirit indwells that person, and he or she receives moral guidance from within. That is why most Christians do not commit murder, even though Satan has significant influence on earthly beings. Satan's presence is why we must learn to live by the Spirit.

BETH. When discussing the topic of homosexuality with my friend Beth, she told me the Bible refers to homosexuality as an *abomination*. Beth's comments gave me the incentive to research the word *abomination* in the Holy Scriptures to discover its true meaning.

Abomination has many meanings: disgusting, loathsome, taboo, forbidden, etc. Abomination can apply to sexual practices, unclean food, idols, and mixed marriages.

The Bible teaches that <u>*God's grace is greater than our sins*</u>.

> *There are six things the LORD hates —*
> *no, seven things he detests:*
> *haughty eyes,*
> *a lying tongue,*
> *hands that kill the innocent,*
> *a heart that plots evil,*
> *feet that race to do wrong,*

> *a false witness who pours out lies,*
>   *a person who sows discord in a family.* Proverbs 6:16-19

Homosexuality did not make this list.

RON. Ron caused me to realize it is imperative to include a chapter teaching that, to be an effective Christian, one must "Die to the Law."

LISA. Thank you so much for motivating me to devote a very thorough exegesis on the misused and misunderstood term *repent*. *Repent* is constantly abused and misunderstood by Christians and Christian teachers, causing confusion for the saved and unsaved.

WANDA. Thank you for encouraging me to emphasize that it is not what we do or say in order to be saved, because we are saved the moment we believe.

JOYCE. You stated in our evangelism class that you don't like the term *born again*. Many Christians don't like this term because of its terrible association with self-righteous, judgmental, bigoted, legalistic Christians. You and I both know not all (born again) Christians are nauseating, but because Jesus used "born again," I have expounded on its meaning to educate those who don't understand.

PASTOR TODD. I was fed up with churches and many church people until I walked through the doors at Good Shepherd. Thankfully, my wife, Loveda, finally convinced me to give your church a try. One visit and I felt welcome and at home. I have never known a pastor who works so hard and who is so committed to providing folks with a *positive* Christian environment. Thank you!

DAVE. Thank you for your faulty teaching regarding James 2:17. It made me realize I should dedicate an entire chapter to the subject *faith without works is dead*, so innocent people won't be misled by misinformed teachers.

PETER. You are the first openly gay Christian (born again) I have had as a close friend. I thank you for your friendship and for your transparency. You and Glenn make a remarkable couple. When you told me you were born gay I believed you. You are not the type to lie. Having been married with children and grandchildren, but realizing your need to be with a male life-companion is proof of your attempt to live the way society dictates. Sadly, mankind is not always man-kind. You are blessed to have friends and a family who loves and respects you.

I appreciate our lengthy conversations about Jesus and his Holy Spirit, who lives in all born again believers. He convicts you in your personal behavior, and he convicts me in my personal behavior. He didn't create us all to be identical, nor does he convict us to behave identically. That is so cool.

WENDY BERNSTEIN. Last, but not least, is my great friend and editor, Wendy Bernstein. Wendy has been my editor for about 10 years, beginning when I first tried my wings as a writer by penning a column in a local newspaper. I didn't realize how bad I was until Wendy made me look good. Sure, I have some creative talent, but Wendy helps me look much better by employing her trade. You are the best!

Any punctuation, grammatical, or layout errors found in this book are not the fault of Wendy. Frequently I choose to use my author's license to think, act, and create outside the box, i.e., Wendy advised me not to underline, but I chose to underline certain important points.

TABLE OF CONTENTS

FOREWORD

By Loveda Knore Finley (the author's wife)

A BIG BOOK FOR A BIG SOCIAL DILEMMA

The United States of America, and many countries throughout the world, are faced with a moral and social dilemma. The numbers of people coming out of the gay closet are overwhelming, leaving government officials, religious leaders, employers, armed forces, moms, dads, sisters, brothers, children, etc., scratching their heads wondering and debating what is right and what is wrong.

The problem is not going away, so it must be addressed intellectually. But what do we use as a point of reference?

Traditionally, the moral values that determine our laws have been based on the moral guidance of the Old and New Testaments, referred to as *the Bible*. Unfortunately, in this era, the majority of the people do not know what is contained in this book of wisdom. The remaining folks oftentimes merely choose their favorite verses and then portray themselves as theological experts.

Those who are coming out of the closet have the overwhelming burden of trying to live fulfilling lives without hurting their non-gay loved ones, while also facing degradation by society.

For the sake of homosexuals and non-homosexuals, Tim has devoted more than a year meticulously writing this book. It is composed of Bible passages systematically arranged to reveal God's word regarding this sensitive topic, primarily focusing on the eternal destination of everybody. We are all here today, but gone tomorrow, so our eternal destinations should be of utmost importance.

> *How do you know what your life will be like tomorrow? Your life is like the morning fog—it's here a little while, then it's gone.* James 4:14

Do not be intimidated by the overwhelming size of this book. Tim's last book — JESUS CHRIST Is the EASY and ONLY Way to HEAVEN — is also a large textbook; however, all who have purchased it have been delighted with its comprehensiveness. Many keep it beside their Bible for reference.

Tim is an uncompromising researcher whose mission is to leave no stones unturned regarding the study of Christian salvation. To ascertain the entire truth, as revealed in God's Word, Tim prays for guidance from the Holy Spirit as he researches all of the passages regarding this crucial topic. Comparing each passage with other parts of the Bible, he establishes an understanding of the language and customs of the time they were written. His painstaking efforts are an attempt to completely comprehend what the original writer(s) intended to communicate.

Tim labors uncompromisingly to ascertain truth for his students; he is a fanatic about explaining what he discovers. The following verse motivates him:

> *Work hard so you can present yourself to God and receive his approval. Be a good worker, one who does not need to be ashamed and who correctly explains the word of truth.* 2 Timothy 2:15

I am confident you will learn from Tim's Holy Spirit-inspired book. I did.

About this Book

This captivating book presents hundreds of Bible passages pertaining to the Doctrine of Christian Salvation, simultaneously answering the many questions that puzzle those not specially trained in the field of soteriology (the study of the Doctrine of Salvation). Ultimately, the book emphasizes God's free gift of salvation by grace through faith.

> *And if by grace, then is it no more of works: otherwise grace is no more grace. But if it be of works, then it is no more grace: otherwise work is no more work.* Romans 11:6 (KJV)

> *God saved you by his grace when you believed. And you can't take credit for this; it is a gift from God. Salvation is not a reward for the good things we have done, so none of us can boast about it.* Ephesians 2:8-9

Once saved — always saved

It is heartbreaking that so many Christians are uncertain of their eternal destiny. This is caused by Christian leaders who erroneously teach that salvation is earned, and can be lost if the individual does not live up to certain standards. Rubbish! Faulty teaching causes countless Christians to live under the sword of Damocles (constant threat; imminent peril). Salvation is an irrevocable gift! Once accepted, it is eternal because it is sealed by the Holy Spirit. The Bible says so. I emphasized important words or phrases in the following passages.

> *"I give them eternal life, and they will never perish. **No one can snatch them away from me**, for my Father has given them to me, and he is more powerful than anyone else. No one can snatch them from the Father's hand."* John 10:28-29, Jesus' words

> *When people work, their wages are not a gift, but something they have earned. But people are counted as righteous, **not because of their work**, but because of their faith in God who forgives sinners.* Romans 4:4-5

*And I am convinced that nothing can ever separate us from God's love. Neither death nor life, neither angels nor demons, neither our fears for today nor our worries about tomorrow—not even the powers of hell can separate us from God's love. No power in the sky above or in the earth below—indeed, **nothing in all creation will ever be able to separate us from the love of God that is revealed in Christ Jesus our Lord**.* Romans 8:38-39

*In him you also, when you heard the word of truth, the gospel of your salvation, and believed in him, were **sealed with the promised Holy Spirit**, who is the guarantee of our inheritance until we acquire possession of it, to the praise of his glory.* Ephesians 1:13-14 (ESV)

But people who aren't spiritual can't receive these truths from God's Spirit. It all sounds foolish to them and they can't understand it, for only those who are spiritual can understand what the Spirit means. 1 Corinthians 2:14

Doubting is natural

Jesus Christ loves mankind so much that he saves us from eternal Hell when we have faith in his finished work on the Cross.

"There is salvation in no one else! God has given no other name under heaven by which we must be saved." Acts 4:12

Afraid you don't have enough faith? Don't worry about it. Jesus understands wavering faith. One of Jesus' greatest apostles was a man named Peter (they were best friends). Peter was in a boat during a storm, when Jesus appeared on the water out of nowhere. Jesus summoned Peter to get out of the boat and come to him.

Enthusiastically, Peter stepped onto the water and miraculously commenced walking toward Jesus (how cool), but when realizing he was only buoyant by faith his conviction waivered and he began to sink. Jesus grabbed him and helped him back into the boat. It must have been hysterical.

Peter was a revering companion of Jesus, yet he lost his faith in the Creator when he focused on the high waves and the deep water.

All have doubts, but the more one fellowships with Jesus, the more his or her faith grows.

Then Jesus told him, "You believe because you have seen me. Blessed are those who believe without seeing me." John 20:29

No need to be a scholar

Millions of people have picked up the Bible, looked through a few pages, and put it down because it appeared too challenging. God is not looking for Bible scholars to be a part of his Kingdom (not that there is anything wrong with being a scholar), but he loves folks of all ages who come to him as seeking babes.

> *But Jesus said, "Let the children come to me. Don't stop them! For the Kingdom of Heaven belongs to those who are like these children."* Matthew 19:14

> *When Jesus saw what was happening, he was angry with his disciples. He said to them, "Let the children come to me. Don't stop them! For the Kingdom of God belongs to those who are like these children. I tell you the truth, anyone who doesn't receive the Kingdom of God like a child will never enter it."* Mark 10:14-15

The Bible can be extremely challenging because it entangles thousands of years of history with an extreme number of topics. *WILL GAYS GO TO HEAVEN?* presents salvation information in a systematic form.

A book for all

WILL GAYS GO TO HEAVEN? was written for a broad spectrum of people, from those who know nothing about Christianity to Christian scholars. Following is a list of those who may benefit from reading this book:

- ➢ Atheists
- ➢ Agnostics
- ➢ Youth who are approaching the age of Christian accountability
- ➢ Those who have a difficult time reading the Bible
- ➢ Christian scholars who don't thoroughly understand salvation
- ➢ Christian evangelists
- ➢ Christian pastors
- ➢ Christian chaplains
- ➢ Roman Catholic priests

- ➢ Roman Catholic bishops
- ➢ Roman Catholic cardinals
- ➢ Roman Catholic nuns
- ➢ Roman Catholic popes
- ➢ Anglicans
- ➢ Jehovah's witnesses
- ➢ Christian Scientists
- ➢ Seventh-Day Adventists
- ➢ Unitarian Universalists
- ➢ Mormons
- ➢ Jews
- ➢ Muslims
- ➢ Buddhists

This list could continue, but you get the point.

For a person to thoroughly understand a Bible topic, a systematic, painstaking analysis must be created. This book presents an exceptionally detailed analysis of the most important topic that exists — salvation. Where will you spend eternity?

About the Author

Timothy Dane "Tim" Finley (born 1946) is an American orthodox Christian, soteriologist (one who studies salvation), evangelist (one who tells folks about the Good News of salvation by grace), and author. Tim grew up in Massillon, OH, in a middle-class family that attended a main stream church on Christmas, Easter, and a few Sundays. There was very little Bible knowledge.

Tim lived most of his adult life in Columbus, OH, where his primary occupation began as a stockbroker, eventually becoming vice president of a New York Stock Exchange member company.

Tim had only a handful of Bible knowledge. It wasn't until he was 34 years of age that he learned the *Good News* of salvation by grace through faith. He was in awe when someone suggested he read Ephesians 2:8-9.

> *God saved you by his grace when you believed. And you can't take credit for this; it is a gift from God. Salvation is not a reward for the good things we have done, so none of us can boast about it.*

Until the *Good News* was explained, and he read the conforming Bible passages, Tim had been under the false impression that people earned their entrance to Heaven. Upon hearing the truth, he accepted Jesus Christ as his Savior.

Immediately upon being saved, Tim felt the calling to share the *Good News* with all who would listen.

Also an accomplished racehorse trainer, Tim is the founder of the Christian Harness Horseman's Association (CHHA), an International Christian fellowship within the horse racing industry. Founded in 1983, the CHHA fellowship still thrives. He was also a board member of the Racetrack Chaplaincy of Ohio. In addition to ministering at racetracks, Tim has ministered at prisons, churches, streets, grocery stores, the beach, or wherever the Lord leads him.

Tim is the author of another Christian book titled *JESUS CHRIST Is the EASY and ONLY Way to HEAVEN*, which has spawned an awakening to *salvation = faith + nothing*.

"Many of the traditional Christian churches have convoluted God's simple plan of salvation, scaring numerous people from accepting this free gift that Jesus died to give to anyone who would accept it," states Tim boldly.

Tim contends that a Christian evangelist is someone who teaches that Jesus Christ, who was God incarnate, is the only way to Heaven, and by believing and trusting in Jesus' finished work (death, burial, and resurrection), an individual is born spiritually, which ultimately results in receiving the free gift of glory in the next life.

A Christian evangelist teaches that a person's good deeds are the spiritually born (saved) individuals' way of thanking Jesus, but good deeds have no effect on one's eternal destiny. He also advocates powerfully that the first priority of the Christian Church should be to make disciples of all people of all nations by introducing them to Jesus, who offers the free gift of eternal life (salvation) by grace through faith.

> ***Then the eleven disciples left for Galilee, going to the mountain where Jesus had told them to go. When they saw him, they worshiped him—but some of them doubted!***
>
> ***Jesus came and told his disciples, "I have been given all authority in heaven and on earth. Therefore, go and make disciples of all the nations, baptizing them in the name of the Father and the Son and the Holy Spirit. Teach these new disciples to obey all the commands I have given you. And be sure of this: I am with you always, even to the end of the age."*** **Matthew 28:16-20**
>
> ***And if by grace, then is it no more of works: otherwise grace is no more grace. But if it be of works, then it is no more grace: otherwise work is no more work.*** **Romans 11:6 (KJV)**

Politically, Tim considers himself to be a compassionate conservative and has called on churches worldwide to focus their efforts on fighting poverty and disease, expanding educational opportunities for the marginalized, and caring for the environment.

Tim married Loveda Knore Edgar in 1977, and they are the proud parents of Tom Finley (1968-2013), Melissa Nino (Patrick), and Lynn Edgar-Smith (Steven), and three grandchildren.

In 2001, Tim and Loveda moved from Columbus, OH, to Lake Worth, FL, where they currently reside.

Notes:

From the Author

I, a messenger of the Good News, am incredibly inspired to write this book informing others about the freedom from "religion" one receives when becoming a Christian. It is my life's purpose.

> *But my life is worth nothing to me unless I use it for finishing the work assigned me by the Lord Jesus—the work of telling others the Good News about the wonderful grace of God.* Acts 20:24

I believe Jesus gave me the assignment of writing this book because he knew I am not afraid to step on the toes of demanding, legalistic, religious people (the types who demanded Jesus' crucifixion). I am opinioned, but thorough and truthful. I tell it the way I interpret it in the Bible, and let the chips fall where they may. At times, the chips are flung at me.

I would rather receive the criticism of 10,000 men than experience the remorse of displeasing God by teaching heresy.

> *"What blessings await you when people hate you and exclude you and mock you and curse you as evil because you follow the Son of Man. When that happens, be happy! Yes, leap for joy! For a great reward awaits you in heaven. And remember, their ancestors treated the ancient prophets that same way."* Luke 6:22-24, Jesus' words

I love, but don't like, all Christians because they can be extremely cruel and demanding. They look for the speck in others' eyes while overlooking the log in their own. These are the *shall-not Christians.*

> *"And why worry about a speck in your friend's eye when you have a log in your own?"* Matthew 7:3, Jesus' words

The Christian churches in America are in trouble!

The problem is not with Jesus, who is the heart of his Church; the problem is the convolution of his simple message. The simplicity of salvation, by grace through faith, has evolved into a massive works-based proposition, which scares folks from the loving Savior. Many Christians want to do Jesus' thinking for him based on how they think it "should" be. Unlearned Christians pick a few of their favorite legalistic Bible verses and pass judgment, considering themselves theologians. The truth is:

JESUS' SHED BLOOD PAID THE PRICE. Many who consider themselves as Christian insist Jesus' shed Blood must be diluted with filthy rags? This is caused by:

1. False teachers.
2. Reading the Bible, but not studying it.
3. The desire to be self-righteousness.

Jesus' shed Blood paid for the consequences of all of the sins of all mankind. No works (filthy rags) are necessary – just faith. The only way one cannot take advantage of this free gift of forgiveness is by rejecting it.

> "The North American Church is at a critical juncture. The gospel of grace is being confused and compromised by silence, seduction, and outright subversion. The vitality of the faith is being jeopardized. The lying slogans of the fixers who carry religion like a sword of judgment pile up with impunity. Let ragamuffins everywhere gather as a confessing Church to cry out in protest. Revoke the licenses of religious leaders who falsify the idea of God. Sentence them to three years in solitude with the Bible as their only companion."
>
> — Brennan Manning, The Ragamuffin Gospel: Good News for the Bedraggled, Beat-Up, and Burnt Out

To ascertain the entire truth of Jesus' death and resurrection, as revealed in God's Word, one must research all passages regarding a topic, using the context around the passage, comparing it with other parts of the Bible, and establishing an understanding of the language and customs of the time it was written — all in an effort to completely comprehend what the original writer(s) intended to communicate. I have done that in this book. It is referred to as an *exegesis*. I guarantee you will learn from my efforts.

Tim Finley
Messenger of the Good News

How to read this Book – Please

This section contains important information you must understand before reading this book.

Because the title of this book — *WILL GAYS GO TO HEAVEN?* — is provocative, you may jump from chapter to chapter attempting to discover answers to your specific questions, rather than reading the book from cover to cover. If you are truly interested in learning about God's Kingdom and how to become a part of it eternally, approach this book in a systematic way, by reading it from front to back. Jumping around is OK, but please be thorough and do not miss anything.

This book is an exegesis of the Christian Doctrine of Salvation. In a biblical sense, *exegesis* is a theological term used to describe an approach to interpreting a Bible passage, topic, or doctrine by critical analysis. A mistake made by most Christians when attempting to understand a Bible topic is they usually employ just one or two passages, while neglecting the many other verses and passages pertaining to that topic. It is an easy mistake to make, but *interpretation must be ascertained using the entire Bible.* There may be dozens of other passages inconsistent with your one or two favorite passages, so be thorough. Establishing a doctrine, or principle, without extensive research is disastrous. The Bible must be studied, not just read.

Proper exegesis includes using the context around the passage and comparing it with other parts of the Bible, while utilizing an understanding of the language and customs of the time it was written — all *in an effort to completely comprehend what the original writer(s) intended to communicate.*

Orthodox evangelical

This book represents the *orthodox* (lower case) *evangelical* perspective.

With a capital O, Orthodox refers to Eastern Orthodox Christians, a division within the early Christian Church that still exists today.

The term *orthodox*, when in lowercase, refers to the traditional/historical Christian belief that the Bible is the Word of God, written by men but inspired by the Holy Spirit. An *orthodox* Christian believes the original manuscripts of the Bible were without error or contradiction, thus the Bible is the complete and sufficient revelation of God, subject to interpretation.

> *All Scripture is inspired by God and is useful to teach us what is true and to make us realize what is wrong in our lives. It corrects us when we are wrong and teaches us to do what is right. God uses it to prepare and equip his people to do every good work.* 2 Timothy 3:16-17

Evangelical is the word used to describe a Christian who believes salvation is only by grace through faith. An evangelical believes that good deeds are a person's way of thanking Jesus, who was God incarnate, for his finished work, but good deeds are not mandatory for one's salvation. The commonly used phrase – "Salvation by grace through faith" – is referred to as the *Good News* or *Gospel of Jesus Christ*.

This book has been written using the Old and New Testament Bibles as the supreme authority. **<u>Any bold or underlined text in Bible passages is my addition to serve as emphasis for certain words or phrases.</u>**

The Five Solas

The Five Solas are five Latin phrases established during the Protestant Reformation in Europe to distinguish between orthodox Christianity and false religions. The Five Solas are the foundation for this book.

Sola, the Latin word for *only,* was used in relation to five key teachings that define the beliefs of Protestants. They are:

1. *Sola Scriptura* (by Scripture alone): belief that the Bible is the only inspired and authoritative Word of God. It is the only source for Christian doctrine and is accessible to all.
2. *Sola Fide* (by faith alone): belief that God declares us righteous only by our faith, and there is no need for good works.
3. *Sola Gratia* (by grace alone): belief that salvation comes by God's grace through faith, and there is no need for good works.

4. *Solus Christus* (Christ alone): belief that Christ is the only mediator between God and man, and that no mediator is necessary.
5. *Soli Deo Gloria* (glory to God alone): belief that all glory is to be given to God for the salvation of man, because salvation is accomplished solely through his will.

Jesus was/is God

Jesus Christ was, is, and always will be the one and only Creator God. He came to this Earth in the form of a man and died on a cross to pay for the sins of all mankind. Three days following his death, he arose from death to prove who he was and to demonstrate he had authority over death, so those who believe in him will have eternal life.

> *"For God loved the world so much that he gave his one and only Son, so that everyone who believes in him will not perish but have eternal life. God sent his Son into the world not to judge the world, but to save the world through him."* John 3:16-17, Jesus' words

The names Jesus and God are interchangeable because they refer to the same deity. God is Jesus, Jesus is God, and both are the Holy Spirit. The names Jesus, Christ, Lord, God, Spirit, and Holy Spirit are synonymous.

Sin, iniquity, and transgression

Most scholars and non-scholars use the term *sin* to describe something that is immoral, but there are two additional biblical words that theologians occasionally use to describe immoral acts. They are *iniquities*, and *transgressions*.

Sin means: to miss the mark.

Iniquity means: premeditated choice or continuing without remorse.

Transgression means: a choice to intentionally disobey. When we deliberately disregard God's authority, we are transgressing.

To avoid confusion, only the term *sin* is used throughout this book when referring to immoral behaviors. Sins, iniquities, and transgressions are lumped into one because Jesus' crucifixion forgave all.

Definitions of frequently used words

Atonement: compensation for a loss. In Christianity the term *atonement,* when used to describe Christ's death on the Cross, signifies his shed Blood as *propitiation* for all sins of all mankind. (Propitiation means: the turning away of wrath by an offering.)

> *He himself is the sacrifice that atones for our sins—and not only our sins but the sins of all the world.* 1 John 2:2

God offers the invitation to all, but it is only those who respond in faith who receive eternal life in Heaven.

Born again (born spiritually, saved, regenerated, justified, and converted): the Spiritual birth that delivers eternal life in Heaven to the recipient by his or her acceptance of Jesus Christ as Savior.

Christian: one indwelt by the Holy Spirit.

> *But you are not controlled by your sinful nature. You are controlled by the Spirit if you have the Spirit of God living in you. (And remember that those who do not have the Spirit of Christ living in them do not belong to him at all.)* Romans 8:9

A person who does not enjoy the indwelling of Holy Spirit is similar to an automobile without an engine. Some may refer to it as an automobile, but it won't go very far. A person void of the Holy Spirit will go to Hell.

Although the word Christian appears only a few times in the Bible, it is the most common word used today to describe someone who is a born-again believer. In the Bible, the terms *disciples, brothers,* and *saints* are used more frequently than *Christian,* but because Christian is the contemporary title, it is the term chosen for this book.

Christian describes those who have accepted Jesus Christ's finished work (sacrificial death and resurrection) as his or her only way of receiving eternal life. It is not used to describe folks who attend church, sing in the church choir, tithe, or do nice things. Those attributes are admirable, but they do not make someone a Christian. The indwelling of the Holy Spirit identifies a Christian.

Dead: referring to those who are spiritually dead (not born again).

Eternal death: the fate that awaits all people who reject Jesus Christ as Savior. Physical death is a one-time experience, but eternal death is everlasting.

> *And anyone whose name was not found recorded in the Book of Life was thrown into the lake of fire.* Revelation 20:15

Eternal life: the reward for those who have been born again. The recipient begins his or her eternal life at the moment of belief.

Grace: God's compassion, kindness, mercy, and charity. *Grace* has several meanings in the Bible, depending on the context of the topic. *Grace* in this book will be primarily in the context of the free gift of salvation (justification).

God's (saving) grace is the formula for one's eternal life beginning at the time of his or her salvation. Eternal life begins on the planet earth, and upon physical death is moved to what is known as the *third Heaven*. This ultimately results in eternal life on the New Earth. This eternal life is the result of God's grace for those who trust in the finished work of Jesus Christ as their only way to the glory that awaits them in the next life. Salvation is an instantaneous occurrence that results in eternal life.

Heaven: the eternal destination of those who are saved from eternal damnation (Hell).

If you are a Christian who died this very moment, you would ascend to the *now* Heaven immediately. This *now* Heaven is an intermediate Heaven where all Christians will reside until Jesus' ultimate creation of the New Earth. You will read about this later.

WARNING: The *now* Heaven is not *purgatory*, because purgatory does not exist.

Hypocrite: one who says one thing but does another; a Christian who claims he or she doesn't sin.

Some folks thrill at criticizing church-goers, alleging they are hypocrites because they (the church-goer) lack perfection. A church is a hospital for sinners, so church attendees are admitting the need for help.

Impute: to lay the responsibility or blame on someone for something bad; or, to give credit for something good — to assign as a characteristic. Synonyms: ascribe, assign, attribute.

Because of imputed sin, everyone is born a sinner. Because of imputed righteousness, all Christians are deemed righteous by God.

Justification: what saves. When justified, we are made righteous through *grace* because of the Blood of Christ. God imputes the Christian's righteousness because of his love for us. It is a gift and it is not earned.

Kingdom of God: includes angels, and all persons who have received salvation by being born again (angels need not be born again). It is eternal, as God is eternal, and it is spiritual — found within all born-again believers. We enter the Kingdom when we are born again, and we remain in the Kingdom eternally.

Kingdom of God is synonymous with *Kingdom of Heaven*. The term *Kingdom of Heaven* appears only in the Gospel of Matthew, and although there is debate among scholars regarding the use of that term, most New Testament scholars believe both refer to the Kingdom of God.

Lake of Fire: the final Hell. The place of eternal punishment for all who reject Jesus Christ as Savior, including humans and demons.

Lamb's Book of Life (Book of Life): God's book containing names of those who have been redeemed by the Blood of the Lord Jesus Christ (born again).

The specifics of the Lamb's Book of Life are debatable. Some scholars believe the names of all saved people were placed in this book in eternity past. Other scholars believe a person's name is entered at the time he or she is saved. Once in this book, a name is never deleted. Once saved — always saved.

Reconciliation: what was accomplished when Christ died on the Cross, and the fact that his shed Blood satisfied God's judgment. Christ's Blood reconciles Christians to God.

Regeneration: the transformation of the believer when he or she is born again via the indwelling of the Holy Spirit. He or she becomes spiritually alive.

Religion: comes from the Latin word religare, meaning "to tie or bind." I will never again allow religious people to put me in bondage. I found freedom, balance, and guidance in the Holy Spirit. You do the same.

Sacrificial Lamb: another name for Jesus. When God established the New Covenant (contract or agreement), it ended the Israelite animal sacrifices (to gain God's favor) forever because Jesus was the ultimate sacrificial lamb.

God's Old Covenant required a lamb to be sacrificed every morning and evening in the Temples for the sins of Israelites.

> *"These are the sacrifices you are to offer regularly on the altar. Each day, offer two lambs that are a year old, one in the morning and the other in the evening. With one of them, offer two quarts of choice flour mixed with one quart of pure oil of pressed olives; also, offer one quart of wine as a liquid offering. Offer the other lamb in the evening, along with the same offerings of flour and wine as in the morning. It will be a pleasing aroma, a special gift presented to the Lord.*
>
> *"These burnt offerings are to be made each day from generation to generation. Offer them in the Lord's presence at the Tabernacle entrance; there I will meet with you and speak with you.* Exodus 29:38-42

Halleluiah, the New Covenant was coming! It was prophesized that the Messiah (Jesus) would be led to slaughter like a lamb to pay for the sins of the world.

> *He was oppressed and treated harshly,*
> *yet he never said a word.*
> *He was led like a lamb to the slaughter.*
> *And as a sheep is silent before the shearers,*
> *he did not open his mouth.* Isaiah 53:7

John the Baptist introduced Jesus as the Messiah.

> *The next day John saw Jesus coming toward him and said, "Look! The Lamb of God who takes away the sin of the world!"* John 1:29

Jesus Christ was crucified during the Passover, as the ultimate and final Passover Lamb (his sacrificial death). Animal sacrifices are no longer necessary.

Saint: synonymous with Christian. In fact, depending on the Bible translation, the term *believer(s)* is used approximately 150 times, *saint(s)* approximately 50 times, but

Christians only three times. Believers, saints, and Christians are synonymous and refer to those who have been born again – God's people.

A Christian is simultaneously a sinner and a saint. All humans are sinners by birth because of the sin of Adam, but only Christians are saints. In the New Testament, the Greek word *hagios* is translated into English as "saint," which means: set apart by and for God as holy/sacred.

Salvation: used to identify the act of being *born again* and being saved from eternal damnation in the Lake of Fire.

Some people may use the term referencing "being saved from addictions or something similar," but for the purpose of this book it is used to describe the act of accepting Jesus as Savior.

Sanctification: the believer's growth process by lessening sinful behavior and yielding one's life to the guidance of the Holy Spirit.

This adaptation takes place after a person has been justified (saved), but is not instantaneous, as is justification. Sanctification is the result of the saved person's efforts combined with the counseling of the Holy Spirit. It is the growth process of a Christian, also referred to as *discipleship.*

Shall-not Christians: Legalistic Christians who compile a list of behaviors they interpret as immoral. This list may be utilized in modifying their personal behavior, but it is usually used to condemn brethren. These Christian policeman do more harm than good.

Redundancy versus repetition

The term *redundant* is defined: something unnecessary. Every effort has been made in this book to avoid redundancy, but ***there is abundant repetition***.

The Holy Bible contains approximately 30,000 verses on many topics, and the same lesson is very often repeated, so the Lord apparently advocates repetition. An example of repetition the first four books of the New Testament (Matthew, Mark, Luke, and John), which are very similar.

<u>We learn by repetition</u>

The trick is to teach by not repeating unnecessarily. God's plan of salvation is so simple, yet the Holy Bible can be so complicated unless energetically and systematically divided by doctrine. This book does that, regarding the Doctrine of Salvation, with its truths and many misunderstandings.

When I taught my children to look both ways before crossing a street, I didn't tell them just once and hope they remembered. I repeated it hundreds of times so they would understand and remember. I am sure they got tired of hearing it, but they were never hit by a car.

An example of repetition in this book is Ephesians 2:8-9:

> *God saved you by his grace when you believed. And you can't take credit for this; it is a gift from God. Salvation is not a reward for the good things we have done, so none of us can boast about it.*

This is such an important verse that you will read it many times. Hopefully, you will memorize it because of the repetition.

Bible translation

Unless otherwise noted, all Scripture in this book comes from the New Living Translation (NLT) Bible. Passages from translations other than the NLT will be noted by the initials used to signify that particular translation. For example, the Amplified Bible will be abbreviated (AMP), and the King James Version (KJV).

Notes:

SECTION ONE
Getting Started

Notes:

The theological term *grace* in this book will be applied primarily in the context of the free gift of salvation (justification).

> *He canceled the record of the charges against us and took it away by nailing it to the cross.* In this way, he disarmed the spiritual rulers and authorities. He shamed them publicly by his victory over them on the cross. Colossians 2:13-14 (Emphasis added by me.)

Chapter 1

Super, Abundant, Radical, Undeserved, Amazing Grace

Would you read a book about how to make a killing in the stock market if it was written by someone who had never invested? I don't think so. How about a book instructing you how to fly an airplane written by someone who had never been in a cockpit? Again, I don't think so.

If you want to thoroughly understand *super, abundant, radical, undeserved, amazing, grace,* then I am the author for you. I am a murderer, an adulterer, a liar, a drunkard, a gambler; I am a selfish, self-centered, greedy, lustful, hot-tempered, foul-mouthed son-of-a gun. If there is anyone who does not deserve to be forgiven by God, it is me. Yet, God has forgiven all the bad I have done, all the bad I am doing, and all the bad I ever will do as his gift to me.

> *God saved you by his **grace** when you believed. And you can't take credit for this; it is a **gift** from God. Salvation is not a reward for the good things we have done, so none of us can boast about it.* Ephesians 2:8-9 (Emphasis added by me.)

If you are a church-goer, you probably hear your pastor mumble something periodically about *grace*, and if you are unchurched, you probably think grace is something you should say before you eat. It is time for someone to stand up and bellow: GRACE, GRACE, GRACE, GRACE! I am that guy.

I am a maverick

I was raised in a moral home, but there was no reference to any religion. As an adolescent, at my request, my dad would drop me off at church on Sunday mornings and then pick me up afterward. I was not welcomed warmly in church because I was very hyper, and I loved to laugh. My activity and laughter branded me as an agitator, so I quit going. **I did not feel worthy.**

In my early teens I began to drink, and play with the ladies — a lot. I was not an alcoholic, but I loved to drink beer in the pubs while looking for a lady. I graduated from high school by the skin of my teeth. Upon graduation (they only graduated me to get me out), I worked full time and attended night school, and continued to drink and pick up the ladies. No church attendance because **I did not feel worthy.**

I was married but only for a very short period (we had two wonderful children despite our differences). Following our separation, I worked, went to school, drank, and continued to pick up the ladies. I was not an evil person, but I loved to party. No more church attendance because **I did not feel worthy.**

While dating my current wife, Loveda, in about 1976, I took her to a local Baptist church — my first time in many years. Nervously (because **I did not feel worthy**), I sat in the very back pew. The atmosphere was very quiet and serene as I squirmed in my seat. When the angelic choir procession began down the aisle, followed by the holy-looking pastors, I panicked because **I did not feel worthy.** As soon as the coast was clear, I grabbed Loveda, and as she gripped my sweaty hand, I pulled her out the front door. **I did not feel worthy.**

In 1980, following my being born again, I began to realize there were many people in that church who were better than me, but there were also many who were worse. Of utmost importance is that we were all sinners housed in a hospital for people who needed healing.

If there is someone reading this who **does not feel worthy,** I pray that my experience of **not feeling worthy** will help. The only qualification for joining the Christian Church is to be **not worthy. I still don't feel worthy.**

I have been chosen by God to write this book, not because I am a good person, but because I am the perfect example of someone who has received *super, abundant, radical, undeserved, amazing, grace.*

*But someone who does not know, and then does something wrong, will be punished only lightly. When someone has been given much, much will be required in return; and when someone has been **<u>entrusted with much</u>**, even more will be required.* Luke 12:48, Jesus' words (Emphasis added by me.)

It is because I have been "entrusted with much" of God's grace, I have been given the responsibility to share my knowledge of Jesus with you.

"O God, make me worthy of this calling, that the name of Jesus may be glorified in me and I in him." Arthur Bennett (1915-1994)

<u>Ripping the veil</u>

The holy temple in Jerusalem was the heart of Jewish religious life. The temple was where animals were sacrificed and worship was conducted according to the laws of Moses. A veil separated the Holy Place (where only the priests could enter) from the Most Holy Place (where only the high priest could enter, and only once a year to atone for the sins of the Jewish nation).

> ***<u>That first covenant between God and Israel</u>*** *had regulations for worship and a place of worship here on earth. There were two rooms in that Tabernacle. In the first room were a lampstand, a table, and sacred loaves of bread on the table. This room was called the Holy Place. Then there was a curtain, and behind the curtain was the second room called the Most Holy Place.* Hebrews 9:1-3 (Emphasis added by me.)

In the passage above, I emphasized "That *first covenant* between God and Israel" because the book you are reading is all about the New Covenant. The old (first) covenant was written in stone, but the new covenant is written on our hearts, made possible only by faith in Christ, who shed his own Blood to atone for the sins of the world.

> *That is why he is the one who mediates a new covenant between God and people, so that all who are called can receive the eternal inheritance God has promised them. For Christ died to set them free from the penalty of the sins they had committed under that first covenant.* Hebrews 9:15

I am going to rip, what may be a veil for you, something that was masked to me until the age of 34. At which time I learned that my salvation was based on Jesus' finished work and not on my behavior. It wasn't until God radically tore the veil of untruth from my blind eyes that I realized my eternal salvation was based solely on my trusting in Jesus' finished work. Until that time, I was under the false impression I was saved by keeping Levitical laws (good behavior; i.e., following the Ten Commandments).

The illusionary *good behavior* veil that exists today, at one time was a physical reality. The veil of good behavior was "torn in two, from top to bottom" by Jesus' death on the Cross.

> *Then Jesus shouted out again, and he released his spirit. At that moment the curtain in the sanctuary of the Temple was **torn in two, from top to bottom**. The earth shook, rocks split apart, and tombs opened. The bodies of many godly men and women who had died were raised from the dead.* Matthew 27:50-52 (Emphasis added by me.)

After that veil was torn, God moved from that temple and its religious system was changed forever. This one act (the veil being torn when Jesus gave up his spirit) changed the course of history. It was at that moment man no longer needed, or needs, a Levitical priest, Roman Catholic priest, Protestant pastor, or anyone else to represent him or her before God. Now, it is a personal relationship with God via the Holy Spirit. As believers in Jesus' finished work, Christ is now our High Priest.

> *And so, dear brothers and sisters, we can boldly enter heaven's Most Holy Place because of the blood of Jesus. <u>By his death, Jesus opened a new and life-giving way through the curtain into the Most Holy Place.</u>* Hebrews 10:19-20 (Emphasis added by me)

That, my friend, is super, abundant, radical, undeserved, amazing grace.

Our radical Lord

The word *radical* has various meanings, but I have chosen that from the Oxford Dictionary: (Especially of change or action) relating to or affecting the fundamental nature of something; far-reaching or thorough. I believe it is accurate to say that God is one of action regarding the fundamental nature of something, is far-reaching, and thorough.

➢ **God is eternal.**
➢ **God created everything that exists.**
➢ **God reigns over all he created.**
➢ **God is omnipresent.**
➢ **God knows all things past, present, and future.**
➢ **God gives life, and he takes it away.**
➢ **God destroyed the Earth with water.**
➢ **God destroyed cities.**
➢ **God sent an army to kill his favorite people.**
➢ **God is so radical that he came to Earth in the form of a man to die on a cross to pay for the sins of all mankind, for all time. After three days of being dead, he arose to prove who he was and to demonstrate that he has power over death. <u>That is radical love and the undeserved grace that accompanies his love.</u>**

God, in the man Jesus, was the Lamb of God.

> *The next day John saw Jesus coming toward him and said, "Look! The Lamb of God who takes away the sin of the world!"* John 1:29

Under the Old Testament Law, every morning and evening, a lamb was sacrificed in the Temple for the sins of the people. That Lamb was thoroughly examined by the priest to assure it had no blemishes. *The individuals whose sins were being forgiven were not examined.*

Now get this: *In this same way, God does not examine us to see if we are acceptable because Jesus was the unblemished Lamb.*

God is gracious, and his grace includes goodness, kindness, mercy, and love. If it were not for God's grace, we would all be doomed. Although most of us agree God is radical, when it comes to the essence of his grace many want to put him in a tightly sealed box, insisting his grace is limited. In order to fully comprehend his grace, it is imperative we study the Scriptures objectively.

One of God's favors is so radical that most refuse to accept its sweeping effect because it scares us to death. Grace does not make sense to our infinitesimal minds. There is a common misunderstanding within Christendom that "too much" grace leads to disobedience. Not so! *Grace produces obedience!*

It is reputed the following verse is the one that freed Martin Luther from the bondage of religious guilt.

> ***This Good News tells us how God makes us right in his sight. This is accomplished from start to finish by faith. As the Scriptures say, "It is through faith that a righteous person has life."*** Romans 1:17 (Emphasis added by me.)

> **"Either sin is with you, lying on your shoulders. Or it is lying on Christ, the Lamb of God." Martin Luther (1483-1546)**

God shows both mercy and grace, but they are not the same. *Mercy withholds a punishment we deserve; grace gives a blessing we don't deserve.* In mercy, God chose to cancel our sin debt by sacrificing his perfect Son in our place. Because of his grace, we who trust in him will inherit eternal life.

> But—***"When God our Savior revealed his kindness and love, he saved us, not because of the righteous things we had done, but because of his mercy. He washed away our sins, giving us a new birth and new life through the Holy Spirit. He generously poured out the Spirit upon us through Jesus Christ our Savior. Because of his grace he declared us righteous and gave us confidence that we will inherit eternal life." This is a trustworthy saying, and I want you to insist on these teachings so that all who trust in God will devote themselves to doing good. These teachings are good and beneficial for everyone.*** Titus 3:4-8 (Emphasis added by me)

> *For God made Christ, who never sinned, to be the offering for our sin, so that we could be made right with God through Christ.* 2 Corinthians 5:21

He extended his grace to us while we were still his enemies. He considers us holy and blameless.

> *But God showed his great love for us by sending Christ to die for us while we were still sinners. And since* **we have been made right in God's sight by the blood of Christ,** *he will certainly save us from God's condemnation. For since our friendship with God was restored by the death of his Son while we were still his enemies, we will certainly be saved through the life of his Son. So now we can rejoice in our wonderful new relationship with God*

because our Lord Jesus Christ has made us friends of God. Romans 5:8-11 (Emphasis added by me.)

This includes you who were once far away from God. You were his enemies, separated from him by your evil thoughts and actions. Yet now he has reconciled you to himself through the death of Christ in his physical body. As a result, he has brought you into his own presence, and you are holy and blameless as you stand before him without a single fault. Colossians 1:21-22

He forgets our sins.

"And I will forgive their wickedness,
  and I will never again remember their sins." Hebrews 8:12

His grace set us free from the bondage of sin, the law, and religion.

He is so rich in kindness and grace that he purchased our freedom with the blood of his Son and forgave our sins. Ephesians 1:7

My deepest desire

I really don't like writing, and that is why I am probably not very good at it, but I love to share great things with my friends, so I am celebrated for my boldness regarding Jesus' finished work.

Grace is so great that I have spent many of the last 30 years telling folks about it. What is so cool about it is that most people only have an inkling of the experience of grace.

Grace has been masked and kept concealed because many Christian leaders are afraid high-testosterone guys like me (maybe you too) might misuse it. Sometimes people do take advantage of grace, but the more you understand it, the better you will typically behave (unless you are an idiot). It is not my desire to encourage you to misbehave, but that is a matter between you and God. Your good behavior benefits you and those around you more than it does him.

Super, abundant, radical, undeserved, amazing grace

I use the Bible as my source of reference because I have not found anything that equals it. Furthermore, my standpoint throughout this book is substantiated by nearly 1,000 Bible verses.

> *"Grace...means the full and free forgiveness of every sin, without God demanding or expecting anything from the one so forgiven—is a principle so opposed to all man's thoughts and ways, so far above man, that he dislikes it. His own heart often secretly calls it injustice. He does not deal in this way and he does not like to think of God doing so."* **J.N. Darby (1800-1882)**

Grace has several meanings in the Bible, depending on the context. When used in the Holy Scriptures, grace is difficult to define because it is one of many complex characteristics of God's sovereignty. The characteristics of God are so vast that volumes have been written by smarter men than me to describe a meticulous comprehension of grace.

The term grace is familiar to most folks, but it's very deep and profound implication is something that must be experienced. There are no words to adequately describe it. *Super, abundant, radical, undeserved, amazing grace* can only be recognized by those who have experienced its soulful penetrating effect.

Grace in the New Testament, translated from the Greek word *charis,* means *favor, kindness, gift, mercy, generosity, blessing, kindness,* etc. Grace is God's endowment to those who do not deserve it. Grace is God's radical compassion, kindness, mercy, and charity to undeserving people.

I am not a Greek scholar or interpreter, but I feel confident in my ability as a Christian to discuss grace. I have studied it for 30 years, but more important is the fact that I personally radically experience it hourly. Volumes can be written about grace, but until you bathe in it you will not totally comprehend or appreciate its cleansing effect. The more someone grasps grace, the more that person will grow in Jesus, which results in dramatically improved moral behavior and bold, enthusiastic evangelization.

Most people saw the movie produced by Mel Gibson in 2004 titled *The Passion of the Christ,* which detailed the final hours and crucifixion of Jesus. The film has been highly controversial and received mixed reviews, with some critics claiming that the extreme violence "obscures its message." Bull!

The extreme violence was necessary to demonstrate the plot. The plot was about bloodshed — blood that was shed for you and for me. Jesus, who was God incarnate, came to earth in the form of a man specifically to die on a cross and bleed to death. His shed Blood was propitiation for our past, present, and future sins. That is radical.

Jesus was spit on, mocked, beaten, and then nailed on a cross to die. Nails were pounded through his wrists and feet. As he hung from the Cross, his crown of thorns dug sharply into his scalp as he forgave his executioners.

> *Jesus said, "Father, forgive them, for they don't know what they are doing."*
> *And the soldiers gambled for his clothes by throwing dice.* Luke 23:34

Jesus was suffering the most horrible, painful death ever devised, but rather than curse those who tortured and killed him, he forgave them — absent their demonstration of *good works.* I italicized good works because that is the false method usually preached as a prerequisite for forgiveness.

The Roman officer and soldiers realized that this **radical forgiveness** was proof of Jesus' divinity. (This one act of forgiveness was the catalyst for Christianity spreading worldwide, as one person told another, who told another, who told another.)

When physical exhaustion took its toll on Jesus, he could not hold himself up to allow blood to reach his vital organs, so he hung his head and died, declaring,

> *"It is finished."* John 19:13, Jesus' words

After being declared dead, one of the soldiers pierced his side with a spear as blood and water oozed from the wound.

More extreme than the physical death of Jesus was the spiritual suffering he experienced as he bore the weight of the sins of all mankind. Jesus did for us what we cannot do for ourselves. He made us righteous by paying the ultimate price for our sinful nature.

> *For God made Christ, who never sinned, to be the offering for our sin, so that we could be made right with God through Christ.* 2 Corinthians 5:21

The story of Jesus final days on earth produces a range of emotions. The account is multi-facetted because Jesus' crucifixion takes us to the depth of grief when we consider our sins, but Jesus' resurrection elevates us to the height of glory when we realize our deliverance from the consequence of that sin. His resurrection gives eternal life to those who trust in his finished work.

Do not be a fool!

If you are placing your confidence for eternal life in your feeble flesh, you are a fool. You are saved only by God's grace. If you don't think grace is *super, abundant, radical, undeserved, and amazing*, I suggest you look at the Cross. Jesus' death on the Cross demonstrated God's favor.

> But now God has shown us a way to be made right with him without keeping the requirements of the law, as was promised in the writings of Moses and the prophets long ago. **We are made right with God by placing our faith in Jesus Christ. And this is true for everyone who believes, no matter who we are.**
>
> For everyone has sinned; we all fall short of God's glorious standard. **Yet God, with undeserved kindness, declares that we are righteous.** He did this through Christ Jesus when he freed us from the penalty for our sins. For God presented Jesus as the sacrifice for sin. **People are made right with God when they believe that Jesus sacrificed his life, shedding his blood.** This sacrifice shows that God was being fair when he held back and did not punish those who sinned in times past, for he was looking ahead and including them in what he would do in this present time. God did this to demonstrate his righteousness, for he himself is fair and just, and **he declares sinners to be right in his sight when they believe in Jesus.**
>
> Can we boast, then, that we have done anything to be accepted by God? No, because **our acquittal is not based on obeying the law.** It is based on faith. So we are made right with God through faith and not by obeying the law. Romans 3:21-28 (Emphasis added by me.)

The only way we could be made perfect is by being washed in the blood of a perfect lamb. Jesus was that perfect and final sacrificial Lamb.

> **So now there is no condemnation for those who belong to Christ Jesus.** And because you belong to him, the power of the life-giving Spirit has freed you from the power of sin that leads to death. **The law of Moses was unable to save us because of the weakness of our sinful nature. So God did what the law could not do. He sent his own Son in a body like the bodies we sinners have. And in that body God declared an end to sin's control over us by giving his Son as a sacrifice for our sins.** He did this so that the just requirement of the law would be fully satisfied for

*us, who no longer follow our sinful nature but instead **follow the Spirit**.* Romans 8:1-4 (Emphasis added by me.)

*For God's will was for us to be made holy by the sacrifice of the body of Jesus Christ, **once for all time**.* Hebrews 10:10 (Emphasis added by me.)

*For you know that God paid a ransom to save you from the empty life you inherited from your ancestors. And the ransom he paid was not mere gold or silver. **It was the precious blood of Christ, the sinless, spotless Lamb of God.*** 1 Peter 1:18-19 (Emphasis added by me.)

Some theologians refer to it as *free grace*, and others more boldly as *hyper-grace*. I don't know if they don't thoroughly understand it, or if they are fearful of offending other theologians by their lack of boldness, but grace needs a standing ovation — not the meekness with which it is usually referred. It is more than just free, or hyper.

Prayerfully, this book rattles the cages of those who the outspoken Apostle Paul calls *fools*.

*I am shocked that you are turning away so soon from God, who called you to himself through the **loving mercy** of Christ. You are following a different way that pretends to be the **Good News** but is not the **Good News** at all. You are being **fooled** by those who deliberately twist the truth concerning Christ.* Galatians 1:6-7 (Emphasis added by me.).

The Amplified Bible states it a little differently, but the meaning is the same.

*I am surprised and astonished that you are so quickly turning renegade and deserting Him Who invited and called you by the **grace (unmerited favor)** of Christ (the Messiah) [and that you are transferring your allegiance] to a different [even an opposition] **gospel**.*

*Not that there is [or could be] any other **[genuine Gospel]**, but there are [obviously] some who are troubling and disturbing and bewildering you [with a different kind of teaching which they offer as a gospel]and want to **pervert and distort the Gospel** of Christ (the Messiah) [into something which it absolutely is not].* Galatians 1:6-7 (AMP) (Emphasis added by me.)

What these passages are referring to is the way in which someone receives eternal life in Heaven, commonly referred to as the *gospel*, *salvation*, and/or *justification*.

Whichever name you wish to use, always remember it is a free gift received by grace through faith. Never pervert or distort it. Never!

> God **saved you by his grace** when you believed. And you can't take credit for this; **it is a gift from God**. Salvation is not a reward for the good things we have done, so none of us can boast about it. Ephesians 2:8-9 (Emphasis added by me)

That, my friend, is radical.

By the Blood of Jesus, God has also forgiven everyone who has ever lived, and everyone who will ever live, for every, and I mean every, sin they have ever committed.

The faith of Abraham

The Old Testament saint Abraham (formerly Abram), the founder of the Jewish nation, is mentioned in the New Testament numerous times. In the following New Testament passage the Great Apostle Paul is using Abraham as proof there has never been a way to salvation other than by grace through faith.

> In the same way, "Abraham believed God, and **God counted him as righteous because of his faith.**" The real children of Abraham, then, are those who put their faith in God. Galatians 3:6-7

Although Abraham demonstrated his faith through his actions, it was his faith in the Creator God that came first. Prior to being a believer in one creator, Abraham had worshiped idols.

Then we have the story of Abraham sacrificing Sarah's safety to save his own neck.

> At that time a severe famine struck the land of Canaan, forcing Abram to go down to Egypt, where he lived as a foreigner. As he was approaching the border of Egypt, Abram said to his wife, Sarai, "Look, you are a very beautiful woman. When the Egyptians see you, they will say, 'This is his wife. Let's kill him; then we can have her!' So please tell them you are my sister. Then they will spare my life and treat me well because of their interest in you."
>
> And sure enough, when Abram arrived in Egypt, everyone noticed Sarai's beauty. When the palace officials saw her, they sang her praises to Pharaoh, their king, and Sarai was taken into his palace. Then Pharaoh gave Abram

many gifts because of her—sheep, goats, cattle, male and female donkeys, male and female servants, and camels. Genesis 12:10-16

Sarai was taken to the Pharaoh's harem, and Abraham was "treated well because of her and received flocks, oxen, donkeys, men and women slaves, she-donkeys and camels."

Nowhere does the text imply that God commanded Abraham to save his own neck by exploiting his wife for slaves and farm animals. It was **Abraham's lack of faith that led to such a cowardly act.**

This man of faith had doubts, as we all do. Abraham and his wife, Sarah (formerly Sarai), were childless but God promised that Abraham would have a son. Because of Sarah's mature age, they had their doubts, so Abraham and Sarah devised a plan in which Abraham would father a child with Sarah's servant, Hagar. **The birth of Ishmael demonstrates the futility of Abraham's lack of faith.**

God comes thru

Yet, God's faithfulness was fulfilled when Sarah, at the age of 90 years, had a son named Isaac. The most recognized story of Abraham's faith is revealed when God commands Abraham to sacrifice Isaac on the top of Mount Moriah. The story has a happy ending when God stopped Abraham almost at the point of no return.

Abraham had his times of faith and doubt, bravery and cowardice — but God protected and blessed Abraham despite his fickleness.

Sola fide (faith alone)

Abraham did his best to obey God, but his faith preceded his good deeds — not the other way around. Abraham began by worshiping idols, but upon his belief in the One Creator God, he began his discipleship.

In the following shining sample of justification by faith alone, Paul uses the example of Abraham because the Jews regarded Abraham as the extreme example of a faithful man. Abraham's faith proves that works-righteousness, as practiced by the Jews, was to be replaced with a new covenant of faith.

> *Abraham was, humanly speaking, the founder of our Jewish nation. What did he discover about being made right with God?* ***If his good deeds had made him acceptable to God, he would have had something to boast***

about. *But that was not God's way. For the Scriptures tell us, "Abraham be-lieved God, and **God counted him as righteous because of his faith."***

When people work, their wages are not a gift, but something they have earned. But people are counted as righteous, not because of their work, but because of their faith in God who forgives sinners. *David also spoke of this when he described the happiness of those who are declared righteous without working for it:*

> ***"Oh, what joy for those***
> > ***Whose disobedience is forgiven,***
> > ***Whose sins are put out of sight.***
> ***Yes, what joy for those***
> > ***Whose record the LORD has cleared of sin."***

*Now, is this blessing only for the Jews, or is it also for uncircumcised Gentiles: Well, we have been saying that **Abraham was counted as righteous by God because of his faith.** But how did this happen? Was he counted as righteous only after he was circumcised, or was it before he was circumcised? Clearly, God accepted Abraham before he was circumcised!*

*Circumcision was a sign that Abraham already had faith and that God had already accepted him and declared him to be righteous—even before he was circumcised. So Abraham is the spiritual father of those who have faith but have not been circumcised. **They are counted as righteous because of their faith.** And Abraham is also the spiritual father of those who have been circumcised, but only if they have the same kind of faith Abraham had before he was circumcised.*

*Clearly, God's promise to give the whole earth to Abraham and his descen-dants was based not on his obedience to God's law, but on a right relation-ship with God that comes by faith. If God's promise is only for those who obey the law, then faith is not necessary and the promise is pointless. **For the law always brings punishment on those who try to obey it. (The only way to avoid breaking the law is to have no law to break!)***

So the promise is received by faith. It is given as a free gift. And we are all certain to receive it, whether or not we live according to the law of Moses, if we have faith like Abraham's. *For Abraham is the father of all who believe. That is what the Scriptures mean when God told him, "I have* *made you the father of many nations." This happened because Abraham believed in the God who brings the dead back to life and who creates new things out of nothing.* Romans 4:1-17 (Emphasis added by me.)

But now God has shown us a way to be made right with him without keeping the requirements of the law, as was promised in the writings of Moses and the prophets long ago. **We are made right with God by placing our faith in Jesus Christ.** *And this is true for everyone who believes, no matter who we are.* Romans 3:21-22 (Emphasis added by me.)

We are confident of all this because of our great trust in God through Christ. It is not that we think we are qualified to do anything on our own. Our qualification comes from God. He has enabled us to be ministers of his new covenant. **This is a covenant not of written laws, but of the Spirit.** *The old written covenant ends in death; but under the new covenant, the Spirit gives life.* 2 Corinthians 3:4-6 (Emphasis added by me.)

Grace for salvation (justification)

God's saving grace is the phrase used to describe God's unmerited favor available to every person who is willing to accept it. It is the method by which one receives eternal life in Heaven. Eternal life begins on the planet Earth, and upon physical death is moved to what is known as the *third Heaven*. This ultimately results in eternal life on the *New Earth*, which I discuss later in this book. Salvation is an instantaneous occurrence resulting in eternal life.

The Great Apostle Paul is a dazzling example of a human being who experienced God's radical amazing grace. Paul, a Roman Jewish tax collector, hated Jesus to the point of being responsible for the deaths of those who accepted Jesus as the Messiah. Upon his encounter with Jesus, and his receiving Jesus' radical grace, Paul devoted his entire life to spreading the Good News of grace through faith.

You know what I was like when I followed the Jewish religion—how I violently persecuted God's church. I did my best to destroy it. I was far ahead of my fellow Jews in my zeal for the traditions of my ancestors. Galatians 1:13-14 (A confession of the Great Apostle Paul)

"Radical grace produces radical devotion to Jesus." Tim Finley (born – 1946)

Jesus chose Paul, a Christian-killing, hard-hearted Roman Jewish tax collector, to be one of his greatest representatives by imparting grace beyond human comprehension. Paul goes on to say:

> **God's law was given so that all people could see how sinful they were. But as people sinned more and more, God's wonderful grace became more abundant.** Romans 5:20 (Emphasis added by me.)

I am sure many of you Modern-day Pharisees (Christian police) hate that verse. Shame on you for attempting to limit the grace of our creator. We humans cannot fathom his might and methods, so quit chasing people from him by putting him in a box.

> *"Can you solve the mysteries of God?*
> *Can you discover everything about the Almighty?*
> *Such knowledge is higher than the heavens—*
> *and who are you?*
> *It is deeper than the underworld—*
> *what do you know? Job 11:7-8*

Many hate grace

Within the Church we have many who are afraid grace will lead to immoral behavior. This is not true if grace is understood. This fear dates back to the time that Jesus was crucified. Those who crucified Jesus were desperately afraid that without written laws, people would behave recklessly, *although God was the one who obliterated the Jewish law by his death on the Cross.*

Paul emphasizes this in his letter to the Roman Church when he emphasized morality comes from the heart and not from laws written on stone given only to the Israelites.

> *Even Gentiles, who do not have God's written law, show that they know his law when they instinctively obey it, even without having heard it. They demonstrate that God's law is written in their hearts, for their own conscience and thoughts either accuse them or tell them they are doing right. Romans 2:14-15*

Paul is explaining that the laws were written in our hearts, which have the capability of distinguishing right from wrong via the Holy Spirit who is the counselor of all Christians.

"This is the new covenant I will make
with my people on that day, says the Lord:
I will put my laws in their hearts,
and I will write them on their minds." Hebrews 10:16

Hebrews 10:16 is a partial quotation from Jeremiah 31:33, when Jesus was prophesized as the coming Messiah, who would usher in a New Covenant (agreement). This *New Covenant* allows God to live in us, and through us. It is a *personal relationship* with God via the Holy Spirit — not laws written on stones. God puts his will in our minds and writes them permanently on our hearts. From this point forward, our relationship with God can grow and expand to meet all that God has purposed and planned for us. Rather than pushing laws down the throats of fellow Christians, legalists should encourage a closer walk with the Spirit. Amen!

"I'm an old, cynical preacher, and sometimes I grow so tired — exhausted, really — from trying to live up to the standards of those who manipulate and manage in the name of Jesus." Steve Brown

Grace experienced

"It has been my experience that folks who have no vices have very few virtues." Abraham Lincoln (1809-1865)

The New Testament oozes with accounts of Jesus' grace, but I have chosen four of my favorites to get you started. Two are Jesus' parables, and two are actual narratives.

The parable of the vineyard workers

"For the Kingdom of Heaven is like the landowner who went out early one morning to hire workers for his vineyard. He agreed to pay the normal daily wage and sent them out to work.

"At nine o'clock in the morning he was passing through the marketplace and saw some people standing around doing nothing. So he hired them, telling them he would pay them whatever was right at the end of the day. So they

went to work in the vineyard. At noon and again at three o'clock he did the same thing.

"At five o'clock that afternoon he was in town again and saw some more people standing around. He asked them, 'Why haven't you been working today?'

"They replied, 'Because no one hired us.'

"The landowner told them, 'Then go out and join the others in my vineyard.'

"That evening he told the foreman to call the workers in and pay them, beginning with the last workers first. **When those hired at five o'clock were paid, each received a full day's wage. When those hired first came to get their pay, they assumed they would receive more. But they, too, were paid a day's wage.** *When they received their pay, they protested to the owner, 'Those people worked only one hour, and yet you've paid them just as much as you paid us who worked all day in the scorching heat.'*

"He answered one of them, 'Friend, I haven't been unfair! Didn't you agree to work all day for the usual wage? Take your money and go. I wanted to pay this last worker the same as you. Is it against the law for me to do what I want with my money? Should you be jealous because I am kind to others?'

"So those who are last now will be first then, and those who are first will be last." Matthew 20:1-16, Jesus words (Emphasis added by me.)

In this parable, God is the landowner and believers are the laborers. The point of the story is that God's grace has no boundaries. The world's way of thinking what is fair is no comparison to what God believes is fair. God makes entry into his kingdom available to even the Johnnies-come-lately. ***That is super, abundant, radical, undeserved, amazing grace.***

The parable of the lost son

To illustrate the point further, Jesus told them this story: "A man had two sons. The younger son told his father, 'I want my share of your estate now before you die.' So his father agreed to divide his wealth between his sons.

"A few days later this younger son packed all his belongings and moved to a distant land, and there he wasted all his money in wild living. About the

time his money ran out, a great famine swept over the land, and he began to starve. He persuaded a local farmer to hire him, and the man sent him into his fields to feed the pigs. The young man became so hungry that even the pods he was feeding the pigs looked good to him. But no one gave him anything.

"When he finally came to his senses, he said to himself, 'At home even the hired servants have food enough to spare, and here I am dying of hunger! I will go home to my father and say, "Father, I have sinned against both heaven and you, and I am no longer worthy of being called your son. Please take me on as a hired servant."'

"So he returned home to his father. And while he was still a long way off, his father saw him coming. Filled with love and compassion, he ran to his son, embraced him, and kissed him. His son said to him, 'Father, I have sinned against both heaven and you, and I am no longer worthy of being called your son.'

"But his father said to the servants, 'Quick! Bring the finest robe in the house and put it on him. Get a ring for his finger and sandals for his feet. And kill the calf we have been fattening. We must celebrate with a feast, for this son of mine was dead and has now returned to life. He was lost, but now he is found.' So the party began.

"Meanwhile, the older son was in the fields working. When he returned home, he heard music and dancing in the house, and he asked one of the servants what was going on. 'Your brother is back,' he was told, 'and your father has killed the fattened calf. We are celebrating because of his safe return.'

"The older brother was angry and wouldn't go in. His father came out and begged him, but he replied, 'All these years I've slaved for you and never once refused to do a single thing you told me to. And in all that time you never gave me even one young goat for a feast with my friends. Yet when this son of yours comes back after squandering your money on prostitutes, you celebrate by killing the fattened calf!'

"His father said to him, 'Look, dear son, you have always stayed by me, and everything I have is yours. We had to celebrate this happy day. For your brother was dead and has come back to life! He was lost, but now he is found!'" Luke 15:11-32

There are two parts to this parable.

1. The crux of the first part is *super, abundant, radical, undeserved, amazing grace*. The father, played by God, runs to welcome home his lost son. The older brother was not lost, yet the younger brother receives the party. This teaches us that God always welcomes us home.
2. The second part regards the jealous obedient behavior of the older brother. As Christians, we should not be jealous or angry because someone less-deserving receives the *super, abundant, radical, undeserved, amazing grace* that we deserve.

The thief on the cross

Two others, both criminals, were led out to be executed with him. When they came to a place called The Skull, they nailed him to the cross. And the criminals were also crucified—one on his right and one on his left.

Jesus said, "Father, forgive them, for they don't know what they are doing." *And the soldiers gambled for his clothes by throwing dice.*

The crowd watched and the leaders scoffed. "He saved others," they said, "let him save himself if he is really God's Messiah, the Chosen One." The soldiers mocked him, too, by offering him a drink of sour wine. They called out to him, "If you are the King of the Jews, save yourself!" A sign was fastened above him with these words: "This is the King of the Jews."

One of the criminals hanging beside him scoffed, "So you're the Messiah, are you? Prove it by saving yourself—and us, too, while you're at it!"

But the other criminal protested, "Don't you fear God even when you have been sentenced to die? We deserve to die for our crimes, but this man hasn't done anything wrong." Then he said, "Jesus, remember me when you come into your Kingdom."

And Jesus replied, "I assure you, today you will be with me in paradise."
Luke 23:32-43 (Emphasis added by me.)

I believe this to be one of the most revealing stories of God's super, abundant, radical, undeserved, amazing grace. At the point of death, the believing thief was welcomed into God's Kingdom, but the non-believer was ignored, revealing that our deeds do not save us, but our faith does. It also divulges that Paradise (the abode of God) is immediate. No purgatory, soul sleep, or any of those other manmade designs.

A sinful woman anoints Jesus' feet

One of the Pharisees asked Jesus to have dinner with him, so Jesus went to his home and sat down to eat. When a certain immoral woman from that city heard he was eating there, she brought a beautiful alabaster jar filled with expensive perfume. Then she knelt behind him at his feet, weeping. Her tears fell on his feet, and she wiped them off with her hair. Then she kept kissing his feet and putting perfume on them.

When the Pharisee who had invited him saw this, he said to himself, "If this man were a prophet, he would know what kind of woman is touching him. She's a sinner!"

Then Jesus answered his thoughts. "Simon," he said to the Pharisee, "I have something to say to you."

"Go ahead, Teacher," Simon replied.

Then Jesus told him this story: "A man loaned money to two people—500 pieces of silver to one and 50 pieces to the other. But neither of them could repay him, so he kindly forgave them both, canceling their debts. Who do you suppose loved him more after that?"

Simon answered, "I suppose the one for whom he canceled the larger debt." "That's right," Jesus said. Then he turned to the woman and said to Simon, "Look at this woman kneeling here. When I entered your home, you didn't offer me water to wash the dust from my feet, but she has washed them with her tears and wiped them with her hair. You didn't greet me with a kiss, but from the time I first came in, she has not stopped kissing my feet. You neglected the courtesy of olive oil to anoint my head, but she has anointed my feet with rare perfume.

"I tell you, her sins—and they are many—have been forgiven, so she has shown me much love. But a person who is forgiven little shows only little love." Then Jesus said to the woman, "Your sins are forgiven."

The men at the table said among themselves, "Who is this man, that he goes around forgiving sins?"

> *And Jesus said to the woman, "__Your faith has saved you__; go in peace."* Luke 7:36-50 (Emphasis added by me.)

This passage demonstrates the difference between how a Pharisee (Jewish law-keeper) treats sinners like you and me, in contrast to how Jesus, by way of his *super, abundant, radical, undeserved amazing grace,* views and treats folks like us. Although the woman was not an invited guest, Jesus elevated her from shame to fellowship with him. ***It was her faith that saved her.***

In review

The passages are uncomplicated illustrations demonstrating it is by *super, abundant, radical, undeserved, amazing grace* that Jesus loves those who come to him clothed in sin, so that he may clothe them in his righteousness. In his kingdom, he is absolutely sovereign and he can deal with all people in whatever way he chooses. He alone makes the decisions regarding his treatment of all people, whether you agree with him or not. So, don't waste your time searching the Scriptures, desperately seeking those few misunderstood verses that make it appear you are the only person worthy of his grace.

The message to each of us is not to be proud of what we have done and expect more than those we think have done less. Does this make grace cheap?

> **"Sure grace is cheap. If it was expensive, you and I couldn't afford it."**
> **Steve Brown.**

Grace produces obedience

It is our sincere appreciation for God's grace that motivates us, with the assistance of the Holy Spirit, to clean up our acts. Throughout my three decades as a Christian evangelist, I can attest to the fact that the more one understands grace, the better one behaves.

> *So I say, let the Holy Spirit guide your lives. Then you won't be doing what your sinful nature craves. The sinful nature wants to do evil, which is just the opposite of what the Spirit wants. And the Spirit gives us desires that are the opposite of what the sinful nature desires. These two forces are constantly fighting each other, so you are not free to carry out your good intentions. But when you are directed by the Spirit, you are not under obligation to the law of Moses.*

When you follow the desires of your sinful nature, the results are very clear: sexual immorality, impurity, lustful pleasures, idolatry, sorcery, hostility, quarreling, jealousy, outbursts of anger, selfish ambition, dissension, division, envy, drunkenness, wild parties, and other sins like these. Let me tell you again, as I have before, that anyone living that sort of life will not inherit the Kingdom of God.

But the Holy Spirit produces this kind of fruit in our lives: love, joy, peace, patience, kindness, goodness, faithfulness, gentleness, and self-control. There is no law against these things!

Those who belong to Christ Jesus have nailed the passions and desires of their sinful nature to his cross and crucified them there. Since we are living by the Spirit, let us follow the Spirit's leading in every part of our lives. Let us not become conceited, or provoke one another, or be jealous of one another.
Galatians 5:16-26

In conclusion

I know I am going to Heaven, but my confidence is based on what Jesus did for me and not based on what I may do for him. I am certainly not worthy of his *super, abundant, radical, undeserved, amazing grace,* so for me to take credit would label me self-righteous. It is my deepest desire that you experience the same forgiveness and eternal life given to me freely by the Jewish carpenter who died on a cross 2,000 years ago to pay for my sins. THANK YOU, JESUS!

Notes:

Chapter 2

Prune the Family Tree!

You may be offended by what you are about to read, but it is not my intention to win friends and influence people. The mission of Heaven Is Easy Ministries is to provide an objective perspective that may have been overlooked due to heritage, laziness, lack of education, stupidity, or stubbornness. Because your parents always drove Fords, it doesn't mean you should not drive a Lexus.

Most people's spiritual beliefs are inherited from their kinfolk. We tend to tag along with what our parents and grandparents believed, whether we truly think it is right or wrong. Usually we think it is correct because it is what we were told to think, or we are too lazy to spend the time and energy to ascertain the truth.

Around the world, billions of *religious* individuals are performing all sorts of rituals, hoping to earn their way to Heaven. You may be one of them.

Some of these folks dress in black, others in white. Some wear cute little caps, some shave their heads, others grow their hair long. Some kneel, some roll, others extend their hands towards the heavens, many fold them on their laps. Some sing, some chant, others holler, and some remain silent. Some sacrifice animals, some refuse to kill anything. Crazies blow up buildings, and passive ones won't lift a finger to protect themselves.

Chances are if you are Christian, it is because you were raised Christian. Catholics are usually Catholic because their family demanded it. If Jewish, it is probably because your family is Jewish. Most Muslims inherit their belief from the family environment. If you fit into the category of *family-hanger-on*, you must stop to consider that perhaps your family is wrong. Your belief, if erroneous, could cause you eternal punishment.

If you are one whose beliefs are fruits of your family tree, you may discover the tree needs pruning, or it may be so diseased it should be pulled up by the roots. Keep in mind that becoming aware of truths in opposition to what you were told as a child does not mean you are deserting your heritage. In most circumstances, it will indicate you are progressing academically and spiritually.

Our ancestors did not have the advantage of the educational resources of our era. Chances are they smoked cigarettes, cooked with animal fat, and attended the same church for five decades. Tradition doesn't make it right. Because your parents attended one particular place of worship, it doesn't mean the teaching was truthful.

Thanks to modern communications and vast educational resources at our fingertips, no one should live in ignorance.

Prayerfully, this book will remove the scales from your eyes.

> *Instantly something like scales fell from Saul's eyes, and he regained his sight. Then he got up and was baptized.* Acts 9:18

Test-drive Jesus

Humans are sometimes reluctant to change. We are also usually afraid of truth because truth can be too convicting. It is much easier to bury our heads in the sand than to accept the challenge of change.

> *"There is salvation in no one else! God has given no other name under heaven by which we must be saved."* Acts 4:12

> *He himself is the sacrifice that atones for our sins—and not only our sins but the sins of all the world.* 1 John 2:2

"Christianity, if false, is of no importance, and if true, of infinite importance. The only thing it cannot be is moderately important." C.S. Lewis (1898-1963)

I am not an easy sell. Before I accepted Christianity as the true faith, I explored other faiths. When I began to study all world religions, most sounded credible and moral. Thankfully, I kept coming back to this Jesus fellow, for he displayed characteristics that all historic major religious leaders lacked. The greatest example of an outstanding characteristic would be when he resurrected himself from being dead. He is the only historic faith leader who is still alive after having been crucified 2000 years ago. The others are dead.

Jesus is freedom from religion

All world belief systems except Christianity involve good behavior to receive God's favor for eternal life. Unlike the others, Christianity is a way that sinful people (and we are all sinful) can spend eternity in the glory that awaits us in the next life with the Creator God, clothed, by faith, in the righteousness of Jesus Christ. Christianity demands nothing more. Good behavior is desirable, *but not mandatory for salvation.*

God created the world and everything in it. Then, he came to earth in the form of a man, for the specific purpose of dying on the Cross to forgive all of mankind for their sins. Then, he arose from the dead so that all who believe in his Divinity will live eternally with him. All that God requires is that a person believes this.

Jesus was God incarnate

> *Christ is the visible image of the invisible God. He existed before God made anything at all and is supreme over all creation. Christ is the one through whom God created everything in heaven and earth. He made the things we can see and the things we can't see—kings, kingdoms, rulers, and authorities. Everything has been created through him and for him. He existed before everything else began, and he holds all creation together.* Colossians 1:15-17

> *Glory and honor to God forever and ever. He is the eternal King. The unseen one who never dies; he alone is God. Amen.* 1 Timothy 1:17

Jesus divides families

Family heritage is important, but if it means choosing between eternity in Heaven or living somewhere else unpleasant, choose Heaven. Eternity is a long time. Don't put off making the decision until it is too late.

Although faith in Jesus Christ provides Christians with peace on earth and eternal life in Heaven, one's faith may cause strains on friendships and within families - but Jesus is very bold, stating that we must choose him.

> *"Don't imagine that I came to bring peace to the earth! No, I came to bring a sword. I have come to set a man against his father, and a daughter against her mother, and a daughter-in-law against her mother-in-law. Your enemies will be right in your own household! If you love your father or mother more than you love me, you are not worthy of being mine; or if you love your son*

*or daughter more than me, you are not worthy of being mine. If you refuse
to take up your cross and follow me, you are not worthy of being mine. If you
cling to your life, you will lose it; but if you give it up for me, you will find it."*
Matthew 10:34-39, Jesus' words

If you value family and friendship more than a relationship with God, then
Christianity may not be for you. But, if you want to live eternally with our Creator in
Heaven, then you may be forced to make a choice. Following Jesus may cause you to
generate enemies, but it can also provide you with the opportunity to be a light for
those living in darkness.

When a person becomes a Christian, it can strain relationships because those who
are unsaved don't understand living in the Spirit.

> ***But people who aren't Christians can't understand these truths from
> God's Spirit.*** *It all sounds foolish to them because only those who have the
> Spirit can understand what the Spirit means. We who have the Spirit under-
> stand these things, but others can't understand us at all. How could they?
> For, "who can know what the Lord is thinking? Who can give Him counsel?"*
> ***But we can understand these things, for we have the mind of Christ.*** 1
> Corinthians 2:14-16 (Emphasis added by me.)

If we are to follow Jesus, many people will get angry with us, argue with us, hurt us,
and mock us. Although this may be unpleasant, the eternal rewards are worth it for
those of us who choose him.

Don't wait until you are dead to discover if your family was wrong.

Chapter 3

Assume the Bible is Trustworthy

"I believe the Bible is the best gift God has ever given to man. All the good from The Savior of the world is communicated to us through this Book."
Abraham Lincoln (1809-1865)

"A thorough understanding of the Bible is better than a college education."
Theodore Roosevelt (1858-1919)

"Of the many influences that have shaped the United States into a distinctive nation and people, none may be said to be more fundamental and enduring than the Bible."
Ronald Reagan (1911-2004)

So distinguished, the Holy Bible has been translated into more than 2,000 languages. The heart of this globally celebrated book is a Jewish carpenter named Jesus, who was God incarnate. He (God) came to Earth in the form of a man to die on a cross to pay for the sins of all mankind.

> *He himself is the sacrifice that atones for our sins—and not only our sins but the sins of all the world.* 1 John 2:2

Three days following his death, he rose from being dead, so all who believe in him as Savior will have the free gift of eternal life in Heaven. This is the central message of the entire New Testament, which has led hundreds of millions worldwide, just like you, to know and love him as the sovereign Lord of grace.

> *"There is salvation in no one else! God has given no other name under heaven by which we must be saved."* Acts 4:12

Because a person's belief in Heaven is usually derived from the Bible, that same book should be used as the source of divine revelation. It is an astonishing point of reference. If someone can direct me to a book that is superior, I will certainly consider changing. But until then, I will trust God's Word.

The Holy Bible of the Christian faith is both the most criticized and loved book in history. The criticism can be blamed on ignorance.

The Bible may be construed as confrontational because it reminds readers of their sins, and may cause them to question their beliefs.

The Bible is the inspired word of God

Yes, mortals wrote the Bible, but God inspired it. Be advised that only the original manuscripts written by the apostles, prophets, etc., are inerrant. The Bible has been copied thousands of times over thousands of years. Though there are some minor differences, the vast majority of the biblical text is identical from one manuscript to another, providing us with a Bible that is 99 percent correct.

> *All Scripture is inspired by God and is useful to teach us what is true and to make us realize what is wrong in our lives. It corrects us when we are wrong and teaches us to do what is right. God uses it to prepare and equip his people to do every good work.* 2 Timothy 3:16-17

The original manuscripts were composed and compiled by individuals chosen by God, and the Holy Spirit inspired and instructed what to write. The Spirit uses the Bible to reveal the purpose, vision, love, and power of God.

> *For the word of God is alive and powerful. It is sharper than the sharpest two-edged sword, cutting between soul and spirit, between joint and marrow. It exposes our innermost thoughts and desires.* Hebrews 4:12

The Word of God has the power to reach the deepest parts of our spirit and soul, and serves as the roadmap for developing strength of character and morals. With the assistance of the Holy Spirit, the Bible instructs us how to live in the world, but not be of the world.

The three tests

When sharing my faith, I am frequently asked by non-believers how I know the Bible is true. The doubter usually refutes my faith in the Scriptures by saying the Bible was written by men. My first response is to ask them which men wrote it; 99.9 percent of them have no clue who wrote it, so my question embarrasses them. It is not my intent to make anyone feel stupid, but I do want them to realize they have much to learn.

Then, I share what I have learned about the reliability of the Bible by the three tests it passes.

The first test

Through the work of many archaeologists, most facts of the Bible have been validated, and each day more proof is discovered, thus validating the history of God's Word. Excavations have uncovered overwhelming, tangible evidence regarding the people and occurrences in the Bible. Archaeology is one of the Bible's best authenticators.

Messianic Jew Zola Levitt produced a documentary titled "The Stones Cry Out," in which he journeyed to Israel and Jordan to photograph archaeological sites and interview experts. This series provides amazing discoveries regarding the truth that archaeology reveals.

The second test

The second evidence of the Bible's validity is its reliability to predict future events.

The Old Testament contains hundreds of prophecies that have come true, and dozens that are currently being revealed. The Bible's ability to prophesize is the irrefutable evidence that differentiates it from all other books. The most important Old Testament prophecies, numbering about 200, are those of the coming Jewish Messiah, revealed in the New Testament to be Jesus. Specific details regarding Jesus' birth, life, death, and resurrection were prophesized centuries before his birth.

The third and most revealing test

The third and most revealing test is its amazing power to affect a person's life.

The Bible is the greatest psychology book ever written. I have read dozens of psychology and positive-thinking books, and have benefited slightly from most, but the greatest book I have read for peace of mind is the New Testament. It reveals why we are here and where we will go following death. If studied, it eliminates all guilt, assists in handling difficult times, and teaches us how to treat others. Millions and millions of people agree with me.

Conclusion

Don't knock it until you have tried it.

Chapter 4

Where will you spend Eternity?

Most people spend more time planning a two-week vacation than thinking about where they will spend eternity. We must face reality and ask ourselves: "Where will I go following my last heartbeat?" This is the most important question one must ask. There are only three plausible answers: Heaven, Hell, or just dead. The latter is a possibility, but I believe in Heaven and Hell.

A book titled *WILL GAYS GO TO HEAVEN?* would be ineffective if it failed to discuss what the Bible teaches about Heaven and its alternative — Hell.

I will get the bad news of a place called *Hell* out of the way so I can present the *Good News* of an incredible place called *Heaven*.

First, the bad news (for some)

Some people believe in Heaven but not in Hell. Their argument is that a loving God would not send a human somewhere to suffer eternally. This is not an educated opinion, but the persuasion of how people *think* it should be. ***Folks like to do God's thinking for him.***

If one believes in Heaven, it makes sense there must be a Hell. According to the Word of Almighty God, the Creator of all that exists, Hell is just as real as Heaven. The Bible clearly teaches that Hell is an actual place for those who reject Jesus' free gift of everlasting life. Watch out!

We know very little about what the existing Hell is like, or the characteristics of the *Lake of Fire* (the future place of eternal torment). We know Hell and the Lake of Fire are eternally hot places where constant torment occurs, but beyond that we know very little. We know for sure Hell and the Lake of Fire are not good places. ***No rational person would desire to live in eternal torment.***

Most Christian scholars agree the miseries of Hell consist of the absence of the love of God, prohibition from happiness, and guilt caused by the sin of rejecting the Lord Jesus as Savior.

> *He is ready to separate the chaff from the wheat with his winnowing fork. Then he will clean up the threshing area, gathering the wheat into his barn but burning the chaff with never-ending fire.* Matthew 3:12

> *"Then the King will turn to those on the left and say, 'Away with you, you cursed ones, into the eternal fire prepared for the devil and his demons.'"* Matthew 25:41, Jesus' words

> *"And they will go away into eternal punishment, but the righteous will go into eternal life."* Matthew 25:46, Jesus' words

> *"If your hand causes you to sin, cut it off. It's better to enter eternal life with only one hand than to go into the unquenchable fires of hell with two hands. If your foot causes you to sin, cut it off. It's better to enter eternal life with only one foot than to be thrown into hell with two feet. And if your eye causes you to sin, gouge it out. It's better to enter the Kingdom of God with only one eye than to have two eyes and be thrown into hell, 'where the maggots never die and the fire never goes out.'*

> *"For everyone will be tested with fire."* Mark 9:43-49, Jesus' words

> *"Finally, the poor man died and was carried by the angels to be with Abraham. The rich man also died and was buried, and his soul went to the place of the dead. There, in torment, he saw Abraham in the far distance with Lazarus at his side.*

> *"The rich man shouted, 'Father Abraham, have some pity! Send Lazarus over here to dip the tip of his finger in water and cool my tongue. I am in anguish in these flames.'"* Luke 16:23-24

> *And God will provide rest for you who are being persecuted and also for us when the Lord Jesus appears from heaven. He will come with his mighty angels, in flaming fire, bringing judgment on those who don't know God and on those who refuse to obey the Good News of our Lord Jesus. They will be punished with eternal destruction, forever separated from the Lord and from his glorious power.* 2 Thessalonians 1:7-9

Then a third angel followed them, shouting, "Anyone who worships the beast and his statue or who accepts his mark on the forehead or on the hand must drink the wine of God's anger. It has been poured full strength into God's cup of wrath. And they will be tormented with fire and burning sulfur in the presence of the holy angels and the Lamb. The smoke of their torment will rise forever and ever, and they will have no relief day or night, for they have worshiped the beast and his statue and have accepted the mark of his name." Revelation 14:10-11

Then the devil, who had deceived them, was thrown into the fiery lake of burning sulfur, joining the beast and the false prophet. There they will be tormented day and night forever and ever. Revelation 20:10

Hell is where those who have rejected Jesus' free gift are now, but that will not be their eternal home. Following the Millennium, the unsaved who have already died will be transferred from Hell (Hades/Sheol) to the Great White Throne Judgment. At that judgment it will be shown that their names are **not** found in the Book of Life, and their departure to the Lake of Fire will be immediate.

And I saw a great white throne and the one sitting on it. The earth and sky fled from his presence, but they found no place to hide. I saw the dead, both great and small, standing before God's throne. And the books were opened, including the Book of Life. And the dead were judged according to what they had done, as recorded in the books. The sea gave up its dead, and death and the grave gave up their dead. And all were judged according to their deeds. Then death and the grave were thrown into the lake of fire. This lake of fire is the second death. And anyone whose name was not found recorded in the Book of Life was thrown into the lake of fire. Revelation 20:11-15

Because God knows everything that has occurred in life, he will punish evil accordingly. There will be different levels of punishment.

He will judge everyone according to what they have done. Romans 2:6

You have just heard the bad news, but thanks to Jesus' free gift there is *Good News*.

Now the *Good News* (for some)

"You're born. You suffer. You die. Fortunately, there's a loophole."
Billy Graham (born 1918)

The loophole Billy is referring to is the *Good News* — Jesus Christ died for all your sins, and was resurrected to guarantee your eternal life in a home called Heaven: all yours just by accepting the loophole.

The Scriptures tell us there is no sin, evil, tears, pain, or sorrow in Heaven.

> *This is what the Lord says: "Heaven is my throne, and the earth is my footstool. Could you build me a temple as good as that? Could you build me such a resting place? My hands have made both heaven and earth; they and everything in them are mine. I, the Lord, have spoken!"* Isaiah 66:1

> *"He will wipe every tear from their eyes, and there will be no more death or sorrow or crying or pain. All these things are gone forever."* Revelation 21:4

The word *Heaven* is used almost 300 times in the New Testament. It is beyond the region of the air, clouds, planets, and stars. It is called the *third Heaven* because it is above the visible heavens.

Paradise — the original *sort-of* Heaven

The Bible informs us that Heaven began in the center of the Earth, but was moved following Jesus' death, and will be moved again following the Millennium.

The first, *Paradise* or *Abraham's Bosom*, was located in the center of the Earth from the beginning of time (although time has no beginning), and is where Jesus went immediately following his death. Paradise was where the righteous people went prior to Jesus' death. ***Until the death of Jesus, there was no absolute forgiveness of sin.***

Until Jesus' death, Satan had the keys to death and Hell, so everyone went into the center of the Earth, where the wicked were tormented but the righteous were protected from pain or suffering. There was a great gap between the two.

After Jesus died, he went to the center of the Earth, took the keys of death and Hell from Satan, and brought out the righteous. ***The Old Testament saints were saved from eternal damnation based on their faith in the coming Messiah!***

> *Then Jesus shouted out again, and he released his spirit. At that moment the curtain in the sanctuary of the Temple was torn in two, from top to bottom. The earth shook, rocks split apart, and tombs opened. The bodies of many godly men and women who had died were raised from the dead.* Matthew 27:50-52

Many people incorrectly believe Jesus went to the center of the Earth to preach to those who were in Hell. Jesus did not preach to those in Hell who were being tormented, because for them it was too late. Their fate and future was sealed. It was the saints being held prisoner to whom Jesus preached. Jesus gives us insight into this in Luke 16:19-26:

> *Jesus said, "There was a certain rich man who was splendidly clothed in purple and fine linen and who lived each day in luxury. At his gate lay a poor man named Lazarus who was covered with sores. As Lazarus lay there longing for scraps from the rich man's table, the dogs would come and lick his open sores.*
>
> *"Finally, the poor man died and was carried by the angels to be with Abraham. The rich man also died and was buried, and his soul went to the place of the dead. There, in torment, he saw Abraham in the far distance with Lazarus at his side.*
>
> *"The rich man shouted, 'Father Abraham, have some pity! Send Lazarus over here to dip the tip of his finger in water and cool my tongue. I am in anguish in these flames.'*
>
> *"But Abraham said to him, 'Son, remember that during your lifetime you had everything you wanted, and Lazarus had nothing. So now he is here being comforted, and you are in anguish. And besides, there is a great chasm separating us. No one can cross over to you from here, and no one can cross over to us from there.'"*

The *now Heaven*

It is only when Jesus gave his life for us on the Cross that the *now Heaven* became the home for Christians (saints). This is the temporary home for all living saints who die before the Millennium.

> *Yes, we are fully confident, and we would rather be away from these earthly bodies, for then we will be at home with the Lord.* 2 Corinthians 5:8

If you are a Christian (saint), upon death you would ascend to the *now Heaven* immediately. This is what theologians consider an intermediate Heaven. It is a transitional period and place between our past lives on earth and our future resurrection to eternity on the *New Earth* (the New Jerusalem). ***Please do not confuse this transitional period with the false doctrine of Purgatory!***

NOTE: The definition of *Purgatory* in the *Roman Catholic Encyclopedia* is: *A place or condition of temporal punishment for those who, departing this life in God's grace, are, not entirely free from venial faults, or have not fully paid the satisfaction due to their transgressions.*

I SAY NONSENSE!

The concept of a place where the dead are imprisoned for cleansing originates from before Christ, when many people would pray to the gods for those who had died. Not only is this continued today in Catholicism, but it is also done in Mormonism and Judaism.

Purgatory may sound fair, except for one thing: Jesus Christ died for all the sins of all mankind on the Cross! He took all the punishment we deserve. Stating that there is something we must do to pay for our transgressions is blasphemy. The belief in a place, or condition, in which a dead Christian must be *cleaned-up* is not biblical. Claiming that a Christian must suffer for sins after death is contrary to everything the Bible says about salvation.

Any religion that claims to be Christian, yet teaches cleansing following death, completely misunderstands the totality and finality of Christ's death. Furthermore, any Christian belief system that teaches anything must be done either while here on Earth or after one's death does not understand that Christ died for all people and all sin.

In that *now Heaven*, we will await the time of Christ's second coming.

The following is a sketch of what most scholars consider the structure of the physical world, whose outer layer is the location of this Heaven.

> ➤ The lower sea of physical waters (our seas and oceans)
> ➤ The first heaven (the atmosphere)
> ➤ The second heaven (outer space)
> ➤ The sea of separation
> ➤ The third Heaven (*now Heaven*)

The third Heaven is the paradise to which Paul was referring in 2 Corinthians, Chapter 12, verses 2-5:

I was caught up to the third heaven fourteen years ago. Whether I was in my body or out of my body, I don't know—only God knows. Yes, only God knows whether I was in my body or outside my body. But I do know that I was caught up to paradise and heard things so astounding that they cannot be expressed in words, things no human is allowed to tell.

That experience is worth boasting about, but I'm not going to do it. I will boast only about my weaknesses.

The Bible is much more explicit about the permanent Heaven than it is regarding this intermediate one.

The New Earth (New Jerusalem) is yet to come

Most people do not understand what the *New Earth* (the permanent Heaven) will be like. The New Earth is where we saints will live following end times.

Following end-time events, the existing heavens and Earth will be destroyed. There will be a new eternal dwelling place created for only those who accepted Jesus as Savior. The *now Heaven*, Earth, and seas will be destroyed by fire.

Then I saw a new heaven and a new earth, for the old heaven and the old earth had disappeared. And the sea was also gone. And I saw the holy city, the new Jerusalem, coming down from God out of heaven like a bride beautifully dressed for her husband. Revelation 21:1-2

The eternal dwelling place of believers (those saved) will be the New Earth — the Heaven on which we will spend eternity. It is where the *New Jerusalem*, a city with pearly gates and streets lined with gold, will be located. God will wipe away every tear from our eyes. Imagine — no more death, mourning, sickness, or pain.

I heard a loud shout from the throne, saying, "Look, God's home is now among his people! He will live with them, and they will be his people. God himself will be with them. He will wipe every tear from their eyes, and there will be no more death or sorrow or crying or pain. All these things are gone forever." Revelation 21:3-4

The city wall will be broad and high, having 12 gates, each guarded by an angel. The names of the 12 tribes of Israel will be written on the gates.

> *The city wall was broad and high, with twelve gates guarded by twelve an-*
> *gels. And the names of the twelve tribes of Israel were written on the gates.*
> Revelation 21:12

This new city will be filled with God's redeemed children. There will be no sun and no moon. Jesus (the Lamb) will be its temple and its light.

> *I saw no temple in the city, for the Lord God Almighty and the Lamb are its*
> *temple. And the city has no need of sun or moon, for the glory of God illumi-*
> *nates the city, and the Lamb is its light.* Revelation 21:22-23

The New Earth (Heaven) is a physical place where those saved from eternal damnation will reside eternally with glorified physical bodies.

> *"Look! I am creating new heavens and a new earth,*
> *and no one will even think about the old ones anymore.*
> *Be glad; rejoice forever in my creation!*
> *And look! I will create Jerusalem as a place of happiness.*
> *Her people will be a source of joy.*
> *I will rejoice over Jerusalem*
> *and delight in my people.*
> *And the sound of weeping and crying*
> *will be heard in it no more.*
> *No longer will babies die when only a few days old.*
> *No longer will adults die before they have lived a full life.*
> *No longer will people be considered old at 100!*
> *Only the cursed will die that young!*
> *In those days people will live in the houses they build*
> *and eat the fruit of their own vineyards.*
> *Unlike the past, invaders will not take their houses*
> *and confiscate their vineyards.*
> *For my people will live as long as trees,*
> *and my chosen ones will have time to enjoy their hard-won gains.*
> *They will not work in vain,*
> *and their children will not be doomed to misfortune.*
> *For they are people blessed by the LORD,*
> *and their children, too, will be blessed.*
> *I will answer them before they even call to me.*
> *While they are still talking about their needs,*
> *I will go ahead and answer their prayers!*

The wolf and the lamb will feed together.
  The lion will eat hay like a cow.
  But the snakes will eat dust.
In those days no one will be hurt or destroyed on my holy mountain.
  I, the LORD, have spoken!" Isaiah 65:17-25

But someone may ask, "How will the dead be raised? What kind of bodies will they have?" What a foolish question! When you put a seed into the ground, it doesn't grow into a plant unless it dies first. And what you put in the ground is not the plant that will grow, but only a bare seed of wheat or whatever you are planting. Then God gives it the new body he wants it to have. A different plant grows from each kind of seed. Similarly there are different kinds of flesh—one kind for humans, another for animals, another for birds, and another for fish.

There are also bodies in the heavens and bodies on the earth. The glory of the heavenly bodies is different from the glory of the earthly bodies. The sun has one kind of glory, while the moon and stars each have another kind. And even the stars differ from each other in their glory.

It is the same way with the resurrection of the dead. Our earthly bodies are planted in the ground when we die, but they will be raised to live forever. Our bodies are buried in brokenness, but they will be raised in glory. They are buried in weakness, but they will be raised in strength. They are buried as natural human bodies, but they will be raised as spiritual bodies. For just as there are natural bodies, there are also spiritual bodies.

The Scriptures tell us, "The first man, Adam, became a living person." But the last Adam—that is, Christ—is a life-giving Spirit. What comes first is the natural body, then the spiritual body comes later. Adam, the first man, was made from the dust of the earth, while Christ, the second man, came from heaven. Earthly people are like the earthly man, and heavenly people are like the heavenly man. Just as we are now like the earthly man, we will someday be like the heavenly man.

What I am saying, dear brothers and sisters, is that our physical bodies cannot inherit the Kingdom of God. These dying bodies cannot inherit what will last forever.

But let me reveal to you a wonderful secret. We will not all die, but we will all be transformed! It will happen in a moment, in the blink of an eye, when

the last trumpet is blown. For when the trumpet sounds, those who have died will be raised to live forever. And we who are living will also be transformed. For our dying bodies must be transformed into bodies that will never die; our mortal bodies must be transformed into immortal bodies.
1 Corinthians 15:35-53

Abraham was confidently looking forward to a city with eternal foundations, a city designed and built by God. Hebrews 11:10

But they were looking for a better place, a heavenly homeland. That is why God is not ashamed to be called their God, for he has prepared a city for them. Hebrews 11:16

No, you have come to Mount Zion, to the city of the living God, the heavenly Jerusalem, and to countless thousands of angels in a joyful gathering. You have come to the assembly of God's firstborn children, whose names are written in heaven. You have come to God himself, who is the judge over all things. You have come to the spirits of the righteous ones in heaven who have now been made perfect. You have come to Jesus, the one who mediates the new covenant between God and people, and to the sprinkled blood, which speaks of forgiveness instead of crying out for vengeance like the blood of Abel. Hebrews 12:22-24

For this world is not our permanent home; we are looking forward to a home yet to come. Hebrews 13:14

Since everything around us is going to be destroyed like this, what holy and godly lives you should live, looking forward to the day of God and hurrying it along. On that day, he will set the heavens on fire, and the elements will melt away in the flames. But we are looking forward to the new heavens and new earth he has promised, a world filled with God's righteousness.
2 Peter 3:11-13

Outside the walls

Its gates will never be closed at the end of day because there is no night there. And all the nations will bring their glory and honor into the city. Nothing evil will be allowed to enter, nor anyone who practices shameful idolatry and dishonesty—but only those whose names are written in the Lamb's Book of Life. Revelation 22:25-27

When the New Earth is created, it will be too late for those who rejected Jesus as Savior to be redeemed.

> *"But many Israelites—those for whom the Kingdom was prepared—will be thrown into outer darkness, where there will be weeping and gnashing of teeth."* Matthew 8:12, Jesus' words

> *"Then death and the grave were thrown into the lake of fire. This lake of fire is the second death. And anyone whose name was not found recorded in the Book of Life was thrown into the lake of fire."* Revelation 22:14-15, Jesus' words

Where will you spend eternity?

> *He will judge everyone according to what they have done.* Romans 2:6

> *"All who are victorious will be clothed in white. I will never erase their names from the Book of Life, but I will announce before my Father and his angels that they are mine."* Revelation 3:5, Jesus' words

"Clothed in white" means to be set apart for God — made pure by the Blood of Jesus. The names of those who have been washed in Jesus' Blood are recorded in the *Lamb's Book of Life.* Will yours be there?

> *God saved you by his grace when you believed. And you can't take credit for this; it is a gift from God. Salvation is not a reward for the good things we have done, so none of us can boast about it.* Ephesians 2:8-9

Eternal life with Jesus is a gift. Accept it!

Notes:

Chapter 5

Free Will versus Predestination

Hey Christians, have you ever wondered why you accepted Jesus Christ as Savior, but a loved one who you want desperately to be saved absolutely refuses? No matter how hard you try, you cannot convince him or her the need to know Jesus. If this leaves you scratching your head, you should become familiar with the differences between *Free Will Theology* (Arminianism) and *Predestination Theology* (Calvinism).

Free Will Theology and Predestination Theology are the two major Christian schools of thought regarding man's ability, or lack thereof, to accept Jesus as Savior. Most people are familiar with the term *free will*, but *predestination*, when used in association with salvation, is unfamiliar to the non-student. Although predestination is unfamiliar to many in Christendom, there are many who embrace this doctrine. A brief explanation of both are, as follows:

Free Will Theology teaches that an individual has the ability to make decisions without God's intervention. Free Will is fairly simple to understand because it seems logical on the surface, but it becomes theologically complicated when studied. I do not have the time or inclination to exegete this doctrine, but I encourage you to educate yourself.

Predestination Theology is slightly more complicated because it teaches that, in eternity past, God chose who he wanted in Heaven. Consequently, the individual has no choice in the matter. Wow, could that be true? Those who embrace Predestination believe that because of humankind's sin, a person will never seek God by his or her own volition, so God chooses those he wants. They believe God's grace is so irresistible that those lucky ones he chooses cannot refuse (referred to as *irresistible grace*). Predestination asserts that no matter how hard you try to convince someone of the need for Jesus' free gift, if that person was not individually selected by God, he or she will go to Hell (the average person cannot fathom that action from a loving God). Many Baptists, Presbyterians, Reformed, and other churches are in this group.

Arminians do not all agree with each other, nor do Calvinists all agree with each other. There are variations in each camp.

The problem with Calvinism

Most Calvinists believe in eternal security (once saved — always saved), but **there is a caveat**: Calvinists believe good works <u>must accompany</u> salvation as evidence of the person's relationship with Jesus. If good works are not present, the person is not saved. This adds works to grace, which is not biblical.

> *And if by grace, then is it no more of works: otherwise grace is no more grace. But if it be of works, then it is no more grace: otherwise work is no more work.* Romans 11:6 (KJV)

This good works stance is referred to as *Lordship Salvation.* This legalistic policy contradicts multiple Bible passages that emphasize salvation as a gift. The entire Bible, from Genesis through Revelation, proves salvation is by grace through faith.

> *God saved you by his grace when you believed. And you can't take credit for this; it is a gift from God. Salvation is not a reward for the good things we have done, so none of us can boast about it.* Ephesians 2:8-9

I believe Calvinists are communally judgmental, which is contrary to Jesus' advice.

> *"Do not judge others, and you will not be judged. For you will be treated as you treat others. The standard you use in judging is the standard by which you will be judged.*
>
> *"And why worry about a speck in your friend's eye when you have a log in your own? How can you think of saying to your friend, 'Let me help you get rid of that speck in your eye,' when you can't see past the log in your own eye? Hypocrite! First get rid of the log in your own eye; then you will see well enough to deal with the speck in your friend's eye."* Matthew 7:1-5, Jesus' words

Certainly, the Bible states that when we are born again we will change, but because everyone's circumstances are different, the Holy Spirit will convict each of us according to the Spirit's timing.

Prominent Calvinist John MacArthur, who pastors a mega-church, is also host of a nationwide radio program and president of a Bible college. I recently read the book *Secure and Sure* by Robert N. Wilkin, in which MacArthur is quoted as saying (page 34), "So to say that you could reach a point that you are one hundred percent sure of your salvation permanently would be very difficult to deal with scripturally." Whoa, I say! You are wrong, MacArthur.

Jesus didn't die on the Cross so we could be unsure. Doubt belittles his finished work. It is not what we do for Jesus that saves us — it is what he did for us.

The Bible states *you may know* you have eternal life. I emphasized the words *you may know* in the following verse.

> *I have written this to you who believe in the name of the Son of God, so that **you may know** you have eternal life.* 1 John 5:13

Shame on you who do not evangelize truth!

The problem with Arminianism

Most Arminians embrace the notion that a saved person can walk away from salvation because he or she has free will, or that salvation can be lost if a person continues to lead a sinful life after being saved. Whoa again, I say!

Christians do not have the free will to walk away from salvation, or become unborn. If one studies the entire Word of God, he or she will agree it is crystal clear that a Christian cannot walk away from being saved. Once saved — always saved! That is a fact.

The Holy Spirit does not come and go, come and go, come and go. **That is silly theology!**

When we are saved, we are given eternal life — not *temporary* eternal life. Christians cannot walk away, nor can they be snatched by Satan (humans belong to either Jesus or Satan).

I have emphasized *No one can snatch them away from me* and *sealed with the promised Holy Spirit* in the passages below.

> *I give them eternal life, and they will never perish. **No one can snatch them away from me**, for my Father has given them to me, and he is more powerful than anyone else. No one can snatch them from the Father's hand.* John 10:28-29, Jesus' words

> *In him you also, when you heard the word of truth, the gospel of your salvation, and believed in him, were* __*sealed with the promised Holy Spirit*__*, who is the guarantee of our inheritance until we acquire possession of it, to the praise of his glory.* Ephesians 1:13-14 (ESV)

In summary, Calvinists believe salvation cannot be lost if one is truly saved, but nobody knows for sure if he or she is truly saved. Arminians believe that salvation can be professed and lost many times, as proven by one's Christian behavior, which results in one never being 100 percent sure if he or she is saved.

Both Arminianism and Calvinism require works, which is not biblical.

Prevenient grace

The Christian theological concept of *prevenient grace* affirms that *divine grace* precedes a person's decision to accept or reject Jesus Christ as Savior. In other words, Jesus' Spirit precedes and inspires his or her decision.

Prevenient grace is embraced by both Arminian and Calvinist Christians; however, the Arminians believe it only assists, but does not guarantee, personal acceptance of the gift of salvation. Calvinists believe the Holy Spirit cannot be resisted (aka *Irresistible Grace*) by the person Jesus chooses to save.

I have talked with thousands of born-again believers, and about 99 percent believe the Holy Spirit sought them, meaning they had no choice in their acceptance of Jesus as Savior. I am a strong proponent of prevenient grace.

Me

Many Bible verses seem to support both *free will* and *predestination*. For several years I vigorously scrutinized all pertinent Bible passages, studied the opinions of scholars, contemplated, and prayed for enlightenment regarding which is correct. I lean toward *predestination*, but unlike many of those Calvinists who support *predestination*, I do not believe one must always demonstrate faith by works.

Chapter 6

God, Jesus, and the Holy Spirit

The triune nature of God

The Christian faith is built on the fundamental belief in one God who has revealed himself in three natures: Father (God), Son (Jesus), and Holy Spirit. These three natures are referred to as the *triune nature of God* (the Trinity).

The triune nature of God means three-in-one. All three have the same nature, power, and authority. The Bible teaches that the Father is God, Jesus is God, and the Holy Spirit is God.

The traditional sequence of the Father mentioned first, the Son second, and the Holy Spirit third does not indicate subordination within the Trinity. For example, because the Father sent the Son, it does not mean the Son is not equal to the Father in essence or divinity. This is also true regarding the Holy Spirit. <u>The order of the names does not mean each is not equal or equally divine.</u> Therefore, it would be appropriate to say Holy Spirit, Son, and God.

It is improbable that mortals can unequivocally understand, or explain, God's three-in-one nature. Because God is infinitely grander than humans, we cannot expect to be able to comprehend his complete nature.

God

Throughout the world most folks believe in *a god*. Most religions believe in a god or multiple gods (folks who believe in multiple gods are called *pluralists*). Many folks invent their own god to fit their liking. The term *god* is probably verbalized millions of times daily throughout the world, both in praise or in a curse word.

As a Christian, I capitalize *God* because I believe the God of Abraham, Isaac, and Jacob (Israelites) is the Creator of all that exists. He is the God of the Old and New

Testament Bibles. His human name was Jesus. Those who accept him as Savior are called *Christians*.

Doubting is normal

Do not beat yourself up for doubting. Most people have doubts about God from time to time, but faith is a leap of acceptance without facts.

Faith

Faith is the confidence that what we hope for will actually happen; it gives us assurance about things we cannot see.

> *By faith we understand that the entire universe was formed at God's command, that what we now see did not come from anything that can be seen.*
> Hebrews 11:1-3

You don't have to like God to be saved

> *Jesus replied, "'You must love the Lord your God with all your heart, all your soul, and all your mind.' This is the first and greatest commandment. A second is equally important: 'Love your neighbor as yourself.'"*
> Matthew 22:37-39

You may be wondering why I would say a person does not have to like God to be saved, when Jesus said we must love him. ***Jesus commanded us to love God, but he didn't say that our salvation was contingent on it. The Bible says we are saved by believing – not by loving.***

As a Christian evangelist for more than 30 years, I have talked with thousands of unsaved people. Many reject the God of the Bible because they cannot fathom a loving God who allows the bad things that happen on Earth. Also, they cannot embrace the biblical God who allows people to go to Hell.

As a "man" in horrific pain, when dying on a cross, Jesus cried out to God, asking why God had forsaken him.

> *"And about the ninth hour Jesus cried with a loud voice, saying, Eli, Eli, lama sabachthani? which means My God, my God, why hast thou forsaken me?"*
> Matthew 27:46, Jesus words

Many times, I have cried out to God asking why he allowed something bad to happen to me, yet I remain saved. The Bible continuously repeats I am saved by my *belief* — not by my love. I love God, but I don't always love his methods because I am a dimwitted human.

Although you may not be pleased with everything God does, and although God may not be pleased with everything you do, he loves you so much that he came to Earth in the form of a baby named Jesus, who grew into a man to die a humiliating death on the Cross, so all your sins would never be remembered. <u>You think about that!</u>

God loves the imperfect

If you believe you are not worthy of God's love, you are right. Yet he loves you anyway. Many people unfamiliar with the Bible believe the pages are filled with the stories of saintly people, thus studying the Bible would cause them terrible feelings about their carnal flaws. Wrong!

The Bible exposes stories of everyday flawed people like you and me. Many of God's favorites were very imperfect, but <u>he loved them for their faith</u>. The more faith they had, the more he appreciated them. Following are examples of very flawed people who God treasured dearly, and used to advance his Kingdom:

> ➤ Abraham sacrificed Sarah's safety to save his own neck.
> ➤ David, although Godly, had an adulterous affair and was a murderer.
> ➤ Jacob was cunning and deceptive.
> ➤ Moses was a murderer.
> ➤ Noah got drunk.
> ➤ Peter denied Jesus three times and periodically lost his faith.
> ➤ Rahab was a prostitute.
> ➤ Samson was a womanizer.
> ➤ Thomas was a doubter.
> ➤ Paul struggled with sin.

Each of these had two distinct commonalities: Each was very imperfect; and each had *faith in God*.

Instead of hiding weaknesses of God's chosen servants, the Bible records them faithfully to reveal there are no perfect humans on Earth. This certainly does not imply

God approves of sinful behavior, but it does prove God loves and uses imperfect, faithful people. ***The lesson here is that every saint has a past and every sinner has a future.*** You may not be as unworthy as you think.

Jesus

ONE SOLITARY LIFE

By Dr. James Allen Francis (1864-1928)

Here is a young man who was born in an obscure village, the child of a peasant woman. He grew up in another village. He worked in a carpenter shop. He was thirty, and then for three years he was an itinerant preacher. He never wrote a book. He never held an office. He never owned a home. He never had a family. He never went to college. He never put his foot inside a big city. He never traveled 200 miles from the place where he was born. He never did one of the things that usually accompany greatness. He had no credentials but himself. While he was still a young man the tide of public opinion turned against him. His friends ran away. He was turned over to his enemies. He went through the mockery of a trial. He was nailed to a cross between two thieves. While he was dying, his executioners gambled for the only piece of property he had on earth, and that was his coat...when he was dead he was laid in a borrowed grave through the pity of a friend. Nineteen centuries wide have come and gone, and today he is the central figure of the human race and the leader of the column of progress. I am far within the mark when I say that all the armies that ever marched, and all the navies that ever sailed, and all the parliaments that ever sat, and all the kings that ever reigned, put together, have not affected the life of man upon this earth as has that One Solitary Life.

Jesus is the focal point of the entire Bible, beginning with the Book of Genesis and ending in Revelation. He appears in every Book.

In Genesis, Jesus was God

In the beginning God created the heavens and the earth. Genesis 1:1

In eternity past God knew Adam would fall, so his plan was to reveal himself as a man named Jesus, who would be born specifically to die for the redemption of all who would trust in his mission.

In Revelation, Jesus is the coming King

> *Then I saw heaven opened, and a white horse was standing there. Its rider was named Faithful and True, for he judges fairly and wages a righteous war. His eyes were like flames of fire, and on his head were many crowns. A name was written on him that no one understood except himself. He wore a robe dipped in blood, and his title was the Word of God. The armies of heaven, dressed in the finest of pure white linen, followed him on white horses. From his mouth came a sharp sword to strike down the nations. He will rule them with an iron rod. He will release the fierce wrath of God, the Almighty, like juice flowing from a winepress. On his robe at his thigh was written this title: King of all kings and Lord of all lords.* Revelation 19:11-16

Jesus was God incarnate

No theologian, scholar, historian, or other knowledgeable person questions the fact that Jesus existed. Atheists, Agnostics, Jews, Muslims, and most other religions recognize Jesus as a true historical figure. The disagreement among beliefs involves Jesus' divinity.

Billions of people believe Jesus was God in the flesh (divine). Contemporary scholars, who endorse the Bible as authoritative, accept the belief that through the power of the Holy Spirit, God became incarnate, was born from the Virgin Mary, died on the Cross for the forgiveness of mankind's sin, and rose from being dead so believers may have eternal life with him in the place he has prepared only for Christians.

✓ Jesus was God incarnate.
✓ He performed multiple miracles, including raising the dead.
✓ Many people witnessed his miracles.
✓ He rose from being dead.
✓ Many people saw him alive and well after he had died.
✓ He said I could go to Heaven just by trusting in his finished work on the Cross.
✓ When I prayed to accept him as my Savior, the Holy Spirit came to live in me.

In the beginning the Word already existed. The Word was with God, and the Word was God. He existed in the beginning with God. God created everything through him, and nothing was created except through him. John 1:1-3

Jesus told him, "I am the way, the truth, and the life. No one can come to the Father except through me. If you had really known me, you would know who my Father is. From now on, you do know him and have seen him!" John 14:6-7

Though he was God,
  he did not think of equality with God
  as something to cling to.
Instead, he gave up his divine privileges;
  he took the humble position of a slave
  and was born as a human being.
When he appeared in human form,
  he humbled himself in obedience to God
  and died a criminal's death on a cross. Philippians 2:6-8

Christ is the visible image of the invisible God.
  He existed before anything was created and is supreme over all creation,
for through him God created everything
  in the heavenly realms and on Earth.
He made the things we can see
  and the things we can't see —
such as thrones, kingdoms, rulers, and authorities in the unseen world.
  Everything was created through him and for him.
He existed before anything else,
  and he holds all creation together. Colossians 1:15-17

And now in these final days, he has spoken to us through his Son. God promised everything to the Son as an inheritance, and through the Son he created the universe. Hebrews 1:2

Because God's children are human beings — made of flesh and blood — the Son also became flesh and blood. For only as a human being could he die, and only by dying could he break the power of the Devil, who had the power of death. Hebrews 2:14

Jesus has two natures as both God and man simultaneously

Jesus' nature as both God and man can be a stumbling block for many; however, once it is accepted based strictly on faith, and not comprehension, it will be understood as the Christian is enlightened by the Holy Spirit.

When Jesus was dying on the Cross, it was the sacrificial man who died. When he arose from being dead, it was his divine nature that allowed him to overcome death.

Hypostasis means "that which lies beneath as basis or foundation." In Christianity, hypostasis is used to describe the reality of the two distinct natures that co-existed in Jesus, as both God and man. Jesus was 100 percent man and 100 percent God simultaneously. Misinformed individuals think of him as half God and half man.

Once Christians know Jesus personally, they comprehend and appreciate his dual nature.

> *But people who aren't spiritual can't receive these truths from God's Spirit. It all sounds foolish to them and they can't understand it, for only those who are spiritual can understand what the Spirit means.* 1 Corinthians 2:14

Jesus performed multiple miracles

> *Everyone tried to touch him, because healing power went out from him, and he healed everyone.* Luke 6:19

> *The disciples saw Jesus do many other miraculous signs in addition to the ones recorded in this book. But these are written so that you may continue to believe that Jesus is the Messiah, the Son of God, and that by believing in him you will have life by the power of his name.* John 20:30-31

Jesus rose from death — witnessed by hundreds

> *After Jesus rose from the dead early on Sunday morning, the first person who saw him was Mary Magdalene, the woman from whom he had cast out seven demons. She went to the disciples, who were grieving and weeping, and told them what had happened. But when she told them that Jesus was alive and she had seen him, they didn't believe her.*

Afterward he appeared in a different form to two of his followers who were walking from Jerusalem into the country. They rushed back to tell the others, but no one believed them.

Still later he appeared to the eleven disciples as they were eating together. He rebuked them for their stubborn unbelief because they refused to believe those who had seen him after he had been raised from the dead. Mark 16:9-14

I passed on to you what was most important and what had also been passed on to me. Christ died for our sins, just as the Scriptures said. He was buried, and he was raised from the dead on the third day, just as the Scriptures said. He was seen by Peter and then by the Twelve. After that, he was seen by more than 500 of his followers at one time, most of whom are still alive, though some have died. 1 Corinthians 15:3-6

He said I could go to Heaven just by believing in him

"For God loved the world so much that he gave his one and only Son, so that everyone who believes in him will not perish but have eternal life. God sent his Son into the world not to judge the world, but to save the world through him." John 3:16-17, Jesus' words

He said if I don't believe in him I won't go to Heaven

"But everyone who denies me here on earth, I will also deny before my Father in heaven." Matthew 10:33, Jesus' words

"The world's sin is that it refuses to believe in me." John 16:9, Jesus' words

I prayed to accept him, and the Holy Spirit came to live in me

And now you Gentiles have also heard the truth, the Good News that God saves you. And when you believed in Christ, he identified you as his own by giving you the Holy Spirit, whom he promised long ago. The Spirit is God's guarantee that he will give us the inheritance he promised and that he has purchased us to be his own people. He did this so we would praise and glorify him. Ephesians 1:13-14

The Spirit of God, who raised Jesus from the dead, lives in you. And just as God raised Christ Jesus from the dead, he will give life to your mortal bodies by this same Spirit living within you. Romans 8:11

Jesus divides families

Although faith in Jesus Christ provides Christians with peace on Earth and eternal life in God's eternal dwelling place, one's faith may cause strains on friendships and within families. However, <u>Jesus is very bold, stating that we must choose him</u>.

NOTE: When Jesus used "sword" in the following passage, it is not to be taken literally, but as a symbol for disagreement rather than violence. He was not advocating that family members feud, but if it comes to choosing him or family members, *he demands we choose him regardless of the effect on our human relationships*.

> *"Don't imagine that I came to bring peace to the earth! I came not to bring peace, but a sword.*
>
> *'I have come to set a man against his father,*
>   *a daughter against her mother,*
> *and a daughter-in-law against her mother-in-law.*
>   *Your enemies will be right in your own household!'*
>
> *"If you love your father or mother more than you love me, you are not worthy of being mine; or if you love your son or daughter more than me, you are not worthy of being mine. If you refuse to take up your cross and follow me, you are not worthy of being mine. If you cling to your life, you will lose it; but if you give up your life for me, you will find it."* Matthew 10:34-39, Jesus' words

At the time Jesus made this proclamation, he knew there would be conflict between Jews who would accept him as Messiah, and their family members who would not. Although Jesus made this statement primarily to Jews, the same problem exists today within Jewish, Gentile, Muslim, Atheist, and other families in which one person accepts Jesus as their personal Savior and others refuse. **When a person becomes a Christian, it can strain relationships because those who are unsaved do not understand living in the Spirit.**

> *But people who aren't spiritual can't receive these truths from God's Spirit. It all sounds foolish to them and they can't understand it, for only those who are spiritual can understand what the Spirit means. Those who are spiritual can evaluate all things, but they themselves cannot be evaluated by others. For,*
>
> > *"Who can know the LORD's thoughts?*
> > *Who knows enough to teach him?"*

But we understand these things, for we have the mind of Christ. 1
Corinthians 2:14-16

Many non-Christians become angry with us, argue, hurt, and mock us.

*"What blessings await you when people hate you and exclude you and mock
you and curse you as evil because you follow the Son of Man. When that
happens, be happy! Yes, leap for joy! For a great reward awaits you in heaven.
And remember, their ancestors treated the ancient prophets that same way."*
Luke 6:22-24, Jesus' words

Although this is unpleasant, the eternal rewards are worth it. When you are ostra-
cized and are tempted to pay back in kind, remember that the Apostle Paul tells us
we must attempt to live peaceably with all men.

*Never pay back evil with more evil. Do things in such a way that everyone
can see you are honorable. Do all that you can to live in peace with everyone.*
Romans 12:17-18

Following Jesus may cause you to generate enemies, but it can also provide you with
the opportunity to be a light for those living in darkness.

Jesus is freedom from religion

All major world belief systems except Christianity involve good behavior to receive
God's favor for eternal life. Unlike the others, Christianity demands nothing more
than faith, although good behavior is desirable and reaps rewards.

Faith without fanaticism

Would-be Christians are often afraid to make the commitment because they fear
they might become extremely zealous — as do some Christians. Many people refer
to me as a "religious fanatic," but I refer to myself as a "freedom from religion fanatic," because it is Jesus' freedom from religion that I evangelize. It was the religious
folks who insisted on Jesus' crucifixion.

Chances are you will not become a fanatic, but even if you do — so what? Quit wor-
rying about what other people think! ***Boldly representing the Creator of all that
exists is cool.***

> **"God proved His love on the Cross. When Christ hung, and bled, and died, it was God saying to the world, 'I love you.'" Billy Graham**

The Holy Spirit

Tragically, the Holy Spirit is not studied or discussed in many Christian churches

This exclusion prevents many Christians from accurately understanding the indwelling of the Holy Spirit who characterizes a person as Christian.

> *But you are not controlled by your sinful nature. You are controlled by the Spirit if you have the Spirit of God living in you. (And remember that those who do not have the Spirit of Christ living in them do not belong to him at all.)* Romans 8:9

The Apostle Paul's statement above makes it clear that *a person must have the Holy Spirit living in them to be considered a Christian*. Without the indwelling of the Holy Spirit, a person may be Christian in name only. Millions believe they are Christians but, probably because of faulty teaching, they lack the indwelling of Jesus' Spirit.

If the Spirit of Jesus is absent from a person, while he or she may attend church regularly, sing in the choir, offer money generously to the church, celebrate Christmas and Easter — they are not a Christian.

The Holy Spirit is on equal level with God

The Holy Spirit as God is clearly seen in many Scriptures.

> *I can never escape from your Spirit!*
> *I can never get away from your presence!*
> *If I go up to heaven, you are there;*
> *if I go down to the grave, you are there.* Psalm 139:7-8

The passage above reveals the Holy Spirit as all-seeing, all-powerful, and omnipresent. God's gift is allowing us to know him via his Spirit.

> *Then Peter said, "Ananias, why have you let Satan fill your heart? You lied to the Holy Spirit, and you kept some of the money for yourself. The property was yours to sell or not sell, as you wished. And after selling it, the money was also yours to give away. How could you do a thing like this? You weren't lying to us but to God!" Acts 5:3-4*

In the passage above, Peter confronts Ananias about why he lied to the Holy Spirit, and tells him *he had not lied to men, but to God.* It is a perfect affirmation that lying to the Holy Spirit is lying to God.

God's deep secrets are revealed to us by his Spirit.

> *But it was to us that God revealed these things by his Spirit. For his Spirit searches out everything and shows us God's deep secrets. No one can know a person's thoughts except that person's own spirit and no one can know God's thoughts except God's own Spirit. 1 Corinthians 2:10-11*

Scripture refers to the Holy Spirit as a person

> *The Spirit of God, who raised Jesus from the dead, lives in you. And just as God raised Christ Jesus from the dead, he will give life to your mortal bodies by this same Spirit living within you. Romans 8:11*

The Holy Spirit grieves

> *But they rebelled against him*
> *   and grieved his Holy Spirit.*
> *So he became their enemy*
> *   and fought against them. Isaiah 63:10*

> *And do not bring sorrow to God's Holy Spirit by the way you live. Remember, he has identified you as his own, guaranteeing that you will be saved on the day of redemption. Ephesians 4:30*

The Holy Spirit loves

> *Dear brothers and sisters, I urge you in the name of our Lord Jesus Christ to join in my struggle by praying to God for me. Do this because of your love for me, given to you by the Holy Spirit. Romans 15:30*

The Holy Spirit has a mind

And the Father who knows all hearts knows what the Spirit is saying, for the Spirit pleads for us believers in harmony with God's own will. Romans 8:27

The Holy Spirit speaks

The Holy Spirit said to Philip, "Go over and walk along beside the carriage." Acts 8:29

One day as these men were worshiping the Lord and fasting, the Holy Spirit said, "Dedicate Barnabas and Saul for the special work to which I have called them." Acts 13:2

The Holy Spirit is the conduit that connects Christians to Jesus

When becoming a Christian, a person needs no intermediary between himself or herself and God. No priest, minister, rabbi, or anyone is needed as a go-between. These professions are essential for educational purposes, but no human is needed as a negotiator in interaction with God. Praying to Mary, or to a saint, is absurd!

People who are not Christians don't understand the Spirit, his power, or his influence.

But people who aren't spiritual can't receive these truths from God's Spirit. It all sounds foolish to them and they can't understand it, for only those who are spiritual can understand what the Spirit means. Those who are spiritual can evaluate all things, but they themselves cannot be evaluated by others. For,

> *"Who can know the LORD's thoughts?*
> *Who knows enough to teach him?"*

But we understand these things, for we have the mind of Christ. 1 Corinthians 2:14-16

After the crucifixion, but before Jesus ascended to Heaven, he promised his followers the Father would send a helper. God honored this on the day of Pentecost, when the Holy Spirit became God's power on Earth. The following are the words of Jesus:

> *"But now I am going away to the One who sent me, and not one of you is asking where I am going. Instead, you grieve because of what I've told you. But in fact, it is best for you that I go away, because if I don't, the Advocate won't come. If I do go away, then I will send him to you. And when he comes, he will convict the world of its sin, and of God's righteousness, and of the coming judgment. The world's sin is that it refuses to believe in me. Righteousness is available because I go to the Father, and you will see me no more. Judgment will come because the ruler of this world has already been judged.*
>
> *"There is so much more I want to tell you, but you can't bear it now. When the Spirit of truth comes, he will guide you into all truth. He will not speak on his own but will tell you what he has heard. He will tell you about the future. He will bring me glory by telling you whatever he receives from me. All that belongs to the Father is mine; this is why I said, 'The Spirit will tell you whatever he receives from me.'"* John 16:5-15, Jesus' words

This is referred to as *Holy Spirit baptism*, which took place on the day of Pentecost, seven weeks after Jesus' resurrection. This is the same baptism that has continuously saved the souls of believers throughout all time.

Holy Spirit baptism

It is the Spirit living in a Christian that provides eternal life in Heaven. Jesus said it best.

> *"Humans can reproduce only human life, but the Holy Spirit gives birth to spiritual life."* John 3:6, Jesus' words

John baptizes Jesus

Although Jesus was baptized in water, it was the baptism of the Holy Spirit that identified Jesus as a part of the Trinity and demonstrated to his followers their need for Spiritual baptism. The Spirit empowered Jesus for ministry, and it will empower the modern-day believer for ministry.

> *After his baptism, as Jesus came up out of the water, the heavens were opened and he saw the Spirit of God descending like a dove and settling on him. And a voice from heaven said, "This is my dearly loved Son, who brings me great joy."* Matthew 3:16-17

The symbol of the Holy Spirit is the dove.

You must also be Holy Spirit baptized (born again)

The term *born again* may be the most intimidating term in the Christian vernacular, although it is used by Jesus to reveal the formula for eternal life.

> *There was a man named Nicodemus, a Jewish religious leader who was a Pharisee. After dark one evening, he came to speak with Jesus. "Rabbi," he said, "we all know that God has sent you to teach us. Your miraculous signs are evidence that God is with you."*
>
> *Jesus replied, "I tell you the truth, unless you are born again, you cannot see the Kingdom of God."*
>
> *"What do you mean?" exclaimed Nicodemus. "How can an old man go back into his mother's womb and be born again?"*
>
> *Jesus replied, "I assure you, no one can enter the Kingdom of God without being born of water and the Spirit. Humans can reproduce only human life, but the Holy Spirit gives birth to spiritual life. So don't be surprised when I say, 'You must be born again.' The wind blows wherever it wants. Just as you can hear the wind but can't tell where it comes from or where it is going, so you can't explain how people are born of the Spirit."* John 3:1-8

The directive you have just read should be the most important you will ever read.

> *But to all who believed him and accepted him, he gave the right to become children of God. They are reborn—not with a physical birth resulting from human passion or plan, but a birth that comes from God.* John 1:12-13
>
> *This means that anyone who belongs to Christ has become a new person. The old life is gone; a new life has begun!* 2 Corinthians 5:17
>
> *For you have been born again, but not to a life that will quickly end. Your new life will last forever because it comes from the eternal, living word of God.* 1 Peter 1:23

Being *born again* is where religion stops and a relationship begins

Being *born again* does not refer to becoming religious. Its meaning is quite the opposite. Religion requires performance from the believer. Christianity is faith in Jesus' finished work.

Judaism, Hinduism, Buddhism, Islam, and certain cults labeling themselves as Christian (i.e., Mormonism, and some believe Catholicism is a cult) are examples of religions. Any organized group or institution with a belief system that embraces or dictates rules for salvation rather than God's grace is a cult. Of the 11 major religions (cults) of the world, 10 teach salvation through human effort. Christianity is the only belief system requiring just faith.

> *God saved you by his grace when you believed. And you can't take credit for this; it is a gift from God. Salvation is not a reward for the good things we have done, so none of us can boast about it.* Ephesians 2:8-9

The moment you believe and trust in the death, burial, and resurrection of Jesus Christ, you instantly become a part of Christ's body of believers. Immediately upon accepting Jesus' finished work on the Cross as your only way to receive eternal life with Jesus, the Holy Spirit will indwell you. ***This may sound scary, but trust me, it is the Holy Spirit that gives you the comfort of knowing you are saved and sealed. The Holy Spirit is your comforter, so do not be afraid.***

> *But the Comforter, which is the Holy Ghost, whom the Father will send in my name, he shall teach you all things, and bring all things to your remembrance, whatsoever I have said unto you.* John 14:26 (KJV)

I was saved in 1980, having only the "seeking" faith of a child. I had years of non-Christian academics, and was vice president of a NYSE member company — yet I was lost regarding God, Jesus, and the Holy Spirit.

> *"I tell you the truth, anyone who doesn't receive the Kingdom of God like a child will never enter it."* Mark 10:15, Jesus' words

My faith was weak, doubtful, and fearful. I wanted to be with God when I died, and I wanted to be pleasing to God, but I was dreadfully petrified of a spirit living inside me. Eek!

The Holy Spirit understood my fear, so was very gentle. I did not roll on the floor, begin speaking in tongues, or do any of those things that I feared. God gradually fed me the power of the Spirit, and he will do what you, as an individual, need and can accept pleasingly.

When does it take place?

At the moment of belief, immediately upon accepting Jesus as Savior, the Holy Spirit baptizes (indwells) the believer.

It is all about the Spirit

When studying the New Testament, you will realize how important the Holy Spirit was in the early Church. That importance remains today.

Jesus came and told his disciples, "I have been given all authority in heaven and on earth. Therefore, go and make disciples of all the nations, baptizing them in the name of the Father and the Son and the Holy Spirit. Matthew 28:18-19

In Chapter 8 of the Book of Romans, Paul mentions the Spirit 22 times.

*So now there is no condemnation for those who belong to Christ Jesus. And because you belong to him, the power of the life-giving **Spirit** has freed you from the power of sin that leads to death. The law of Moses was unable to save us because of the weakness of our sinful nature. So God did what the law could not do. He sent his own Son in a body like the bodies we sinners have. And in that body God declared an end to sin's control over us by giving his Son as a sacrifice for our sins. He did this so that the just requirement of the law would be fully satisfied for us, who no longer follow our sinful nature but instead follow the **Spirit**.*

*Those who are dominated by the sinful nature think about sinful things, but those who are controlled by the **Holy Spirit** think about things that please the **Spirit**. So letting your sinful nature control your mind leads to death. But letting the **Spirit** control your mind leads to life and peace. For the sinful nature is always hostile to God. It never did obey God's laws, and it never will. That's why those who are still under the control of their sinful nature can never please God.*

*But you are not controlled by your sinful nature. You are controlled by the **Spirit** if you have the **Spirit** of God living in you. (And remember that those who do not have the **Spirit** of Christ living in them do not belong to him at all.) And Christ lives within you, so even though your body will die because of sin, the **Spirit** gives you life because you have been made right with God. The **Spirit** of God, who raised Jesus from the dead, lives in you. And just as God raised Christ Jesus from the dead, he will give life to your mortal bodies by this same **Spirit** living within you.*

Therefore, dear brothers and sisters, you have no obligation to do what your sinful nature urges you to do. For if you live by its dictates, you will die. But if *through the power of the **<u>Spirit</u>** you put to death the deeds of your sinful nature, you will live. For all who are led by the **<u>Spirit</u>** of God are children of God.*

*So you have not received a **<u>spirit</u>** that makes you fearful slaves. Instead, you received God's **<u>Spirit</u>** when he adopted you as his own children. Now we call him, "Abba, Father." For his **<u>Spirit</u>** joins with our **<u>spirit</u>** to affirm that we are God's children. And since we are his children, we are his heirs. In fact, together with Christ we are heirs of God's glory. But if we are to share his glory, we must also share his suffering.*

*Yet what we suffer now is nothing compared to the glory he will reveal to us later. For all creation is waiting eagerly for that future day when God will reveal who his children really are. Against its will, all creation was subjected to God's curse. But with eager hope, the creation looks forward to the day when it will join God's children in glorious freedom from death and decay. For we know that all creation has been groaning as in the pains of childbirth right up to the present time. And we believers also groan, even though we have the **<u>Holy Spirit</u>** within us as a foretaste of future glory, for we long for our bodies to be released from sin and suffering. We, too, wait with eager hope for the day when God will give us our full rights as his adopted children, including the new bodies he has promised us. We were given this hope when we were saved. (If we already have something, we don't need to hope for it. But if we look forward to something we don't yet have, we must wait patiently and confidently.)*

*And the **<u>Holy Spirit</u>** helps us in our weakness. For example, we don't know what God wants us to pray for. But the **<u>Holy Spirit</u>** prays for us with groanings that cannot be expressed in words. And the Father who knows all hearts knows what the **<u>Spirit</u>** is saying, for the **<u>Spirit</u>** pleads for us believers in harmony with God's own will. And we know that God causes everything to work together for the good of those who love God and are called according to his purpose for them. For God knew his people in advance, and he chose them to become like his Son, so that his Son would be the firstborn among many brothers and sisters. And having chosen them, he called them to come to him. And having called them, he gave them right standing with himself. And having given them right standing, he gave them his glory.*

What shall we say about such wonderful things as these? If God is for us, who can ever be against us? Since he did not spare even his own Son but gave him up for us all, won't he also give us everything else? Who dares accuse us whom God has chosen for his own? No one—for God himself has given us right standing with himself. Who then will condemn us? No one—for Christ Jesus died for us and was raised to life for us, and he is sitting in the place of honor at God's right hand, pleading for us.

Can anything ever separate us from Christ's love? Does it mean he no longer loves us if we have trouble or calamity, or are persecuted, or hungry, or destitute, or in danger, or threatened with death? (As the Scriptures say, "For your sake we are killed every day; we are being slaughtered like sheep.") No, despite all these things, overwhelming victory is ours through Christ, who loved us.

And I am convinced that nothing can ever separate us from God's love. Neither death nor life, neither angels nor demons, neither our fears for today nor our worries about tomorrow—not even the powers of hell can separate us from God's love. No power in the sky above or in the earth below—indeed, nothing in all creation will ever be able to separate us from the love of God that is revealed in Christ Jesus our Lord. Romans 8:1-39

The following two passages describe the beginning of the Christian Church. The emphasis was added by me.

*Then Peter said to them, "Repent, and let every one of you be baptized in the name of Jesus Christ for the remission of sins; and **you shall receive the gift of the Holy Spirit**."* Acts 2:38 (KJV)

*Even as Peter was saying these things, the **Holy Spirit fell upon all** who were listening to the message. The Jewish believers who came with Peter were amazed that the gift of the Holy Spirit had been poured out on the Gentiles, too.* Acts 10:44-45

Paul instructs us (author emphasis):

*But you are not controlled by your sinful nature. **You are controlled by the Spirit if you have the Spirit of God living in you. (And remember that those who do not have the Spirit of Christ living in them do not belong to him at all.)** And Christ lives within you, so even though your body will die because of sin, **the Spirit gives you life** because you have been made right with God. The Spirit of God, who raised Jesus from the dead, lives in you. And just as God raised Christ Jesus from the dead, he will give life to your mortal bodies by this same Spirit living within you.* Romans 8:9-11

Let me ask you this one question: Did you receive the Holy Spirit by obeying the law of Moses? Of course not! You received the Spirit because you believed the message you heard about Christ. How foolish can you be? After starting your Christian lives in the Spirit, why are you now trying to become perfect by your own human effort? Galatians 3:2-3

*And all who have been **<u>united with Christ in baptism</u>** have put on Christ, like putting on new clothes. There is no longer Jew or Gentile, slave or free, male and female. For you are all one in Christ Jesus.* Galatians 3:27-28

*And now you Gentiles have also heard the truth, the Good News that God saves you. **<u>And when you believed in Christ, he identified you as his own by giving you the Holy Spirit</u>**, whom he promised long ago. The **<u>Spirit is God's guarantee</u>** that he will give us the inheritance he promised and that he has purchased us to be his own people. He did this so we would praise and glorify him.* Ephesians 1:13-14

For you were buried with Christ when you were baptized. And with him you were raised to new life because you trusted the mighty power of God, who raised Christ from the dead. Colossians 2:12

*He saved us, not because of the good things we did, but because of his mercy. He washed away our sins and gave us a new life through the Holy Spirit. **<u>He generously poured out the Spirit upon us because of what Jesus Christ our Savior did.</u>** He declared us not guilty because of his great kindness. And now we **<u>know</u>** that we will inherit eternal life.* Titus 3:5-7 (NLT 1996)

Notice in the last passage, I have emphasized the word *know*. It does not say *hope* or *guess*. Once baptized by the Holy Spirit, a person <u>knows</u> he or she has <u>eternal life in Heaven.</u> It is guaranteed.

<u>Gifts of the Holy Spirit</u>

Spiritual gifts are those bestowed upon Christians supernaturally by the Holy Spirit to strengthen the Church:

There are different kinds of spiritual gifts, but the same Spirit is the source of them all. There are different kinds of service, but we serve the same Lord. God works in different ways, but it is the same God who does the work in all of us.

A spiritual gift is given to each of us so we can help each other. To one person the Spirit gives the ability to give wise advice; to another the same Spirit gives a message of special knowledge. The same Spirit gives great faith to another, and to someone else the one Spirit gives the gift of healing. He gives one person the power to perform miracles, and another the ability to prophesy. He gives someone else the ability to discern whether a message is from the Spirit of God or from another spirit. Still another person is given the ability to speak in unknown languages, while another is given the ability to interpret what is being said. It is the one and only Spirit who distributes all these gifts. He alone decides which gift each person should have. 1 Corinthians 12: 4-11

Although no one doubts the numerous Spiritual gifts in the early Church, many believe their operation was limited to that period. Numerous scholars maintain these gifts were evident for only a short time and practiced only by Jesus' followers to prove his divinity.

Many Christians insist the Spiritual gifts ceased at the time of the completion of the last book of the New Testament, or upon the death of the last apostle. They argue the only source of knowledge needed today is the Scriptures. These Christians are referred to as *Cessationists*. Although some stand firm there are no miracles or miracle workers today, there are different degrees of Cessationalism. Some feel God occasionally performs miracles or uses individuals to perform miracles, healings, and so forth. Cessationists are usually flexible.

Christians contending Spiritual gifts continued are appropriately referred to as *Continuationists* — usually affiliated with the Charismatic movement, which includes Pentecostals, Apostolics, and other similar denominations. Continuationists are generally not flexible.

The debate between both camps is hotter than hot, thus can be a major divider of Christ's body. Both sides use Bible passages to substantiate their opinions. I haven't spoken in gibberish since infancy, but if some folks do — God bless them.

Fear and a cause

The possibility of losing control because there was a ghost living inside me was a gigantic fear. I heard stories about church people who would holler, wave their arms, jump over pews, and roll down church aisles as a result of the Holy Ghost. Before I thoroughly understood this behavior, I went to one of these spirit-filled churches, but quickly exited. One guy was jerking around so much that his false teeth fell out.

The mere mention of a Holy Ghost and being *born again* is frightening to many un-saved people, and causes them to resist listening to God's simple plan of salvation.

I have shared my pre-Christian fears with others who have not been born again and they admit their lack of knowledge causes fear. Few people welcome the thought of becoming a new creature because a ghost lives inside them. The Holy Spirit (the Holy Ghost) is probably the scariest part of Christianity because it is the least understood.

As a Christian, I have never lost control — I have more control. My teeth are still in-tact, and I never rolled down a church isle. The indwelling of the Holy Spirit has been a great comfort to me because I find my life is much more peaceful. Rest assured the Holy Spirit is a good guy. Tens of millions of people agree with me.

If you are not yet a Christian, I am sure you have other fears and objections about making the commitment, but I assure you: In my 30 years as an active Christian evangelist, I have never met one person who has regretted the choice of making Jesus Christ his or her Savior. Jesus' love vaporizes fear.

How to know the Holy Spirit lives in you

Most Christians know they have been saved because they feel the presence of the Holy Spirit in them. This is particularly true with Christians who were adults when they accepted Jesus. With this mature group, their conversion to Christianity is usu-ally accompanied by a unique change in behavior, which usually includes a passion to serve Jesus.

Sometimes adults question their salvation, particularly if they accepted Jesus as a youth. Youthful Christians are frequently led away from discipleship by new life ex-periences and attractive alternatives; however, if the young person was sincere in his or her proclamation of faith, their salvation was not lost (just put on hold while the hormones took over). Having weak young flesh does not result in lost salvation. If a youth's acceptance of Jesus was sincere, he or she is secure.

If you are unsure of your salvation, take God's word for it.

> *On the last day, the climax of the festival, Jesus stood and shouted to the crowds, "Anyone who is thirsty may come to me! Anyone who believes in me may come and drink! For the Scriptures declare, 'Rivers of living water will flow from his heart.'" (When he said "living water," he was speaking of*

*the Spirit, who would be given to everyone believing in him. But the Spirit
had not yet been given, because Jesus had not yet entered into his glory.)*
John 7:37-39

You were sealed with the promised Holy Spirit.

> *It is God who enables us, along with you, to stand firm for Christ. He has
> commissioned us, and he has identified us as his own by placing the Holy
> Spirit in our hearts as the first installment that guarantees everything he has
> promised us.* 2 Corinthians 1:22

> *God himself has prepared us for this, and as a guarantee he has given us his
> Holy Spirit.* 2 Corinthians 5:5

> *And now you Gentiles have also heard the truth, the Good News that God
> saves you. And when you believed in Christ, he identified you as his own by
> giving you the Holy Spirit, whom he promised long ago. The Spirit is God's
> guarantee that he will give us the inheritance he promised and that he has
> purchased us to be his own people. He did this so we would praise and glorify
> him.* Ephesians 1:13-14

The gift of the Spirit is God's guarantee that we belong to him. The indwelling of
God's Spirit is not questionable if you believe Jesus was God incarnate, who came to
Earth in the form of a man, who died on a cross to forgive mankind for their sins,
and who rose from being dead.

Sealed — sealed — sealed!

It's never too late

If you still question the Holy Spirit's indwelling, it is never too late to make the faith
proclamation. Many people choose to be water baptized a second time. Although
water baptism does not save anyone, it is an outward expression of the inward
confession.

Listen to the Holy Spirit, and allow him to be the guiding force in your life. The Spirit
will guide you into all truth, and agitate your conscience as to what you should and
should not do. Although the Holy Spirit may not always present himself in a con-
spicuous way, he lives within all Christians, all of the time. He does not take coffee
breaks, go on vacation, or leave when you sin — and you will sin.

> # CAUTION!
>
> Do not allow anyone to influence you regarding what you must do to prove you are a Christian. Christianity is not something you do; it is something Jesus Christ did for you.

Speaking in tongues

Many people insist the indwelling of the Holy Spirit must be evidenced by speaking in *tongues*, because it was an ability given to Jesus' disciples. Hooey! It was a charm used to edify the original Church until the completed New Testament became available. The Apostle Paul declared in 1 Corinthians 13:8 this "unknown language" would become useless:

> *Prophecy and speaking in unknown languages and special knowledge will become useless. But love will last forever!*

Just because someone speaks in gibberish does not mean it is the Holy Spirit speaking through him or her. If I turn cartwheels, I can say it was the Holy Spirit working through me, and it may be. But unless it has a fruitful result, it was probably just me turning cartwheels. It makes people feel spiritual to do unusual things, and then they blame or credit the Holy Spirit.

Many Christians believe praying in tongues is necessary. It is not! Do not feel uneasy if you are unable or uncomfortable with this practice. God understands English.

If the gift of tongues does exist, a believer does not have to possess that particular gift to be a Spirit-filled Christian, says Paul.

> *All of you together are Christ's body, and each of you is a part of it. Here are some of the parts God has appointed for the church:*
>
> *first are apostles,*
> *second are prophets,*
> *third are teachers,*
> *then those who do miracles,*
> *those who have the gift of healing,*
> *those who can help others,*

those who have the gift of leadership,
those who speak in unknown languages.

Are we all apostles? Are we all prophets? Are we all teachers? Do we all have the power to do miracles? Do we all have the gift of healing? Do we all have the ability to speak in unknown languages? Do we all have the ability to interpret unknown languages? Of course not! So you should earnestly desire the most helpful gifts.

But now let me show you a way of life that is best of all. 1 Corinthians 12:27-31

Dear brothers and sisters, if I should come to you speaking in an unknown language, how would that help you? But if I bring you a revelation or some special knowledge or prophecy or teaching, that will be helpful. Even lifeless instruments like the flute or the harp must play the notes clearly, or no one will recognize the melody. 1 Corinthians 14:6-7

Paul claims there is something greater than any of the Holy Spirit gifts listed above — the choice to love!

If I could speak all the languages of earth and of angels, but didn't love others, I would only be a noisy gong or a clanging cymbal. If I had the gift of prophecy, and if I understood all of God's secret plans and possessed all knowledge, and if I had such faith that I could move mountains, but didn't love others, I would be nothing. If I gave everything I have to the poor and even sacrificed my body, I could boast about it; but if I didn't love others, I would have gained nothing. 1 Corinthians 13:1-3

There is nothing physical you must do to prove the Holy Spirit lives in you; just believe.

"For God loved the world so much that he gave his one and only Son, so that everyone who believes in him will not perish but have eternal life." John 3:16, Jesus' words

Ready – Set – Go!

The believer's prayer

Although it is a person's faith alone in Jesus' finished work that saves, many Christians repeat a prayer as their acknowledgement. Also, oftentimes people have neglected their Christian life, so they want to begin again. Saying a prayer is not necessary, but God loves it when we pray. Prayer can be done aloud, silently, publicly, or privately. It is not the intellectual content of the prayer, but its sincerity. Say something like this:

> God,
>
> I believe you came to Earth in the form of a man named Jesus and died on a cross as payment for my sins. Many people saw you come back from being dead, which proved you are God and that you can overcome death. I know you are living in me, which is my assurance I will live eternally with you. I am saying this prayer to reinforce my relationship with you, and I am praying that I will grow in my Christian faith.
>
> Amen.

The Bible says because you are a believer in Jesus' finished work, you were saved the moment you believed. This is also known as: *justified, born spiritually, regenerated,* or *born again.*

The seeker's prayer

> God,
>
> I am not yet convinced, but I want to be. If you are for real, and if you came to Earth in the form of a man, I invite your Spirit to live in me and to show me truths as you guide me through my life.
>
> Amen.

I believe if you say the seeker's prayer, God will reveal the truth to you. At the very moment you trust Jesus as your only means of salvation, you will be saved. Now find a church and purchase an easy-to-read New Testament Bible.

Chapter 7

Satan is Real

Satan is a key personality throughout the Scriptures. He is introduced in the beginning of the Book of Genesis, but his fate is sealed in the Book of Revelation.

A few of Satan's many names are: Adversary, Devil, False Accuser, Slanderer, Beelzebub, Tempter, Wicked One, Lucifer, Prince of the World, Prince of Darkness, Liar, Father of Lies, Deceiver, Old Serpent, God of this World, The Enemy, Dragon, Piercing Serpent, Angel of Light, Murderer, Roaring Lion, Oppressor, and Son of the Morning.

Most of my life I had a difficult time believing in a devil. I understood evil, but not in the form of a red being with horns and a pitchfork. This doubt continued until shortly after I accepted Jesus as my Lord and Savior. I asked a friend what he thought, and he simply replied, "If you believe in God, you must believe in Satan." Bingo! I became a believer (absent the red color, horns, and pitchfork).

Satan's origin

Satan did not begin as a devil. He began as an angel named Lucifer, but because he was given free will he rebelled against God, so was cast from Heaven to Earth, where he can disguise himself as an angel of light. The word *Lucifer* means "the light bringer."

> *These people are false apostles. They are deceitful workers who disguise themselves as apostles of Christ. But I am not surprised! Even Satan disguises himself as an angel of light. So it is no wonder that his servants also disguise themselves as servants of righteousness. In the end they will get the punishment their wicked deeds deserve.* 2 Corinthians 11:13-15

God did not create a devil, but with his power of free choice, Lucifer transformed himself into a devil by his own free choice of rebellion against God.

Facts about Satan

> ➢ Satan instigates false doctrine.
> ➢ Satan influences misinterpretation of Scripture.
> ➢ Satan cannot be two places at one time, but dispatches demons.
> ➢ Satan cannot tempt a believer without God's permission.
> ➢ Satan is the author of confusion.
> ➢ Satan wants people to think salvation is difficult because he wants folks in Hell with him.

Satan has tremendous power

We know that God's children do not make a practice of sinning, for God's Son holds them securely, and the evil one cannot touch them. We know that we are children of God and that the world around us is under the control of the evil one. 1 John 5:18-19

He prowls around like a roaring lion.

Stay alert! Watch out for your great enemy, the devil. He prowls around like a roaring lion, looking for someone to devour. 1 Peter 5:8

We have hope.

"I have told you all this so that you may have peace in me. Here on earth you will have many trials and sorrows. But take heart, because I have overcome the world." John 16:33, Jesus' words

But you belong to God, my dear children. You have already won a victory over those people, because the Spirit who lives in you is greater than the spirit who lives in the world. 1 John 4:4

Satan is the father of the big lie that salvation is obtained by good behavior!

The most important question one should ask oneself is: How do I receive eternal life in Heaven?

For centuries, under the influence of Satan, religious leaders (sometimes in ignorance) have lied to their followers insisting Heaven is an eternal reward for people who live moral lives. Tragically, this lie will cause many worthy folks to spend eternity in Hell.

This book drives home what the Great Apostle Paul stated in Romans:

> *And if by grace, then it is no more of works, otherwise grace is no more grace. But if it be of works, then it is no more grace; otherwise work is no more work.* Romans 11:6 (KJV)

Eternal life with Jesus is a gift to all who will accept it. A gift is free!

For an in-depth study of the Christian Doctrine of Salvation, please read all of the chapters in Section Three.

Beware of deceptive spirits

Many people have told me they are *spiritual*, but I warn them to beware of demonic spirits. When Satan, who was once Lucifer, rebelled against God and fell from Heaven, one-third of the angels joined his rebellion. These fallen angels are now known as *demons*.

In the following passage, Paul warns Timothy that false teachings come from demons. Emphasis was added by me.

> *Now the Holy Spirit tells us clearly that in the last times some will turn away from the true faith;* ***they will follow deceptive spirits and teachings that come from demons.*** 1 Timothy 4:1

Be certain if you are spiritual that it is the Holy Spirit of Jesus who lives in you, and not one of Satan's spirits.

Resist him

Soon after accepting Jesus' free gift, I discovered a short, powerful Bible verse that freed me from the overwhelming anxiety caused by sensing the two opposite forces — good and evil —influencing my thoughts and behavior.

> *So humble yourselves before God. **Resist the devil**, and he will flee from you.*
> James 4:7

I emphasized the words *Resist the devil* because I believe that if you constantly resist him, he will eventually flee. I refuse to accept him into my presence. Whenever I feel the presence of Satan (evil), I boldly say, "Get out of here, Satan," and he flees.

The Lake of Fire

> *Then I saw an angel coming down from heaven with the key to the bottomless pit and a heavy chain in his hand. He seized the dragon—that old serpent, who is the devil, Satan—and bound him in chains for a thousand years. The angel threw him into the bottomless pit, which he then shut and locked so Satan could not deceive the nations anymore until the thousand years were finished. Afterward he must be released for a little while.*
>
> *Then I saw thrones, and the people sitting on them had been given the authority to judge. And I saw the souls of those who had been beheaded for their testimony about Jesus and for proclaiming the word of God. They had not worshiped the beast or his statue, nor accepted his mark on their foreheads or their hands. They all came to life again, and they reigned with Christ for a thousand years.*
>
> *This is the first resurrection. (The rest of the dead did not come back to life until the thousand years had ended.) Blessed and holy are those who share in the first resurrection. For them the second death holds no power, but they will be priests of God and of Christ and will reign with him a thousand years.*
> Revelation 20:1-6

The thousand years mentioned in the passage above is also known as the Millennium (Millennial Kingdom), which is the period when Jesus will rule over the entire Earth, taking place between the Tribulation and the destruction of the world. The specifics of this period differ among Christian scholars, although most interpret that Christ will return, defeat Satan, and reign forever on the New Earth.

At the end of the Millennium, Jesus will show no mercy. At that time he will be quick to judge, and the final rebellion of Satan and unsaved people will be over in a flash of fire. After this, the final judgment of the dead will take place.

Then the devil, who had deceived them, was thrown into the fiery lake of burning sulfur, joining the beast and the false prophet. There they will be tormented day and night forever and ever. And I saw a great white throne and the one sitting on it. The earth and sky fled from his presence, but they found no place to hide. I saw the dead, both great and small, standing before God's throne. And the books were opened, including the Book of Life. And the dead were judged according to what they had done, as recorded in the books. The sea gave up its dead, and death and the grave gave up their dead. And all were judged according to their deeds. Then death and the grave were thrown into the lake of fire. This lake of fire is the second death. And anyone whose name was not found recorded in the Book of Life was thrown into the lake of fire. Revelation 20:10-15

A commonly accepted interpretation is the *lake of fire* and *second death* both are representative of the eternal pain and punishment for rejecting Jesus as Savior.

Multitudes of people will have died thinking their good deeds would save them, only to realize that <u>one's behavior is not what saves</u>.

For no one can ever be made right with God by doing what the law commands. The law simply shows us how sinful we are.

But now God has shown us a way to be made right with him without keeping the requirements of the law, as was promised in the writings of Moses and the prophets long ago. We are made right with God by placing our faith in Jesus Christ. And this is true for everyone who believes, no matter who we are. Romans 3:20-22

Don't be one of them!

Notes:

SECTION TWO
Understanding Sin

Notes:

NOTE: For a comprehensive understanding of the complex subject of sin, please read this chapter, and refer to the chapters titled "Old and New Covenants" and "Die to the Law and live by the Spirit."

Chapter 8

What is Sin?

As a messenger of the Good News for more than three decades, I have determined the word sin is the favorite term used relentlessly by people to criticize others. Sinners love to call other sinners, sinners.

> **"You can never tell the sinner from the Christian. They drink the same drinks and smoke the same cigars." Aimee Semple McPherson (1890-1944)**

Who said having a drink and smoking a cigar is a sin? I didn't. One of the most famous and effective preachers in history, Charles Haddon Spurgeon (1834-1892), enjoyed a cigar while he walked to church Sunday mornings (on his way to preach) until some of his stiff-necked critics complained. He then quit, at least in public.

Hamartiology, which comes from the Greek word *hamartos* (meaning "sin"), is the study of sin.

The term *sin* is tossed around a lot. When I encounter someone who uses it frequently, I ask him or her to define it. So far, each has been dumbfounded. It is an easy word to use, especially when condemning others, but difficult to elucidate. I once heard it said, "If you laid all of the tens of thousands of theologians, both contemporary and historical, end to end, they still would not reach a conclusion."

The three greatest misconceptions regarding sin

1. Probably the most misunderstood viewpoint of sin is that there are big and little sins.

For the person who keeps all of the laws except one is as guilty as a person who has broken all of God's laws. For the same God who said, "You must not commit adultery," also said, "You must not murder." So if you murder someone but do not commit adultery, you have still broken the law. James 2:10-11

The passage above reminds us we are all sinners, regardless of the sins we have committed or how often. In our mortal minds, most of us believe there are little and big sins. But in God's mind, all sins are equal because we are all sinners. **God does not differentiate between one sin and another.** Cheating on one's income tax is just as serious as murder, because both are immoral.

We think cheating on our income tax is the American thing to do, but consider adultery as the act of an immoral person. In God's Kingdom both are equal, just as stealing a pencil from work is as sinful as murder. Whether it is telling a little fib, lusting, robbing a bank, or murder — sin is sin.

2. **The false belief that sin sends someone to Hell comes in second.**

   The Good News is: Sinning does not send someone to Hell. That debt has been paid in full by Jesus' shed Blood on the Cross. Religious folks usually describe smoking, drinking, swearing, and gambling as sins, but these behaviors are not always considered sinful to God. Mankind is not always *man kind.* Sometimes Christians impose their interpretations of morality on one another in an unkindly way. <u>Christian judgmentalism is the reason I am so adamant about thoroughly understand the meaning of sin.</u>

3. **Disobeying one or more of the Ten Commandments may be sinful, but not because you are disobeying an Old Testament commandment. Think about that before you proceed.**

   One must understand the Ten Commandments were given only to the Israelites, along with 603 other laws. These laws were impossible to keep, which is the reason God offered himself in the form of a man, named Jesus, to be brutalized and sacrificed, and whose shed Blood would be the propitiation for all who believed in him and accepted his free gift of salvation. <u>See the chapter titled "Die to the Law and live by the Spirit."</u>

How sin was introduced into the world – *imputed sin*

The word *sin* is used hundreds of times throughout the Old and New Testaments, yet **nowhere in the Scriptures do we find a precise dictionary definition**. To ascertain the actual meaning of sin, one must understand both the history and the future of mankind as revealed by the Creator.

Adam and Eve were the first two humans. From the very beginning, God differentiated between what was right and wrong, but Adam and Eve disobeyed. This is known as *original sin*. The immediate effect of Adam and Eve's sin was they died spiritually. Because all people are descendants of Adam and Eve, sin entered the entire human race. This is referred to as *imputed sin* (the verb *impute* means to lay the responsibility or blame on someone for something bad; or, to give credit for something good — to assign as a characteristic. Synonyms: ascribe, assign, attribute). *Because of imputed sin, everyone is born a sinner.*

> **"If you have doubts that original sin is not a reality, just look at the history of the world." Tullian Tchividjian (born 1972)**

The implication of sin

Based on the account of Adam and Eve, the Bible indicates that **sin is disobeying God**. The moment Adam and Eve ate from the tree of forbidden fruit, sin was born. The sin was the act of disobeying. From that point until the very last chapter of the New Testament, examples of sin are found continuously and condemned.

Defining sin is very tricky and can become very complicated. To completely understand the Bible, you need to learn Hebrew, Greek, and Aramaic.

The Old Testament was originally written in Hebrew, with a few portions written in Aramaic. The New Testament was originally written in Greek. Despite many modern English translations that closely represent the original languages, it is impossible to convert the original words into a precise meaning. Translating is not an exact science.

A number of words used in the original Greek New Testament translate to *sin* or *sins*. These are *hamartia*, *hamartema*, and *hamartano*. In the original Greek New

Testament, the most common word translated as *sin* or *sins* is the word *hamartia*. *Vine's Complete Expository Dictionary of Old and New Testament Words* says *hamartia* means "missing of the mark."

The subject of sin is somewhat difficult to write about because it has so many implications. "To miss the mark" is the standard of perfection established by God and evidenced by Jesus. Viewed in that light, it is clear that we are all sinners because none can hit the bull's eye.

> *For everyone has sinned; we all fall short of God's glorious standard.*
> Romans 3:23

Sin is an offense against God. When a sin is deliberate in action — such as murder, stealing, lying, or adultery — it is referred to as a *sin of commission*. If it is something we should have done, but did not, such as feeding a poor person, it is referred to as a *sin of omission. All sins <u>are punishable by death and eternal damnation.</u>*

In a nutshell, sinning means doing something contrary to the will of God, who speaks to us via the Bible and his Spirit. Even though we know better, it is impossible not to sin, primarily because we are imperfect creations. **No matter how hard we try, we are going to sin.**

The consequences of sin

> *For the wages of sin is death, but the free gift of God is eternal life through Christ Jesus our Lord.* Romans 6:23

Without Jesus, sin results in eternal death. Sin can also result in overwhelming feelings of guilt and anxieties, but our *guilt is a tool of Satan.*

Because there are so many ways to sin, it is easy to feel like giving up or not even trying. These feelings of shortcomings are what Jesus uses to show us the need for him as Savior.

With Jesus, Christians receive the free gift of glory that awaits all Christians in the next life; plus, Christian life on Earth becomes amazing when the Holy Spirit supernaturally transforms each of us. When a person receives and yields to the Spirit, he or she receives new power.

The more aware we are of our moral defects, the more we depend on Jesus' power to keep us morally responsible.

Many churches have invented sins that are not biblical

We depend on our church leaders to be biblically accurate. Sadly, throughout the centuries, self-appointed Christian moralists have invented non-biblical sins based on what they consider personally offensive and what they think should be offensive to God, regardless of biblical accuracy. **They compile continuous lists of human behaviors and label them sinful for everyone.** This is a disastrous blunder on the part of church leaders because it causes many people to reject Jesus based on false information. Creating undeserved guilt and unworthiness in people should not be the function of the Church. ***Guilt is a tool of Satan.***

To compound this problem, many churches neglect discussing the role of the Holy Spirit in the Christian's life. The Bible states that we are to learn from one another, but makes it clear that a Christian's ultimate counselor is the Holy Spirit. Church leaders make leadership errors, but the Holy Spirit's guidance is flawless. Therefore, sin for one person may be different from sin for another, as defined by the Holy Spirit.

What is sin for one Christian, may not be sin for another

Each Christian has a *personal relationship* with the Lord Jesus Christ via the in-dwelling of the Holy Spirit. What the Holy Spirit communicates to one may be different from what the Holy Spirit communicates to another. That is what defines a personal relationship with Jesus Christ.

The Holy Spirit works differently in each person's life, convicting each individual to the path he or she is to follow. For example, having a couple beers (the Bible says not to get drunk) may not be sin for the person who has control of his alcohol consumption and who has _not_ been convicted by the Holy Spirit not to drink.

> **"Whoever drinks beer, he is quick to sleep; whoever sleeps long, does not sin; whoever does not sin, enters Heaven! Thus, let us drink beer!" Martin Luther (1483-1546)**

Another individual may have a drinking problem, so _is_ convicted by the Spirit to totally abstain. It is not a sin to drink for the first person, but it is for the second. There are many more examples.

Example: The Holy Spirit may convict me to volunteer in helping to feed the poor, but may not convict you to help in that same mission. The Holy Spirit treats and convicts each person individually. For me not to feed the poor would be a sin, but may not be a sin for you.

Example: One person may be convicted by the Holy Spirit to go to war and fight for his or her country, while another Christian is convicted to serve by working in a hospital. Killing on the battlefield would not be a sin for one Christian, but it would be a sin for the other.

Social issues

Many social issues labeled sinful in Christendom may not be sinful to Jesus, despite what is preached by legalists. A few of these social issues include: the playing of musical instruments, dancing, uttering an occasional swear word, drinking a few beers, or buying a lottery ticket.

I am guilty of all of the above, but I am a person of moderation, so God and I do not consider them personal sinful behavior for me.

The Lord allows me certain liberties. He has convicted me to change my behavior in some areas, but allowed me those liberties in others. A Mormon friend bragged to me that her church dictates how all Mormons must behave, so she behaves accordingly. I told her Jesus tells me how to behave, and I behave accordingly. Then I told her cults demand conformity, and she hasn't spoken to me since.

I understand conviction because this book is the result of my being convicted. For me to *not* write this book would be a sin. I have been convicted to participate in other Christian endeavors and activities in which I had no choice. I fought the convictions, but the Lord won. My ignoring God's convictions would have been a sin.

The Good News

The Good News is: Jesus' crucifixion forgives all sins, iniquities, and transgressions — except one. Murder, sexual sins, lying, lust, drunkenness, compulsive gambling, swearing, cheating on one's income tax, and even selling a used car that has problems are all forgivable.

There is only one sin not pardonable.

The world's unpardonable sin is disbelief in Jesus

He came into the very world he created, but the world didn't recognize him. He came to his own people, and even they rejected him. But to all who believed him and accepted him, he gave the right to become children of God. They are reborn—not with a physical birth resulting from human passion or plan, but a birth that comes from God. John 1:10-14

"The world's sin is that it refuses to believe in me." John 16:9, Jesus' words

He that believeth on the Son hath everlasting life: and he that believeth not the Son shall not see life; but the wrath of God abideth on him. John 3:36

The unpardonable sin is the refusal to acknowledge God's power in Jesus, which is rejecting Jesus as divine. Whoever rejects Jesus as God is guilty of blaspheming the Holy Spirit because Jesus is the Holy Spirit.

All of mankind's sins except rejecting the Holy Spirit of Jesus were forgiven on the Cross.

"So I tell you, every sin and blasphemy can be forgiven—except blasphemy against the Holy Spirit, which will never be forgiven. Anyone who speaks against the Son of Man can be forgiven, but anyone who speaks against the Holy Spirit will never be forgiven, either in this world or in the world to come." Matthew 12:31-32, Jesus' words

Accept the Holy Spirit now.

Imputed sin

Adam's sin became our sin (imputed sin). *Imputed sin* is the reason none are worthy of the glory of God.

Imputed righteousness

The Good News is: Jesus' righteousness became our righteousness — hence, *imputed righteousness.*

Jesus' imputed righteousness finds the Christian not guilty. Therefore, the punishment of death and eternity in Hell is exchanged for eternal life with Jesus in Heaven.

> *When people work, their wages are not a gift, but something they have earned. But people are counted as righteous, not because of their work, but because of their faith in God who forgives sinners. David also spoke of this when he described the happiness of those who are declared righteous without working for it:*
>
> *"Oh, what joy for those*
>   *whose disobedience is forgiven,*
>   *whose sins are put out of sight.*
> *Yes, what joy for those*
>   *whose record the LORD has cleared of sin."* Romans 4:7-8

"Abounding sin is the terror of the world, but abounding grace is the hope of mankind." A. W. Tozer (1897-1963)

More about imputed righteousness is discussed throughout this book.

Chapter 9

Is Homosexuality a Sin?

"Do not judge others, and you will not be judged. For you will be treated as you treat others. The standard you use in judging is the standard by which you will be judged.

"And why worry about a speck in your friend's eye when you have a log in your own? How can you think of saying to your friend, 'Let me help you get rid of that speck in your eye,' when you can't see past the log in your own eye? Hypocrite! First get rid of the log in your own eye; then you will see well enough to deal with the speck in your friend's eye." Matthew 7:1-5, Jesus' words

This book is an exegesis. In a Biblical sense *exegesis* is a theological term describing an approach to establish doctrine by critical Bible analysis. One of the mistakes frequently made by Christians is they employ just one or two passages to establish doctrines without studying the other verses and passages that pertain to a doctrinal topic.

Doctrine must be established using the entire Bible and other resources. Establishing a doctrine, or principle, without extensive research is disastrous. All biblical evidence regarding a topic must be used — not just one's favorite verses. There may be dozens of other passages inconsistent with your one or two favorite passages. The Bible must be studied, not just read.

Proper exegesis includes using the context around the passage, and comparing it with other parts of the Bible, while utilizing an understanding of the language and customs of the time it was written — all in an effort to completely comprehend what the original writer(s) intended to communicate.

I am writing this exegetical chapter very humbly and with compassion toward everyone. As a messenger of the Good News of salvation by grace through faith, I was given the mandate of reconciling (uniting) people to Jesus the Messiah.

And it is all from God, who through the Messiah has reconciled us to himself and has given us the work of that reconciliation, which is that God in the Messiah was reconciling mankind to himself, not counting their sins against them, and entrusting to us the message of reconciliation. Therefore we are ambassadors of the Messiah; in effect, God is making his appeal through us. What we do is appeal on behalf of the Messiah, "Be reconciled to God! God made this sinless man be a sin offering on our behalf, so that in union with him we might fully share in God's righteousness." 2 Corinthians 5:18-21 (CJB)

That is the *Good News!* The bad news is that as a messenger of the Good News, I am put in a position of having to answer questions outside my comfort zone. "Is homosexuality a sin?" is one of those questions because Jesus is the final authority and judge. I teach salvation and allow the Holy Spirit to implant morals.

As a Christian salvation teacher, I use two divine sources: The Holy Scriptures and the Holy Spirit. It doesn't get better than that.

First, let's study the Old Testament passages

Genesis is a good place to begin our study because it is the first mention of a man and a woman in a relationship that will reproduce (Adam and Steve couldn't reproduce).

> *This explains why a man leaves his father and mother and is joined to his wife, and the two are united into one.* Genesis 2:24

Genesis is an explanation of origins, so it would be lazy theology to use this single verse as the only source for the Doctrine of Homophobia. This verse does not address homosexuality.

Fast forward to Sodom and Gomorrah

> *That evening two angels came to the entrance of the city of Sodom. Lot was sitting there, and when he saw them, he stood up to meet them. Then he welcomed them and bowed with his face to the ground. "My lords," he said, "come to my home to wash your feet, and be my guests for the night. You may then get up early in the morning and be on your way again."*
>
> *"Oh no," they replied. "We'll just spend the night out here in the city square."*

But Lot insisted, so at last they went home with him. Lot prepared a feast for them, complete with fresh bread made without yeast, and they ate. But before they retired for the night, all the men of Sodom, young and old, came from all over the city and surrounded the house. They shouted to Lot, "Where are the men who came to spend the night with you? Bring them out to us so we can have sex with them!"

So Lot stepped outside to talk to them, shutting the door behind him. "Please, my brothers," he begged, "don't do such a wicked thing. Look, I have two virgin daughters. Let me bring them out to you, and you can do with them as you wish. But please, leave these men alone, for they are my guests and are under my protection."

"Stand back!" they shouted. "This fellow came to town as an outsider, and now he's acting like our judge! We'll treat you far worse than those other men!" And they lunged toward Lot to break down the door.

But the two angels reached out, pulled Lot into the house, and bolted the door. Then they blinded all the men, young and old, who were at the door of the house, so they gave up trying to get inside.

Meanwhile, the angels questioned Lot. "Do you have any other relatives here in the city?" they asked. "Get them out of this place—your sons-in-law, sons, daughters, or anyone else. For we are about to destroy this city completely. The outcry against this place is so great it has reached the LORD, and he has sent us to destroy it." Genesis 19:1-13

The passage above is commonly used as a story condemning homosexuality, but it never clearly identifies homosexuality as the sin for which Sodom was destroyed.

In Ezekiel 16:49-50, the specific sin for which Sodom was destroyed is identified as arrogance and apathy toward the poor.

"Sodom's sins were pride, gluttony and laziness, while the poor and needy suffered outside her door. She was proud and committed detestable sins, so I wiped her out, as you have seen." Ezekiel 16:49-50

The passage above is in the NLT, which states Sodom committed detestable sins; however, the same passage appearing in the KJV (below) does not use the term *sin*, but indicates behavior not pleasing to God. I doubt if God was pleased with what appeared to be the desired lust of a gang rape of the angels, nor was he pleased with Lot's willingness to sacrifice his virgin daughters.

> *Behold, this was the iniquity of thy sister Sodom, pride, fulness of bread, and abundance of idleness was in her and in her daughters, neither did she strengthen the hand of the poor and needy.*
>
> *And they were haughty, and committed abomination before me: therefore I took them away as I saw good.* Ezekiel 16:49-50 (KJV)

Peter wrote to the Church at large the following:

> *Later, God condemned the cities of Sodom and Gomorrah and turned them into heaps of ashes. He made them an example of what will happen to ungodly people. But God also rescued Lot out of Sodom because he was a righteous man who was sick of the shameful immorality of the wicked people around him. Yes, Lot was a righteous man who was tormented in his soul by the wickedness he saw and heard day after day. So you see, the Lord knows how to rescue godly people from their trials, even while keeping the wicked under punishment until the day of final judgment. He is especially hard on those who follow their own **twisted sexual desire**, and who despise authority.*
>
> *These people are proud and arrogant, daring even to scoff at supernatural beings without so much as trembling.* 2 Peter 2:6-10 (Emphasis added by me.)

The NLT is used above, but other translations use other phrases instead of "twisted sexual desire." They are: *walk after the flesh; follow their old natures; follow their filthy bodily lusts;* and *indulge the flesh in its corrupt desires.*

The Book of Jude, written by Jude, a brother to Jesus and James, has a different take regarding the destruction of Sodom.

> *And I remind you of the angels who did not stay within the limits of authority God gave them but left the place where they belonged. God has kept them securely chained in prisons of darkness, waiting for the great day of judgment. And don't forget Sodom and Gomorrah and their neighboring towns, which were filled with immorality and every kind of sexual perversion. Those cities were destroyed by fire and serve as a warning of the eternal fire of God's judgment.* Jude 1:6-7

Levitical laws!

When the Israelites moved from Egypt, God forewarned them how tempting it would be to become involved in the carnal practices of the Canaanites. Because the Israelites are God's chosen people, he did not want them charmed by immorality, so he gave them laws, as detailed in the Book of Leviticus. Notice Leviticus 18:22, which I emphasized.

> *Then the Lord said to Moses, 2 "Give the following instructions to the people of Israel. I am the Lord your God. 3 So do not act like the people in Egypt, where you used to live, or like the people of Canaan, where I am taking you. You must not imitate their way of life. 4 You must obey all my regulations and be careful to obey my decrees, for I am the Lord your God. 5 If you obey my decrees and my regulations, you will find life through them. I am the Lord.*

> *6 "You must never have sexual relations with a close relative, for I am the Lord.*

> *7 "Do not violate your father by having sexual relations with your mother. She is your mother; you must not have sexual relations with her.*

> *8 "Do not have sexual relations with any of your father's wives, for this would violate your father.*

> *9 "Do not have sexual relations with your sister or half sister, whether she is your father's daughter or your mother's daughter, whether she was born into your household or someone else's.*

> *10 "Do not have sexual relations with your granddaughter, whether she is your son's daughter or your daughter's daughter, for this would violate yourself.*

> *11 "Do not have sexual relations with your stepsister, the daughter of any of your father's wives, for she is your sister.*

> *12 "Do not have sexual relations with your father's sister, for she is your father's close relative.*

> *13 "Do not have sexual relations with your mother's sister, for she is your mother's close relative.*

14 "Do not violate your uncle, your father's brother, by having sexual relations with his wife, for she is your aunt.

15 "Do not have sexual relations with your daughter-in-law; she is your son's wife, so you must not have sexual relations with her.

16 "Do not have sexual relations with your brother's wife, for this would violate your brother.

17 "Do not have sexual relations with both a woman and her daughter. And do not take her granddaughter, whether her son's daughter or her daughter's daughter, and have sexual relations with her. They are close relatives, and this would be a wicked act.

18 "While your wife is living, do not marry her sister and have sexual relations with her, for they would be rivals.

19 "Do not have sexual relations with a woman during her period of menstrual impurity.

20 "Do not defile yourself by having sexual intercourse with your neighbor's wife.

21 "Do not permit any of your children to be offered as a sacrifice to Molech, for you must not bring shame on the name of your God. I am the Lord.

22 "Do not practice homosexuality, having sex with another man as with a woman. It is a detestable sin.

23 "A man must not defile himself by having sex with an animal. And a woman must not offer herself to a male animal to have intercourse with it. This is a perverse act.

24 "Do not defile yourselves in any of these ways, for the people I am driving out before you have defiled themselves in all these ways. 25 Because the entire land has become defiled, I am punishing the people who live there. I will cause the land to vomit them out. 26 You must obey all my decrees and regulations. You must not commit any of these detestable sins. This applies both to native-born Israelites and to the foreigners living among you.

27 "All these detestable activities are practiced by the people of the land where I am taking you, and this is how the land has become defiled. 28 So do not defile the land and give it a reason to vomit you out, as it will vomit out the people who live there now. 29 Whoever commits any of these detestable sins will be cut off from the community of Israel. 30 So obey my instructions, and do not defile yourselves by committing any of these detestable practices that were committed by the people who lived in the land before you. I am the Lord your God." Leviticus 18:1-30

Also from the Book of Leviticus.

"If a man practices homosexuality, having sex with another man as with a woman, both men have committed a detestable act. They must both be put to death, for they are guilty of a capital offense." Leviticus 20:13

Leviticus 18:22 and 20:13 are the two passages most often used to declare homosexuality immoral.

In the Canaanite religion (cult), the main emphasis was on fertility and sex. The inhabitants of Canaan were obsessed with worshiping Baal. The Semitic word *baal* means *lord*. The Canaanites believed Baal was in absolute control over nature and over people.

> **Only two passages in Leviticus prohibit male homosexual conduct. Leviticus also stipulates that any man who touches a woman during her menstrual period is to be stoned to death, adulterers are to be executed, interracial marriage is sinful, two types of cloth are not to be worn together, and certain foods must never be eaten.**

Are Christians bound by Levitical laws?

Levitical laws were God's requirements for righteousness for the Israelites. The question is: Were they for all mankind — for all time?

*When the Gentiles sin, they will be destroyed, even though **they never had God's written law**. And the Jews, who do have God's law, will be judged by that law when they fail to obey it.* Romans 2:12 (Emphasis added by me.)

The passage above makes it clear the Gentiles (non-Israelites) never were under the law.

The Old Covenant (covenant means *agreement*) laws that God had established with the Israelites required performing rituals and sacrifices in order to gain favor with God. The Israelites received some righteousness by attempting (it was humanly impossible for them to abide by them all) to adhere to the law(s), but this law-biding was only temporary. God knew when he imposed the old laws that mankind was too weak to walk the straight-and-narrow, but he did it to show the need for the coming Savior.

> *"The day is coming," says the Lord, "when I will make a new covenant with the people of Israel and Judah. This covenant will not be like the one I made with their ancestors when I took them by the hand and brought them out of the land of Egypt. They broke that covenant, though I loved them as a husband loves his wife," says the Lord.*

> *"But this is the new covenant I will make with the people of Israel on that day," says the Lord. "I will put my instructions deep within them, and I will write them on their hearts. I will be their God, and they will be my people.* Jeremiah 31:31-33

The Old Covenant was replaced by the righteousness attained when people accepted the indwelling of the Holy Spirit of Jesus Christ.

> *If the first covenant had been faultless, there would have been no need for a second covenant to replace it.* Hebrews 8:7

> *For Christ has already accomplished the purpose for which the law was given. As a result, all who believe in him are made right with God.* Romans 10:4

The New Covenant of *grace* does not insinuate that God condones immorality. God's reason for wanting us to live moral lives is primarily because our uncontrolled carnal desires can result in disastrous consequences. Marrying close relatives can cause birth defects; promiscuity can cause unwanted children, disease, jealousy, death; improper sexual behavior can destroy people. God's rules benefit us.

Let's look at the new rules.

The glorious New Covenant

The New replaces the Old! (Emphasis added by me.)

> ***The old way, with laws etched in stone, led to death***, *though it began with such glory that the people of Israel could not bear to look at Moses' face. For his face shone with the glory of God, even though the brightness was already fading away. Shouldn't we expect far greater glory under the new way, now that the Holy Spirit is giving life?* ***If the old way, which brings condemnation, was glorious, how much more glorious is the new way, which makes us right with God!*** *In fact, that first glory was not glorious at all compared with the overwhelming glory of the new way. So if the old way, which has been replaced, was glorious, how much more glorious is the new, which remains forever!*

> ***Since this new way gives us such confidence, we can be very bold.*** *We are not like Moses, who put a veil over his face so the people of Israel would not see the glory, even though it was destined to fade away.* ***But the people's minds were hardened, and to this day whenever the old covenant is being read, the same veil covers their minds so they cannot understand the truth. And this veil can be removed only by believing in Christ.*** *Yes, even today when they read Moses' writings, their hearts are covered with that veil, and they do not understand.*

> *But whenever someone turns to the Lord, the veil is taken away.* ***For the Lord is the Spirit, and wherever the Spirit of the Lord is, there is freedom***. *So all of us who have had that veil removed can see and reflect the glory of the Lord. And the Lord—who is the Spirit—makes us more and more like him as* ***we are changed into his glorious image***. 2 Corinthians 3:7-18

We learned from the Old Testament that God had exclusive laws for only the Israelites, but the New Testament states boldly they are not applicable today.

> *But now Jesus, our High Priest, has been given a ministry that is far superior to the old priesthood, for he is the one who mediates for us a far better covenant with God, based on better promises.* Hebrews 8:6

For the last 2,000 years, to please God one must receive the indwelling of Jesus' Spirit. This is his New Covenant, which replaces the Old Covenant of adhering to laws.

But you are not controlled by your sinful nature. You are controlled by the Spirit if you have the Spirit of God living in you. (And remember that those who do not have the Spirit of Christ living in them do not belong to him at all.) Romans 8:9

And now, just as you accepted Christ Jesus as your Lord, you must continue to follow him. Let your roots grow down into him, and let your lives be built on him. Then your faith will grow strong in the truth you were taught, and you will overflow with thankfulness. Colossians 2:6-7

Jesus' sacrifice for our sins fulfilled both the letter of the law and God's intent behind all those laws; but does that mean we are free to live carnally?

Those who are dominated by the sinful nature think about sinful things, but those who are controlled by the Holy Spirit think about things that please the Spirit. So letting your sinful nature control your mind leads to death. But letting the Spirit control your mind leads to life and peace. For the sinful nature is always hostile to God. It never did obey God's laws, and it never will. That's why those who are still under the control of their sinful nature can never please God. Romans 8:5-8

You say, "I am allowed to do anything"—but not everything is good for you. You say, "I am allowed to do anything"—but not everything is beneficial. 1 Corinthians 10:23

Our initial acceptance of Jesus as Savior is a relationship in which we are to grow. As Jesus' disciples, we are to follow his teachings by studying the Holy Scriptures and by allowing the Holy Spirit to live through us.

Jesus said nothing regarding homosexuality in the Scriptures. His ministry spoke more about the sins of the spirit than the sins of the body, although he also gave us moral guidelines.

Jesus spent his entire life befriending the poor, the marginalized, and folks called unclean by their society — demonstrating that his love included them. He treated them with compassion. He said to love your neighbor as yourself, but he didn't say, "Love your neighbor, unless he or she happens to be gay." His harshest words concerned the Pharisees, who were the ruling class of Israel that regulated the religious law.

We have ascertained that mankind is not under the Old Testament law, and to receive God's favor we must individually live in harmony with the indwelling Holy Spirit.

New Testament passages

A passage from the Great Apostle Paul (I emphasized categorical verses):

> For I am not ashamed of this Good News about Christ. It is the power of God at work, saving everyone who believes—the Jew first and also the Gentile. This Good News tells us how God makes us right in his sight. This is accomplished from start to finish by faith. As the Scriptures say, "It is through faith that a righteous person has life."

> But God shows his anger from heaven against all sinful, wicked people who suppress the truth by their wickedness. They know the truth about God because he has made it obvious to them. For ever since the world was created, people have seen the earth and sky. Through everything God made, they can clearly see his invisible qualities—his eternal power and divine nature. So they have no excuse for not knowing God.

> Yes, they knew God, but they wouldn't worship him as God or even give him thanks. And they began to think up foolish ideas of what God was like. As a result, their minds became dark and confused. Claiming to be wise, they instead became utter fools. And instead of worshiping the glorious, ever-living God, they worshiped idols made to look like mere people and birds and animals and reptiles.

> So God abandoned them to do whatever shameful things their hearts desired. As a result, they did vile and degrading things with each other's bodies. They traded the truth about God for a lie. So they worshiped and served the things God created instead of the Creator himself, who is worthy of eternal praise! Amen. That is why God abandoned them to their shameful desires. **_Even the women turned against the natural way to have sex and instead indulged in sex with each other. And the men, instead of having normal sexual relations with women, burned with lust for each other. Men did shameful things with other men, and as a result of this sin, they suffered within themselves the penalty they deserved._**

> Since they thought it foolish to acknowledge God, he abandoned them to their foolish thinking and let them do things that should never be done. Their lives

became full of every kind of wickedness, sin, greed, hate, envy, murder, quar-
reling, deception, malicious behavior, and gossip. They are backstabbers,
haters of God, insolent, proud, and boastful. They invent new ways of sin-
ning, and they disobey their parents. They refuse to understand, break their
promises, are heartless, and have no mercy. They know God's justice requires
that those who do these things deserve to die, yet they do them anyway. Worse
yet, they encourage others to do them, too. Romans 1:16-32

In 1 Corinthians 6:9-20, in a letter from the Great Apostle Paul, the term *homo-*
sexuality (Emphasis added by me.) is used. This passage is from the NLT, which is a
newer translation of the New Testament. Older translations of the New Testament
do not use *homosexual* or *homosexuality*, as I have presented in **Selected passages**.

Don't you realize that those who do wrong will not inherit the Kingdom of
God? Don't fool yourselves. Those who indulge in sexual sin, or who worship
*idols, or commit adultery, or are male prostitutes, or **practice homosexual-***
***ity**, or are thieves, or greedy people, or drunkards, or are abusive, or cheat*
people—none of these will inherit the Kingdom of God. Some of you were once
like that. But you were cleansed; you were made holy; you were made right
with God by calling on the name of the Lord Jesus Christ and by the Spirit of
our God.

You say, "I am allowed to do anything"—but not everything is good for you.
And even though "I am allowed to do anything," I must not become a slave
to anything. You say, "Food was made for the stomach, and the stomach for
food." (This is true, though someday God will do away with both of them.)
But you can't say that our bodies were made for sexual immorality. They
were made for the Lord, and the Lord cares about our bodies. And God will
raise us from the dead by his power, just as he raised our Lord from the
dead.

Don't you realize that your bodies are actually parts of Christ? Should a man
take his body, which is part of Christ, and join it to a prostitute? Never! And
don't you realize that if a man joins himself to a prostitute, he becomes one
body with her? For the Scriptures say, "The two are united into one." But the
person who is joined to the Lord is one spirit with him.

Run from sexual sin! No other sin so clearly affects the body as this one does.
For sexual immorality is a sin against your own body. Don't you realize that
your body is the temple of the Holy Spirit, who lives in you and was given to

you by God? You do not belong to yourself, for God bought you with a high price. So you must honor God with your body. 1 Corinthians 6:9-20

Most Bible references throughout this book are from the NLT because I believe it to be very reliable, and easy to understand, but not perfect. My craving to be theologically correct steered me to several other Bible translations for their vernacular. Keep in mind, the original manuscripts for our modern-day Bibles are no longer in existence, so Bible publishers must use alternative resources. Furthermore, because Bibles are copyrighted, each Bible publishing company must not copy the exact work of another. Hence, Bibles do not always agree.

To ascertain truth, we must compare translations, research words and their origins, seek the opinions of scholars, and listen to the Holy Spirit.

Homosexual is a new English term, not used until about 1900, and it wasn't used in any English Bible translation until about 1950. Other Bible words used throughout history in the context of sinful behaviors were: *malakoi, neische, letchouris ayen kinde, weaklings, weichlinge, wantons, those who make women of themselves, catamites* (boys who have sex with men), *men who lie down with males, sodomites, and sexual perverts.*

Selected passages

1599 Geneva Bible (GNV)

9 Know ye not that the unrighteous shall not inherit the kingdom of God? Be not deceived: neither fornicators, nor idolaters, nor adulterers, nor **wantons***, nor buggerers,*

10 Nor thieves, nor covetous, nor drunkards, nor railers, nor extortioners shall inherit the kingdom of God. 1 Corinthians 6:9-10

King James Version (KJV)

9 Know ye not that the unrighteous shall not inherit the kingdom of God? Be not deceived: neither fornicators, nor idolaters, nor adulterers, nor **effeminate***, nor abusers of themselves with mankind,*

10 Nor thieves, nor covetous, nor drunkards, nor revilers, nor extortioners, shall inherit the kingdom of God. 1 Corinthians 6:9-10

Douay-Rheims 1899 American Edition (DRA)

9 Know you not that the unjust shall not possess the kingdom of God? Do not err: neither fornicators, nor idolaters, nor adulterers,

*10 Nor the **effeminate**, nor liers with mankind, nor thieves, nor covetous, nor drunkards, nor railers, nor extortioners, shall possess the kingdom of God. 1* Corinthians 6:9-10

American Standard Version (ASV)

*9 Or know ye not that the unrighteous shall not inherit the kingdom of God? Be not deceived: neither fornicators, nor idolaters, nor adulterers, nor **effeminate**, nor abusers of themselves with men,*

10 nor thieves, nor covetous, nor drunkards, nor revilers, nor extortioners, shall inherit the kingdom of God. 1 Corinthians 6:9-10

Authorized (King James) Version (AKJV)

*9 Know ye not that the unrighteous shall not inherit the kingdom of God? Be not deceived: neither fornicators, nor idolaters, nor adulterers, nor **effeminate**, nor abusers of themselves with mankind, 10 nor thieves, nor covetous, nor drunkards, nor revilers, nor extortioners, shall inherit the kingdom of God. 1* Corinthians 6:9-10

Wycliffe Bible (WYC)

*9 Whether ye know not, that wicked men shall not wield the kingdom of God? Do not ye err; neither lechers, neither men that serve maumets [neither men serving to idols], neither adulterers, **neither lechers against kind**, neither they that do lechery with men,*

10 neither thieves, neither avaricious men [neither covetous men, or niggards], neither men full of drunkenness, neither cursers, neither raveners, shall wield the kingdom of God. 1 Corinthians 6:9-10

Another passage from the Great Apostle Paul (Emphasis added by me.):

I don't want you to forget, dear brothers and sisters, about our ancestors in the wilderness long ago. All of them were guided by a cloud that moved ahead of them, and all of them walked through the sea on dry ground. In the cloud and in the sea, all of them were baptized as followers of Moses. All of them ate the same spiritual food, and all of them drank the same spiritual water. For they drank from the spiritual rock that traveled with them, and that rock was Christ. Yet God was not pleased with most of them, and their bodies were scattered in the wilderness.

*These things happened as a warning to us, so that we would not crave evil things as they did, or worship idols as some of them did. As the Scriptures say, "The people celebrated with feasting and drinking, and they indulged in pagan revelry." **And we must not engage in sexual immorality** as some of them did, causing 23,000 of them to die in one day.*

Nor should we put Christ to the test, as some of them did and then died from snakebites. And don't grumble as some of them did, and then were destroyed by the angel of death. These things happened to them as examples for us. They were written down to warn us who live at the end of the age.

If you think you are standing strong, be careful not to fall. The temptations in your life are no different from what others experience. And God is faithful. He will not allow the temptation to be more than you can stand. When you are tempted, he will show you a way out so that you can endure. 1 Corinthians 10:1-13

And this from the Book of Ephesians (Ephesians authorship has traditionally been credited to Paul, but there are some who believe it is Deutero-Pauline, meaning it was written in Paul's name by a later author influenced by Paul's teachings):

With the Lord's authority I say this: Live no longer as the Gentiles do, for they are hopelessly confused. Their minds are full of darkness; they wander far from the life God gives because they have closed their minds and hardened their hearts against him. They have no sense of shame. They live for lustful pleasure and eagerly practice every kind of impurity.

But that isn't what you learned about Christ. Since you have heard about Jesus and have learned the truth that comes from him, throw off your old sinful nature and your former way of life, which is corrupted by lust and deception. Instead, let the Spirit renew your thoughts and attitudes. Put on your new nature, created to be like God—truly righteous and holy.

So stop telling lies. Let us tell our neighbors the truth, for we are all parts of the same body. And "don't sin by letting anger control you." Don't let the sun go down while you are still angry, for anger gives a foothold to the devil.

If you are a thief, quit stealing. Instead, use your hands for good hard work, and then give generously to others in need. Don't use foul or abusive language. Let everything you say be good and helpful, so that your words will be an encouragement to those who hear them.

And do not bring sorrow to God's Holy Spirit by the way you live. Remember, he has identified you as his own, guaranteeing that you will be saved on the day of redemption. Ephesians 4:17-30

> **It appears Paul condemned all forms of homosexual behavior. In other parts of the Bible he also told slaves to obey their masters not once, but five times. He instructed women not to teach, not to cut their hair, and not to speak in church.**

IMPORTANT: To ascertain the entire truth, as revealed in God's Word, one must pray for guidance from the Holy Spirit, research all of the passages regarding a topic, using the context around the passage, comparing it with other parts of the Bible, and establishing an understanding of the language and customs of the time it was written — all in an effort to completely comprehend what the original writer(s) intended to communicate.

I work hard to ascertain truth and am a fanatic about explaining what I discover.

> *Work hard so you can present yourself to God and receive his approval. Be a good worker, one who does not need to be ashamed and who **correctly explains the word of truth**.* 2 Timothy 2:15 (Emphasis added by me.)

> **The topic of homosexuality is complex. There are many places that condemn it, and none I have found that condone it. We could argue and analyze the subject of homosexuality until Hell freezes over, and gain little ground, but there is one thing the Bible makes clear — The Good News.**

The Good News

The Bible clearly states we are all sinners in need of a savior. Jesus Christ is that Savior because his shed Blood on the Cross paid for the past, present, and future sins of all mankind. Regardless of the sin, it has been paid for. It is a gift.

> *God saved you by his grace when you believed. And you can't take credit for this; it is a gift from God. Salvation is not a reward for the good things we have done, so none of us can boast about it.* Ephesians 2:8-9

> *So now there is no condemnation for those who belong to Christ Jesus.* Romans 8:1

This verse declares Christians **not guilty**. Jesus, by way of his finished work on the Cross, has paid the price for our sins and has offered us freedom to live our lives in a way that is either pleasing to our flesh, or pleasing to his Spirit.

If you haven't accepted Jesus Christ as your only way to receive eternal life in Heaven, and then on the New Earth, I beg you do that now. Don't wait. Of the thousands of Christians I have personally met, none have said they regret it.

> **Being gay will not send someone to Hell, but rejecting the Lord Jesus as one's Savior will.**

If you consider yourself a sinner, and we are all sinners, please read this book in its entirety, but pay particular attention to **Section Three: Christian Salvation**.

The bottom line

If you are a practicing homosexual who has not been born again, you should be more concerned about knowing Jesus than the morality of being gay. Sexual preference is secondary.

> *"But everyone who denies me here on earth, I will also deny before my Father in heaven."* Matthew 10:33, Jesus' words

Then he said to the disciples, "Anyone who accepts your message is also accepting me. And anyone who rejects you is rejecting me. And anyone who rejects me is rejecting God, who sent me." Luke 10:16

"For God loved the world so much that he gave his one and only Son, so that everyone who believes in him will not perish but have eternal life. God sent his Son into the world not to judge the world, but to save the world through him.

There is no judgment against anyone who believes in him. But anyone who does not believe in him has already been judged for not believing in God's one and only Son." John 3:16-18, Jesus' words

He that believeth on the Son hath everlasting life: and he that believeth not the Son shall not see life; but the wrath of God abideth on him. John 3:36

"The world's sin is that it refuses to believe in me." John 16:9, Jesus' words

Do not reject Jesus as your only way to receive eternal life in Heaven!

The believer's prayer

Although it is a person's faith alone in Jesus' finished work that saves, many Christians repeat a prayer as their acknowledgement. Also, oftentimes people have neglected their Christian life, so they want to begin again. Saying a prayer is not necessary, but God loves it when we pray. Prayer can be done aloud, silently, publicly, or privately. It is not the intellectual content of the prayer, but its sincerity. Say something like this:

God,

I believe you came to Earth in the form of a man named Jesus and died on a cross as payment for my sins. Many people saw you come back from being dead, which proved you are God and that you can overcome death. I know you are living in me, which is my assurance I will live eternally with you. I am saying this prayer to reinforce my relationship with you, and I am praying that I will grow in my Christian faith.

Amen.

The Bible says because you are a believer in Jesus' finished work, you were saved the moment you believed. This is also known as *justified, born spiritually, regenerated,* or *born again.*

The seeker's prayer

God,

I am not yet convinced, but I want to be. If you are for real, and if you came to Earth in the form of a man, I invite your Spirit to live in me and to show me truths as you guide me through my life.

Amen.

I believe if you say the seeker's prayer God will reveal the truth to you. At the very moment you trust Jesus as your only means of salvation, you will be saved. Now find a church and purchase an easy-to-read New Testament Bible.

Do not judge others

If you are one of those who believes Jesus Christ died on a cross as payment for your gossiping about your homosexual neighbor, but believe Jesus' death was not effective enough to forgive that gay neighbor, you don't thoroughly understand Jesus' death. <u>God forgave gossips and gays.</u>

> *You may think you can condemn such people, but you are just as bad, and you have no excuse! When you say they are wicked and should be punished, you are condemning yourself, for you who judge others do these very same things.* Romans 2:1

Notes:

Chapter 10

What Jesus said about Homosexuality

Notes:

Chapter 11

Are People Born Gay?

Did you really think I am smart enough to answer a question that is contemplated, deliberated, and debated by millions of intellects who cannot come to a scientific determination?

It is beyond my pay grade to understand and analyze the miracles that take place when babies are being created in their mothers' wombs. I could pretend to understand the functions of DNA, testosterone, estrogen, progesterone, androgens, chromosomes, adrenal hyperplasia, and all of those other hundred-dollar medical terms; but regarding God's recipe to create a human, I am as dumb as a stump — perhaps dumber. God's creation of a body, mind, personality, soul, and spirit is a mystery to me.

A thoughtless Christian statement

I have had hundreds of folks tell me God would not allow someone to be born gay because we are made in God's image. Baloney, I say!

> *Then God said, "Let us make human beings in our image, to be like us. They will reign over the fish in the sea, the birds in the sky, the livestock, all the wild animals on the earth, and the small animals that scurry along the ground."*
>
> *So God created human beings in his own image.*
> *In the image of God he created them;*
> *male and female he created them.* Genesis 1:26-27

Most folks do not take the time to analyze Genesis 1:26-27 to gain an intelligent awareness of our image versus God's image. A well-thought-out analysis reveals we have attributes similar to the Creator of all things, but we are not like God.

1. God created everything in existence. We humans cannot cure the common cold effectively.
2. God was of a triune nature. We are not.

3. We are sinners.
4. God doesn't make bad choices. Adam did.

Adam was created with perfect health and eternal life, but he had the capacity to make free choices. Although created as righteous, Adam made a sinful choice to rebel against God's instructions. Thus, Adam inflicted sin and imperfection into all mankind. This is why we must be re-made in the likeness of Jesus by the indwelling of the Holy Spirit.

In Genesis 1:27, God stated, "...male and female he created them." In the beginning, humans were created as male or female, but that is no longer applicable today. Genesis 1:27 was before Adam sinned, which changed God's Kingdom to be less than perfect. Mankind is no longer as were Adam (male) and Eve (female). Approximately one in every 2,000 babies is born with both male and female sexual organs, or characteristics of both sexes' organs — called *intersex*.

> **From the fact that some children are born with both male and female sex organs, one must also intellectually conclude that some can be born with varying sexual preferences. To deny this would be similar to burying one's head in the sand.**

Because I am not smart enough to understand what takes place in a mother's womb, when my gay friends tell me they were born gay, I believe them. I am not in the practice of calling my friends liars, especially when it is a statement that cannot be proven otherwise.

I am an evangelist. My specialty is helping folks to receive eternal life in God's eternal dwelling place — not judging them.

Sexual preference does not affect a person's eternal destiny

My factual declaration that *sexual preference does not affect a person's destiny* angers many judgmental and legalistic Christians. The Bible says we are all born sinners, and our sinful natures differ.

> *When Adam sinned, sin entered the world. Adam's sin brought death, so death spread to everyone, for everyone sinned. Yes, people sinned even before the law was given. But it was not counted as sin because there was*

not yet any law to break. Still, everyone died—from the time of Adam to the time of Moses—even those who did not disobey an explicit commandment of God, as Adam did. Now Adam is a symbol, a representation of Christ, who was yet to come. But there is a great difference between Adam's sin and God's gracious gift. For the sin of this one man, Adam, brought death to many. But even greater is **God's wonderful grace and his gift of forgiveness to many through this other man, Jesus Christ.** *And the result of God's gracious gift is very different from the result of that one man's sin. For Adam's sin led to condemnation, but* **God's free gift leads to our being made right with God, even though we are guilty of many sins.** *For the sin of this one man, Adam, caused death to rule over many. But even greater is God's wonderful grace and his gift of righteousness, for all who receive it will live in triumph over sin and death through this one man, Jesus Christ.*

Yes, Adam's one sin brings condemnation for everyone, but Christ's one act of righteousness brings a right relationship with God and new life for everyone. *Because one person disobeyed God, many became sinners. But because one other person obeyed God, many will be made righteous.*

God's law was given so that all people could see how sinful they were. But as people sinned more and more, God's wonderful grace became more abundant. *So just as sin ruled over all people and brought them to death, now God's wonderful grace rules instead, giving us right standing with God and resulting in eternal life through Jesus Christ our Lord.* Romans 5:12-21 (Emphasis added by me.)

God's gift is *justification*, and being justified is what determines a person's eternal destiny.

God's grace is greater than our sins

God saved you by his grace when you believed. And you can't take credit for this; it is a gift from God. Salvation is not a reward for the good things we have done, so none of us can boast about it. Ephesians 2:8-9

Faith comes from hearing the *Good News.*

So faith comes from hearing, that is, hearing the Good News about Christ. Romans 10:17

If you lack faith, I suggest you ask.

> *"And so I tell you, keep on asking, and you will receive what you ask for. Keep on seeking, and you will find. Keep on knocking, and the door will be opened to you. For everyone who asks, receives. Everyone who seeks, finds. And to everyone who knocks, the door will be opened."* Luke 11:9-12, Jesus' words

As with any gift from God, it is our responsibility to exercise the gift and not become complacent, lazy, or apathetic.

> *And so, dear brothers and sisters, I plead with you to give your bodies to God because of all he has done for you. Let them be a living and holy sacrifice—the kind he will find acceptable. This is truly the way to worship him. Don't copy the behavior and customs of this world, but let God transform you into a new person by changing the way you think. Then you will learn to know God's will for you, which is good and pleasing and perfect.* Romans 12:1-2

> *Therefore, since we are surrounded by such a huge crowd of witnesses to the life of faith, let us strip off every weight that slows us down, especially the sin that so easily trips us up. And let us run with endurance the race God has set before us. We do this by keeping our eyes on Jesus, the champion who initiates and perfects our faith. Because of the joy awaiting him, he endured the cross, disregarding its shame. Now he is seated in the place of honor beside God's throne.* Hebrews 12:1-2

If you are behaving in a way that offends the Holy Spirit, you must use every resource to abstain.

> *You say, "I am allowed to do anything"—but not everything is good for you. And even though "I am allowed to do anything," **I must not become a slave** to anything.* 1 Corinthians 6:12

> *You say, "I am allowed to do anything"—but not everything is good for you. You say, "I am allowed to do anything"—but **not everything is beneficial**.* 1 Corinthians 10:23

I emphasized words in the above passages that stress we cannot become slaves to sin, and as Christians, although we are free from laws, not all behavior is beneficial.

Because we were born with a predisposition, it does not give us permission to become addicted to anything that will have harmful consequences.

Many people are born with a disposition to commit adultery, and most are born with the predisposition to lie — but that doesn't mean it is OK.

I am guilty of having a sinful nature. At 68, I am a very happily married man. I have always appreciated the female gender, so it wouldn't be impossible to be tempted into an adulterous situation under certain circumstances. Could it be I was born with a tendency to be promiscuous? Perhaps, but I don't use that as an excuse to cheat on my wife.

Many couples use the excuse that what takes place between two people is their business. That is a poor excuse for bad behavior. There are always innocent bystanders.

> **We are all born so imperfect that if we constantly acted on all of our desires we would be a world gone mad.**

Notes:

Chapter 12

You can't Stop Sinning

According to the Scriptures, it is impossible to live without sinning.

> As the Scriptures say,
> "No one is righteous—
>   not even one." Romans 3:10

> If we claim we have no sin, we are only fooling ourselves and not living in the truth. 1 John 1:8

If possible to live a sinless life, then Jesus Christ died for nothing!

Needlessly, most believers periodically punish themselves for the inability to stop sinning. *We were born with the predisposition to live a flawed life.* Even the Apostle Paul, possibly the greatest Christian of all time, struggled with sin.

> So the trouble is not with the law, for it is spiritual and good. The trouble is with me, for I am all too human, a slave to sin. I don't really understand myself, for I want to do what is right, but I don't do it. Instead, I do what I hate. But if I know that what I am doing is wrong, this shows that I agree that the law is good. So I am not the one doing wrong; it is sin living in me that does it.

> And I know that nothing good lives in me, that is, in my sinful nature. I want to do what is right, but I can't. I want to do what is good, but I don't. I don't want to do what is wrong, but I do it anyway. But if I do what I don't want to do, I am not really the one doing wrong; it is sin living in me that does it.

> I have discovered this principle of life—that when I want to do what is right, I inevitably do what is wrong. I love God's law with all my heart. But there

*is another power within me that is at war with my mind. This power makes
me a slave to the sin that is still within me. Oh, what a miserable person
I am! Who will free me from this life that is dominated by sin and death?*
Romans 7:14-24

Give yourself permission to sin — a little

WOW! I'll bet my statement to give yourself permission to sin will drive some of you
religious nuts crazy. I said what I did because it is a fact that you will sin. Everyone
does, including the Great Apostle Paul – the chief of sinners.

> *But suppose we seek to be made right with God through faith in Christ and
> then we are found guilty because we have abandoned the law. Would that
> mean Christ has led us into sin? Absolutely not! Rather, I am a sinner if I
> rebuild the old system of law I already tore down. **For when I tried to keep
> the law, it condemned me.** So I died to the law—I stopped trying to meet all
> its requirements—so that I might live for God. My old self has been crucified
> with Christ. It is no longer I who live, but Christ lives in me. So I live in this
> earthly body by trusting in the Son of God, who loved me and gave himself
> for me. I do not treat the grace of God as meaningless. **For if keeping the law
> could make us right with God, then there was no need for Christ to die.***
> Galatians 2:17-21 (Emphasis added by me.)

If you do not give yourself permission to be human, you may possibly be one of those
millions who depend on anti-anxiety, or anti-depression, medications to function.
Also, you may become so self-righteous that you reject the idea of needing Jesus as
your savior (many do).

We must allow ourselves to be human, and to accept Jesus' free gift of grace! That is
why he died.

> **"Be a sinner and sin strongly, but more strongly have faith and rejoice in
> Christ." Martin Luther (1483-1546)**

We are all weak, so we all sin. Luther's point is not whether sin is OK, but whether
sin is a real fact. Luther is acknowledging the reality that most people, including
Christians, struggle with some sort of sinful behavior repeatedly. Luther is remind-
ing us that *God's grace is greater than our sins.*

> "The greatest enemy to human souls is the self-righteous spirit which makes men look to themselves for salvation." Charles Haddon Spurgeon (1834-1892)

A license to sin?

> God's law was given so that all people could see how sinful they were. **But as people sinned more and more, God's wonderful grace became more abundant.** Romans 5:20 (Emphasis added by me.)

The passage above makes it clear that God's grace is greater than our sins. But, that does not mean we should sin more.

> Well then, should we keep on sinning so that God can show us more and more of his wonderful grace? Of course not! Since we have died to sin, how can we continue to live in it? Or have you forgotten that when we were joined with Christ Jesus in baptism, we joined him in his death? For we died and were buried with Christ by baptism. And just as Christ was raised from the dead by the glorious power of the Father, now we also may live new lives.

> Since we have been united with him in his death, we will also be raised to life as he was. We know that our old sinful selves were crucified with Christ so that sin might lose its power in our lives. We are no longer slaves to sin. For when we died with Christ we were set free from the power of sin. And since we died with Christ, we know we will also live with him. We are sure of this because Christ was raised from the dead, and he will never die again. Death no longer has any power over him. When he died, he died once to break the power of sin. But now that he lives, he lives for the glory of God. So you also should consider yourselves to be dead to the power of sin and alive to God through Christ Jesus.

> Do not let sin control the way you live; do not give in to sinful desires. Do not let any part of your body become an instrument of evil to serve sin. Instead, give yourselves completely to God, for you were dead, but now you have new life. So use your whole body as an instrument to do what is right for the glory of God. Sin is no longer your master, for you no longer live under the requirements of the law. Instead, you live under the freedom of God's grace. Well then, since God's grace has set us free from the law, does that mean we can go on sinning? Of course not! Don't you realize that you become the slave of

whatever you choose to obey? You can be a slave to sin, which leads to death, or you can choose to obey God, which leads to righteous living. Thank God! Once you were slaves of sin, but now you wholeheartedly obey this teaching we have given you. Now you are free from your slavery to sin, and you have become slaves to righteous living.

Because of the weakness of your human nature, I am using the illustration of slavery to help you understand all this. Previously, you let yourselves be slaves to impurity and lawlessness, which led ever deeper into sin. Now you must give yourselves to be slaves to righteous living so that you will become holy.

When you were slaves to sin, you were free from the obligation to do right. And what was the result? You are now ashamed of the things you used to do, things that end in eternal doom. But now you are free from the power of sin and have become slaves of God. Now you do those things that lead to holiness and result in eternal life. For the wages of sin is death, but the free gift of God is eternal life through Christ Jesus our Lord. Romans 6:1-23

Paul is not advocating sinful behavior, but suggesting we think of our sinful life as dead and buried.

Too much freedom has consequences

"So if the Son sets you free, you are truly free." John 8:36, Jesus' words

Habitual sinning is ignoring the Holy Spirit who lives in each Christian. Don't be stupid and allow your freedom to hurt yourself or others.

You say, "I am allowed to do anything"—but not everything is good for you. And even though "I am allowed to do anything," I must not become a slave to anything. 1 Corinthians 6:12

You say, "I am allowed to do anything"—but not everything is good for you. You say, "I am allowed to do anything"—but not everything is beneficial. 1 Corinthians 10:23

Jesus Christ is the answer for sins

Christian salvation does not depend on our lack of sin, or our good works. <u>Salvation is entirely a product of God's grace.</u>

Thank God! The answer is in Jesus Christ our Lord. So you see how it is: In my mind I really want to obey God's law, but because of my sinful nature I am a slave to sin. Romans 7:25

So now there is no condemnation for those who belong to Christ Jesus. And because you belong to him, the power of the life-giving Spirit has freed you from the power of sin that leads to death. The law of Moses was unable to save us because of the weakness of our sinful nature. So God did what the law could not do. He sent his own Son in a body like the bodies we sinners have. And in that body God declared an end to sin's control over us by giving his Son as a sacrifice for our sins. He did this so that the just requirement of the law would be fully satisfied for us, who no longer follow our sinful nature but instead follow the Spirit. Romans 8:1-4

God saved you by his grace when you believed. And you can't take credit for this; it is a gift from God. Salvation is not a reward for the good things we have done, so none of us can boast about it. Ephesians 2:8-9

For God's will was for us to be made holy by the sacrifice of the body of Jesus Christ, once for all time. Hebrews 10:10

Jesus became sin

The Bible teaches that Jesus took *all* of our sins to the Cross in his body. Christ became sin for us so we would have absolute righteousness. This is called *justification,* and it is what saves a person from eternal damnation. When we are justified, it means that we are made righteous through grace because of the Blood of Christ. The Christian's righteousness is imputed (credited) by God because of his love for us. It is free and is not earned. ***It is by grace alone that we are justified, and the Bible says it has nothing to do with our behavior.***

> *God made him who had no sin to be sin for us, so that in him we might become the righteousness of God.* 2 Corinthians 5:21 (NIV)

> *He canceled the record of the charges against us and took it away by nailing it to the cross.* Colossians 2:14

Guilt-filled Christian lives are the result of not understanding the truth. Guilt is a tool of Satan. The truth is that God does not remember our sins because they were nailed to the Cross with Jesus!

But now God has shown us a way to be made right with him without keeping the requirements of the law, as was promised in the writings of Moses and the prophets long ago. We are made right with God by placing our faith in Jesus Christ. And this is true for everyone who believes, no matter who we are. Romans 3:21-22

"Oh, what joy for those
whose disobedience is forgiven,
whose sins are put out of sight.
Yes, what joy for those
whose record the LORD has cleared of sin." Romans 4:7-8

And since it is through God's kindness, then it is not by their good works. For in that case, God's grace would not be what it really is—free and undeserved. Romans 11:6

God saved you by his grace when you believed. And you can't take credit for this; it is a gift from God. Salvation is not a reward for the good things we have done, so none of us can boast about it. Ephesians 2:8-9

The Old Testament prepared the world for the forthcoming Messiah — a baby named Jesus.

Jesus provides an advocate

The New Testament is dedicated to teaching the grace of Jesus Christ and the Counselor (Holy Spirit) he would send on our behalf.

"But when the Father sends the Advocate as my representative—that is, the Holy Spirit—he will teach you everything and will remind you of everything I have told you." John 14:26, Jesus' words

"O Holy Spirit, descend plentifully into my heart. Enlighten the dark corners of this neglected dwelling and scatter there Thy cheerful beams." Saint Augustine (354-430)

Do not give Satan a stronghold

A final word: Be strong in the Lord and in his mighty power. Put on all of God's armor so that you will be able to stand firm against all strategies of the

devil. For we are not fighting against flesh-and-blood enemies, but against evil rulers and authorities of the unseen world, against mighty powers in this dark world, and against evil spirits in the heavenly places.

Therefore, put on every piece of God's armor so you will be able to resist the enemy in the time of evil. Then after the battle you will still be standing firm. Stand your ground, putting on the belt of truth and the body armor of God's righteousness. For shoes, put on the peace that comes from the Good News so that you will be fully prepared. In addition to all of these, hold up the shield of faith to stop the fiery arrows of the devil. Put on salvation as your helmet, and take the sword of the Spirit, which is the word of God.

Pray in the Spirit at all times and on every occasion. Stay alert and be persistent in your prayers for all believers everywhere. Ephesians 6:10-18

Following the Spirit improves behavior

To show their appreciation for what God provided through Jesus Christ, most Christians make moral improvements, though this is not always easy.

The best way for a person to change is to replace the bad behavior with something superior. There is nothing more superior than allowing Jesus' Spirit to be one's personal counselor. ***People need to allow Jesus to live through them via the Holy Spirit, rather than struggling to make feeble attempts at changing their own behavior.*** The flesh is weak, but the Spirit is strong.

> *"Keep watch and pray, so that you will not give in to temptation. For the spirit is willing, but the body is weak!"* Matthew 26:41, Jesus' words

Once a person begins to allow the Holy Spirit to work through them, the more moral they become, and the less they enjoy immorality.

For more information regarding how a Christian improves his or her behavior, I beg that you read the remainder of this book.

Notes:

SECTION THREE
Christian Salvation

Notes:

Chapter 13

Old and New Covenants

Adam and Eve were the first two humans. From the very beginning, God established right from wrong, but Adam and Eve disobeyed. You know that story. This failure to obey God is known as *original sin.* The immediate effect of Adam and Eve's sin was they died spiritually.

Because all mankind are descendants of Adam and Eve, sin entered the entire human race. This is referred to as *imputed sin.* The verb *impute* means to lay the responsibility or blame on someone for something bad; or, to give credit for something good. To assign as a characteristic. Synonyms: ascribe, assign, attribute. Because of imputed sin, everyone is born a sinner.

God had many behavioral covenants with mankind, beginning with Adam. Because of the weakness of humans, they all failed.

The Old Covenant

Approximately 2,500 years after creation, when God's chosen people, the Israelites, came out of Egypt, God gave them the Ten Commandments. These were just the beginning of God's given laws. An additional 603 laws were given for the Israelites to obey in order to gain favor with God. Of those laws, 365 were the *shall-not* kind. These laws, all described in the Old Testament Bible, are known as the Old Covenant (covenant means *agreement*).

Old Testament (pre-Jesus) believers in God offered him continuous sacrifices in attempts to have their sins forgiven, but these sacrifices served only as a temporary cleansing of sins, thus provided only temporary forgiveness. God foreknew it would be impossible for anyone to obey these laws, but that was part of his plan.

> *Why, then, was the law given? It was given alongside the promise to show people their sins. But the law was designed to last only until the coming of the child who was promised. God gave his law through angels to Moses, who was*

the mediator between God and the people. Now a mediator is helpful if more than one party must reach an agreement. But God, who is one, did not use a mediator when he gave his promise to Abraham.

Is there a conflict, then, between God's law and God's promises? Absolutely not! If the law could give us new life, we could be made right with God by obeying it. But the Scriptures declare that we are all prisoners of sin, so we receive God's promise of freedom only by believing in Jesus Christ. Galatians 3:19-22

God is infinitely holy and righteous, and he wants his human creation to be just as holy and righteous. ***It is humanly impossible to use the laws given to the Israelites as the evaluation or evidence of holiness.*** If a conscientious person attempts to compile a list of his or her sins based on Old Testament laws, he or she will be overcome with guilt and failure. Guilt is a tool of Satan.

But those who depend on the law to make them right with God are under his curse, for the Scriptures say, "Cursed is everyone who does not observe and obey all the commands that are written in God's Book of the Law." Galatians 3:10

The blood of animals was commonly used for these temporary forgiveness sacrifices.

Animal blood temporarily forgave sins

God's prerequisite in the Old Testament for the forgiveness of sins was attained by the Israelites shedding the blood of animals. The term *blood* has a special meaning in the Bible. Blood is the evidence of life, thus considered sacred, just as life is considered sacred. Because of this, Israel's priests used the blood of animals when preparing the sacrifices to God for the benefit of the people.

Then slaughter the young bull in the Lord's presence, and Aaron's sons, the priests, will present the animal's blood by splattering it against all sides of the alter that stands at the entrance to the Tabernacle. Leviticus 1:5

Then the priest must remove all the animal's fat and burn it on the altar, just as he does with the bull offered as a sin offering for the high priest. Through this process, the priest will purify the people, making them right with the Lord, and they will be forgiven. Leviticus 4:19-20

In fact, according to the law of Moses, nearly everything was purified with blood. For without the shedding of blood, there is no forgiveness. Hebrews 9:22

Tens of thousands of animals were ceremonially slaughtered by Israelite priests for centuries, illustrating the seriousness of sin. *Still, these repetitive sacrifices were nothing more than a bandage, only acting as a covering for sin.*

One example is in the Old Testament Book of Exodus. God helped the Israelites escape from their slavery in Egypt by inflicting 10 plagues upon the Egyptians before Pharaoh would release his Israelite slaves. The last and worst of the plagues resulted in the death of the Egyptian firstborn. The Israelites were instructed to paint the sides and tops of the doorframes of their homes with the blood of a slaughtered one-year-old lamb so the Lord knew to "pass over" the firstborn in those homes — hence Passover, the holiday to celebrate Israel's deliverance from Egypt.

Another example took place at Mount Sinai. Blood was poured out to sanction the covenant between God and the Israelite people.

> *Then Moses took the blood from the basins and splattered it over the people, declaring, "Look, this blood confirms the covenant the Lord has made with you in giving you these instructions."* Exodus 24:8

Because the blood of the sacrificed animals served as only temporary forgiveness, the animal sacrifices needed to be a continuous practice.

God introduced a new plan!

The God of the Israelites (the God of Abraham, Isaac, and Jacob) is the one and only God, the Creator of all that exists. He is also the same God of Christians. But he introduced a new plan that would change the course of history.

God's new plan, the *New Covenant*, would end God's required animal sacrifice forever, and put an end to laws etched in stone and impossible for humans to obey.

The New Covenant (*contract* or *agreement*) was established only by <u>the shed Blood of Jesus, who was the ultimate and final Sacrificial Lamb.</u>

The old way, with laws etched in stone, led to death, though it began with such glory that the people of Israel could not bear to look at Moses' face. For his face shone with the glory of God, even though the brightness was already fading away. Shouldn't we expect far greater glory under the new way, now that the Holy Spirit is giving life? If the old way, which brings condemnation, was glorious, how much more glorious is the new way, which makes us right with God! In fact, that first glory was not glorious at all compared with the overwhelming glory of the new way. So if the old way, which has been replaced, was glorious, how much more glorious is the new, which remains forever!

Since this new way gives us such confidence, we can be very bold. We are not like Moses, who put a veil over his face so the people of Israel would not see the glory, even though it was destined to fade away. But the people's minds were hardened, and to this day whenever the old covenant is being read, the same veil covers their minds so they cannot understand the truth. And this veil can be removed only by believing in Christ. Yes, even today when they read Moses' writings, their hearts are covered with that veil, and they do not understand.

But whenever someone turns to the Lord, the veil is taken away. For the Lord is the Spirit, and wherever the Spirit of the Lord is, there is freedom. So all of us who have had that veil removed can see and reflect the glory of the Lord. And the Lord—who is the Spirit—makes us more and more like him as we are changed into his glorious image.
2 Corinthians 3:7-18

The New Covenant is the Good News

*Let me now remind you, dear brothers and sisters, of the **Good News** I preached to you before. You welcomed it then, and you still stand firm in it. **It is this Good News that saves you** if you continue to believe the message I told you—unless, of course, you believed something that was never true in the first place.*

*I passed on to you what was most important and what had also been passed on to me. **Christ died for our sins, just as the Scriptures said. He was buried, and he was raised from the dead on the third day,** just as the Scriptures said.* 1 Corinthians 15:1-4 (Emphasis added by me.)

> **The *New Covenant* is God's agreement that replaces the Old Covenant. It is not only for the Jews, but for all mankind. Those who accept the New Covenant with God are referred to as *Christians*.**

When one accepts Jesus as Savior, righteousness is imputed, termed *imputed righteousness*.

The following passage explains the Old Testament (Old Covenant) and New Testament (New Covenant):

> *When Adam sinned, sin entered the world. Adam's sin brought death, so death spread to everyone, for everyone sinned. Yes, people sinned even before the law was given. But it was not counted as sin because there was not yet any law to break. Still, everyone died—from the time of Adam to the time of Moses—even those who did not disobey an explicit commandment of God, as Adam did. Now Adam is a symbol, a representation of Christ, who was yet to come. But there is a great difference between Adam's sin and God's gracious gift. For the sin of this one man, Adam, brought death to many. But even greater is God's wonderful grace and his gift of forgiveness to many through this other man, Jesus Christ. And the result of God's gracious gift is very different from the result of that one man's sin. For Adam's sin led to condemnation, but God's free gift leads to our being made right with God, even though we are guilty of many sins. For the sin of this one man, Adam, caused death to rule over many. But even greater is God's wonderful grace and his gift of righteousness, for all who receive it will live in triumph over sin and death through this one man, Jesus Christ.*
>
> *Yes, Adam's one sin brings condemnation for everyone, but Christ's one act of righteousness brings a right relationship with God and new life for everyone. Because one person disobeyed God, many became sinners. But because one other person obeyed God, many will be made righteous.*
>
> *God's law was given so that all people could see how sinful they were. But as people sinned more and more, God's wonderful grace became more abundant. So just as sin ruled over all people and brought them to death, now God's wonderful grace rules instead, giving us right standing with God and resulting in eternal life through Jesus Christ our Lord.* Romans 5:12-21

No distinction between Jew, Gentile, slave, free, male, or female

The term *Israelites* refers to both the direct descendants of the patriarch Jacob (Israel) and the historical populations of the United Kingdom of Israel. For the post-exilic period, beginning in the 5th century BC, the fragments of the Israelite tribes came to be referred to as Jews (tribes of Judah, Simeon, Benjamin, and partially Levi), named for the kingdom of Judah.

According to the Old Testament, the Israelites were the "chosen people" of God; however, the New Testament Bible teaches the Christian Church is the Israel of God. Another way of putting it would be that Christians are now God's chosen people.

> *There is no longer Jew or Gentile, slave or free, male and female. For you are all one in Christ Jesus.* Galatians 3:28

The walls of distinction were broken down by the Blood (New Covenant) of Jesus. Those who belong to Jesus are part of his glorious eternal Kingdom. Those who don't belong to Jesus — are lost.

Chapter 14

Christian Salvation

Salvation, in the eternal sense, describes the experience of being saved from eternal punishment in Hell, and the gift of receiving eternal life with Jesus (and then on the New Earth), by trusting in Jesus Christ's finished work as payment for all sins — past, present, and future.

> **You were dead because of your sins and because your sinful nature was not yet cut away. Then, God made you alive with Christ, for <u>he forgave all our sins. He canceled the record of the charges against us and took it away by nailing it to the cross</u>. Colossians 2:13-14 (Emphasis added by me.)**

The *finished work* not only includes Jesus' death, which resulted in forgiveness for all sin, but also his resurrection, which gives believers eternal life.

Our Savior Jesus

"And she will have a son, and you are to name him Jesus, for he will save his people from their sins." Matthew 1:21

Jesus means: the Lord saves, as translated from the Hebrew word *Yeshua.*

For God made Christ, who never sinned, to be the offering for our sin, so that we could be made right with God through Christ. 2 Corinthians 5:21

Christ means "Anointed One, Messiah."

Jesus was God incarnate

You learned in the chapter titled "God, Jesus, and the Holy Spirit" that Jesus was God incarnate. It is important to believe this so you fully comprehend it was God who came to Earth in the form of a man to die on a cross to pay for all of the sins of all mankind.

> *The next day John saw Jesus coming toward him and said, "Look! The Lamb of God who takes away the sin of the world!"* John 1:29

In the verse above, John the Baptist refers to Jesus as the *Lamb of God* because a lamb sacrifice was very familiar to the Jews. You read earlier in this book, when studying about the Old Covenant, that God's prerequisite for the forgiveness of sins was attained only by the shedding of blood. However, the blood of the sacrificed animal served only as a temporary forgiveness for the sinner, meaning animal sacrifice needed to be a continuous practice.

John referred to Jesus as the *Lamb of God* because Jesus would be the ultimate and final sacrifice (also referred to as the *Sacrificial Lamb*).

Jesus became sin and was crucified

The Bible teaches that Jesus loved mankind so much that he took *all* of our sins to the Cross in his body. Jesus was a sinless man who was miraculously capable of transferring the sin of the world into his body immediately before he died.

> *"There is no greater love than to lay down one's life for one's friends."*
> John 15:13, Jesus' words

Christ became sin for us so we could have absolute and permanent righteousness. When we acknowledge Jesus as God incarnate and accept his sacrificial death as propitiation for mankind's sins, we immediately receive his Spirit, which makes us righteous. This *imputed* (credited) *righteousness* is called *justification*. When we are justified, it guarantees we are made righteous by the grace of God because of the Blood of Christ. The Christian's righteousness is imputed by God because of his love for us. It is free and is not earned. It is by grace alone that we are justified, and the Bible says it has nothing to do with our behavior.

> *For God made Christ, who never sinned, to be the offering for our sin, so that we could be made right with God through Christ.* 2 Corinthians 5:21

He canceled the record of the charges against us and took it away by nailing it to the cross. Colossians 2:14

> **Many Christians live guilt-filled lives because they don't understand the truth. The truth is that God does not remember our past, present, or future sins because they were nailed to the Cross with Jesus!**

Jesus took our place on the Cross. Jesus was the perfect sacrificial Lamb of God, who experienced death for all of the sins of mankind.

> *Surely he hath borne our griefs, and carried our sorrows: yet we did esteem him stricken, smitten of God, and afflicted.*
>
> *But he was wounded for our transgressions, he was bruised for our iniquities: the chastisement of our peace was upon him; and with his stripes we are healed.* Isaiah 53:4-5 (KJV)
>
> *The next day John saw Jesus coming toward him and said, "Look! The Lamb of God who takes away the sin of the world!"* John 1:29
>
> *Christ suffered for our sins once for all time. He never sinned, but he died for sinners to bring you safely home to God. He suffered physical death, but he was raised to life in the Spirit.* 1 Peter 3:18
>
> *Who his own self bare our sins in his own body on the tree, that we, being dead to sins, should live unto righteousness: by whose stripes ye were healed.* 1 Peter 2:24 (KJV)

Super, abundant, radical, undeserved, amazing, grace

The term *grace* has several meanings in the Bible depending on the context of the topic. When used in the context of salvation it means *God's compassion, kindness, mercy, charity.*

God's grace is the formula for one's eternal life beginning instantaneously at the time of his or her belief in Jesus as Savior. The Christian's eternal life begins on Earth, and then upon physical death is moved to what is known as the *third Heaven,* and ultimately results in eternal life on the *New Earth.*

> *"For God loved the world so much that he gave his one and only Son, so that everyone who believes in him will not perish but have eternal life. God sent his Son into the world not to judge the world, but to save the world through him."* John 3:16-17, Jesus' words

> *For God presented Jesus as the sacrifice for sin. People are made right with God when they believe that Jesus sacrificed his life, shedding his blood. This sacrifice shows that God was being fair when he held back and did not punish those who sinned in times past, for he was looking ahead and including them in what he would do in this present time. God did this to demonstrate his righteousness, for he himself is fair and just, and he declares sinners to be right in his sight when they believe in Jesus.* Romans 3:25-26

> *God saved you by his grace when you believed. And you can't take credit for this; it is a gift from God. Salvation is not a reward for the good things we have done, so none of us can boast about it.* Ephesians 2:8-9

Because your salvation is guaranteed, you should make every attempt to follow the Holy Spirit's guidance. This is referred to as *discipleship*, which will be discussed in the chapter **Salvation versus Discipleship.**

Jesus' plan is simple

> *"For God loved the world so much that he gave his one and only Son, so that everyone who **believes** in him will not perish but have eternal life. God sent his Son into the world not to judge the world, but to save the world through him.*

> *There is no judgment against anyone who **believes** in him. But anyone who does not **believe** in him has already been judged for not believing in God's one and only Son."* John 3:16-18, Jesus' words (Emphasis added by me.)

The passage you just read explains Christian salvation concisely and perfectly. I emphasized the word *believe(s)* because belief in Jesus as Savior is what saves a person. Believers, being saved by faith, are what differentiate Christianity from the religions that necessitate works to please their god(s).

The unique quality of Christianity is: Most religions insist their followers must perform in order to reach up to their god, but Christianity embraces the fact that God loved mankind so much *he came down to us* in the form of a man

named Jesus, and he made all the sacrifices necessary for those who *believe.* Christians are saved by faith.

> *"I tell you the truth, those who listen to my message and believe in God who sent me have eternal life. They will never be condemned for their sins, but they have already passed from death into life."* John 5:24, Jesus' words

> *We are made right with God by placing our faith in Jesus Christ. And this is true for everyone who believes, no matter who we are.* Romans 3:22

Christianity is the way immoral people (we are all immoral) can spend eternity in Heaven with the Creator God, clothed in the righteousness of Jesus Christ. Christianity demands nothing more than faith. Good behavior is desirable, but not mandatory for salvation.

> **"Christ died for men precisely because men are not worth dying for; to make them worth it." C.S. Lewis (1898-1963)**

Jesus is the only way

> *Jesus told him, "I am the way, the truth, and the life. No one can come to the Father except through me. If you had really known me, you would know who my Father is. From now on, you do know him and have seen him!"* John 14:6-7

> **"There is but one Church in which men find salvation, just as outside the ark of Noah it was not possible for anyone to be saved." Saint Thomas Aquinas (1225-1274)**

Many people become intolerant of we Christians who boldly proclaim Christ as the only way to Heaven. The "Jesus only" attitude makes Christians seem narrow-minded, bigoted, extreme, radical, prejudiced, and fanatical. So what! I would rather be called narrow-minded than gamble with my eternal destination.

Why would anyone want to look elsewhere when Jesus is so readily available, and historically credible? Not only is Jesus credible — he is incredible!

You say: What about all of those well-behaved, moral people around the world who are not familiar with Jesus? God knows all things, including who will and won't accept Jesus Christ as Savior. We must have faith that his decision will be fair and just to all who have not been exposed to Jesus.

Although God is a loving God, he also destroyed the world with water once, destroyed two cities, and will come back to destroy the world again. He also allowed himself, as the man Jesus, to be humiliated, brutalized, and nailed to the Cross to die so those who believe in his finished work may have eternal life. God has reasons for everything he does, and I decided years ago not to question his methods.

Jesus' Blood was our atonement

Atonement means "compensation for a loss."

In Christianity, *atonement*, when used to describe Christ's death on the Cross, means Jesus' shed Blood was the propitiation (a gesture of reconciliation to gain or regain the favor of someone or something) for the sin of mankind.

Because of the Old Testament blood sacrifices, the shed Blood of Jesus did what the blood of animals could not do.

> *For everyone has sinned; we all fall short of God's glorious standard. Yet God, with undeserved kindness, declares that we are righteous. He did this through Christ Jesus when he freed us from the penalty for our sins. For God presented Jesus as the sacrifice for sin. People are made right with God when they believe that Jesus sacrificed his life, shedding his blood. This sacrifice shows that God was being fair when he held back and did not punish those who sinned in times past, for he was looking ahead and including them in what he would do in this present time. God did this to demonstrate his righteousness, for he himself is fair and just, and he declares sinners to be right in his sight when they believe in Jesus.* Romans 3:23-26

Everyone in the entire human race has sinned and is sinning. The only way a person can be redeemed is through a blood sacrifice. Because the Old Testament blood sacrifice only covered sin, not being sufficient to completely and permanently cleanse a person of their sinful nature, God came to Earth in the form of a baby named Jesus, foreknowing that non-believers would crucify him as a man. They did.

The righteousness of Christ

When Jesus allowed himself to be crucified on a cross, he did so to offer his own Blood once for all time, making future sacrifices unnecessary. This is what Jesus meant by his dying words on the Cross: "It is finished" (John 19:30). Never again would the blood of bulls and goats be used to cover the sins of people. Only by trusting in Jesus' finished work as our **only** way to experience the eternal place Christ has prepared for Christians can we stand before God covered in the righteousness of Christ. *Our righteousness is received only as a result of our faith*.

> *God has united you with Christ Jesus. For our benefit God made him to be wisdom itself. Christ made us right with God; he made us pure and holy, and he freed us from sin.* 1 Corinthians 1:30

What a powerful passage! Our union with Christ Jesus results in our being acceptable to God because of our imputed righteousness.

> *This Good News tells us how God makes us right in his sight. This is accomplished from start to finish by faith. As the Scriptures say, "It is through faith that a righteous person has life."* Romans 1:17

> *But now God has shown us a way to be made right with him without keeping the requirements of the law, as was promised in the writings of Moses and the prophets long ago. We are made right with God by placing our faith in Jesus Christ. And this is true for everyone who believes, no matter who we are.* Romans 3:21-22

> *For the Scriptures tell us, "Abraham believed God, and God counted him as righteous because of his faith."*

> *When people work, their wages are not a gift, but something they have earned. But people are counted as righteous, not because of their work, but because of their faith in God who forgives sinners. David also spoke of this when he described the happiness of those who are declared righteous without working for it:*

> > *"Oh, what joy for those*
> >   *whose disobedience is forgiven,*
> > *whose sins are put out of sight.*
> >   *Yes, what joy for those*
> >   *whose record the LORD has cleared of sin."* Romans 4:3-8

For God made Christ, who never sinned, to be the offering for our sin, so that we could be made right with God through Christ. 2 Corinthians 5:21

The old system under the Law of Moses was only a shadow, a dim preview of the good things to come, not the good things themselves. The sacrifices under that system were repeated again and again, year after year, but they were never able to provide perfect cleansing for those who came to worship. If they could have provided perfect cleansing, the sacrifices would have stopped, for the worshipers would have been purified once for all time, and their feelings of guilt would have disappeared.

But instead, those sacrifices actually reminded them of their sins year after year. For it is not possible for the blood of bulls and goats to take away sins. That is why, when Christ came into the world, he said to God,

> *"You did not want animal sacrifices or sin offerings*
> *But you have given me a body to offer.*
> *You were not pleased with burnt offerings*
> *or other offerings for sin.*
> *Then I said, 'Look, I have come to do your will, O God—*
> *as is written about me in the Scriptures.'"*

First, Christ said, "You did not want animal sacrifices or sin offerings or burnt offerings or other offerings for sin, nor were you pleased with them" (though they are required by the law of Moses). Then he said, "Look, I have come to do your will." He cancels the first covenant in order to put the second into effect. For God's will was for us to be made holy by the sacrifice of the body of Jesus Christ, once for all time.

Under the old covenant, the priest stands and ministers before the altar day after day, offering the same sacrifices again and again, which can never take away sins. But our High Priest offered himself to God as a single sacrifice for sins, good for all time. Then he sat down in the place of honor at God's right hand. There he waits until his enemies are humbled and made a footstool under his feet. For by that one offering he forever made perfect those who are being made holy

And the Holy Spirit also testifies that this is so. For he says,

> *"This is the new covenant I will make*
> *with my people on that day, says the Lord:*

I will put my laws in their hearts,
and I will write them on their minds."

Then he says,

"I will never again remember
their sins and lawless deeds."

And when sins have been forgiven, there is no need to offer any more sacrifices. Hebrews 10:1-18

And now you Gentiles have also heard the truth, the Good News that God saves you. And when you believed in Christ, he identified you as his own by giving you the Holy Spirit, whom he promised long ago. Ephesians 1:13

For his Spirit joins with our spirit to affirm that we are God's children. Romans 8:16

We are saved only by our faith

Approximately 100 times in the Book of John, the term believe is used. Repeatedly, Jesus states that those who believe in him have everlasting life. I have emphasized the word believe in the following passages.

*"For God loved the world so much that he gave his one and only Son, so that everyone who **believes** in him will not perish but have eternal life. God sent his Son into the world not to judge the world, but to save the world through him.*

*There is no judgment against anyone who **believes** in him. But anyone who does not **believe** in him has already been judged for not believing in God's one and only Son."* John 3:16-18, Jesus' words

*"I tell you the truth, those who listen to my message and **<u>believe</u>** in God who sent me have eternal life. They will never be condemned for their sins, but they have already passed from death into life."* John 5:24, Jesus' words

*Jesus replied, "I am the bread of life. Whoever comes to me will never be hungry again. Whoever **<u>believes</u>** in me will never be thirsty."* John 6:35

*"And this is the will of God, that I should not lose even one of all those he has given me, but that I should raise them up at the last day. For it is my Father's will that all who see his Son and **believe** in him should have eternal life. I will raise them up at the last day."* John 6:39-40, Jesus' words

*"I tell you the truth, anyone who **believes** has eternal life."* John 6:47, Jesus' words

*Jesus told her, "I am the resurrection and the life. Anyone who **believes** in me will live, even after dying. Everyone who lives in me and **believes** in me will never ever die. Do you **believe** this, Martha?"*

*"Yes, Lord," she told him. "I have always **believed** you are the Messiah, the Son of God, the one who has come into the world from God."* John 11:25-27

One must study the Scriptures to get the complete and true message.

A great example of someone who was saved by his faith is the thief on the Cross

One of the criminals hanging beside him scoffed, "So you're the Messiah, are you? Prove it by saving yourself—and us, too, while you're at it!"

But the other criminal protested, "Don't you fear God even when you have been sentenced to die? We deserve to die for our crimes, but this man hasn't done anything wrong." Then he said, "Jesus, remember me when you come into your Kingdom."

And Jesus replied, "I assure you, today you will be with me in paradise." Luke 23:39-43

The thief, a sinner like you and me, was instantly saved by his faith. He accepted Jesus as the Jewish Messiah, so in return, Jesus demonstrated his mercy for the thief because he **believed**.

It is guaranteed

As a messenger of the Good News for three decades, I have spoken personally with several thousand people regarding their salvation. Sadly, most did not understand their salvation is guaranteed. I emphasized *guarantee* and *guaranteeing* in the following passages.

*The Spirit is God's **guarantee** that he will give us the inheritance he prom-ised and that he has purchased us to be his own people. He did this so we would praise and glorify him.* Ephesians 1:14

*And do not bring sorrow to God's Holy Spirit by the way you live. Remember, he has identified you as his own, **guaranteeing** that you will be saved on the day of redemption.* Ephesians 4:30

The Holy Spirit living in a person guarantees his or her salvation from eternal dam-nation because he or she belongs to God. No more wondering.

What doesn't save us

Receiving eternal life in the place Jesus prepared for Christians (Heaven), and then on the New Earth, is <u>NOT</u> received by doing religious things. The Bible ***does not*** say one must:

1. Repent of sin. (*Repent of sin* is a manmade phrase, not biblical. *Repent* means "change of mind." To receive eternal life in the place Jesus has prepared for Christians, a person must *repent* of the notion of working his or her way there, and accept Jesus as Savior.) NOBODY HAS EVER RECEIVED THE FREE GIFT OF ETERNAL LIFE BY REPENTING OF SIN!
2. Make Jesus Lord of your life. Like it or not, Jesus, as God, is already Lord of all lives. (But to receive the free gift of salvation you must "trust" Jesus as your Savior, at which time you will be baptized by the Holy Spirit, who will be your counselor. *Don't be drunk with wine, because it will ruin your life. Instead, be filled with the Holy Spirit.* Ephesians 5:18)
3. Confess with your mouth that Jesus is Lord. (This was a one-time instruction from Paul to a certain group of Jews.)
4. Give your life to the Lord. (This is a phrase that is used, but it doesn't save. A person is saved by his or her faith.)
5. Be sorry for sinning. (Only a fool would not be sorry for sinning, but sorrow does not save. Only faith in Jesus saves.)
6. Ask forgiveness for sins. (All sins were forgiven on the Cross.)
7. Stop sinning. (Nobody can quit sinning.)
8. Invite Jesus into your heart. (Not necessary, but it demonstrates faith.)
9. Go forward in an alter call. (Although going forward demonstrates faith.)
10. Become water baptized. (Water baptism is an outward expression of an in-ward confession.)

11. Say a prayer. (Saying a prayer shows sincerity, but it is not the prayer that saves. We are saved by our faith.)
12. Obey Jesus' two commands. (He did say to obey his commands if you love him.)
13. Do good deeds. (Good deeds are discipleship. Be a disciple.)
14. Attend or join a church. (Jesus likes to see people in church.)
15. Give money to a church. (Monetary contributions are good deeds, but not necessary.)
16. Participate in Communion. (Communion is done in remembrance, but it doesn't save.)
17. Confess sins. (He already knows everyone's sins and they were all forgiven at the Cross.)
18. Repeat Hail Marys. (Nonsense!)
19. Light candles. (Pretty, but an unnecessary ritual.)
20. Perform rituals. (Make sure your rituals aren't pagan.)
21. Receive Last Rites. (More nonsense!)
    …and the list goes on and on.

Know what you believe and why you believe it! If a person believes that any of the actions listed above must be added to Jesus' finished work, he or she is adding works to faith. To be saved, a person must believe and trust in Jesus as Savior. It is a gift to those who believe.

> *And if by grace, then is it no more of works: otherwise grace is no more grace. But if it be of works, then it is no more grace: otherwise work is no more work.* Romans 11:6 (KJV)

> *God saved you by his grace when you believed. And you can't take credit for this; it is a gift from God. Salvation is not a reward for the good things we have done, so none of us can boast about it.* Ephesians 2:8-9

Christians are saved by *super, abundant, radical, undeserved, amazing, grace* through faith. It is not how much faith a person has, or how he or she behaves — it is faith that saves. It's a gift — it's a gift — it's a gift!

> *Let God's curse fall on anyone, including us or even an angel from heaven, who preaches a different kind of Good News than the one we preached to you. I say again what we have said before: If anyone preaches any other Good News than the one you welcomed, let that person be cursed.* Galatians 1:8-9

According to God's standard of perfection, a person cannot do anything to make himself or herself blameless.

A few religions, including some that label themselves as Christian, still have priests who continue to stand before the altar day after day performing religious sacrifices in the hope of sins being forgiven. This monotonous act is not only futile, but blasphemous. Those who participate in this ritual are claiming that the Blood of Jesus was insufficient in cleansing sins once and for all.

> *Unlike those other high priests, he does not need to offer sacrifices every day. They did this for their own sins first and then for the sins of the people. But Jesus did this once for all when he offered himself as the sacrifice for the people's sins. The law appointed high priests who were limited by human weakness. But after the law was given, God appointed his Son with an oath, and his Son has been made the perfect High Priest forever.* Hebrews 7:27-28

Half way there

The first half of Jesus' finished work was: As God, he came to Earth to die on a cross to forgive all sins of all mankind.

Belief in Jesus' resurrection is the second half

On the third day after his crucifixion, Jesus rose from death. *The resurrection of Jesus constitutes the most magnificent proof of his deity.*

> *Early on Sunday morning, as the new day was dawning, Mary Magdalene and the other Mary went out to visit the tomb.*
>
> *Suddenly there was a great earthquake! For an angel of the Lord came down from heaven, rolled aside the stone, and sat on it. His face shone like lightning, and his clothing was as white as snow. The guards shook with fear when they saw him, and they fell into a dead faint.*
>
> *Then the angel spoke to the women. "Don't be afraid!" he said. "I know you are looking for Jesus, who was crucified. He isn't here! He is risen from the dead, just as he said would happen. Come, see where his body was lying. And now, go quickly and tell his disciples he has risen from the dead, and he is going ahead of you to Galilee. You will see him there. Remember what I have told you."* Matthew 28:1-7

The resurrection gives Christians eternal life

The resurrection of Jesus Christ displayed the immeasurable power of God — who became a man, was crucified on a cross, but miraculously had the power to resurrect himself. Jesus' resurrection substantiated the fact he is God, and that, my friends, is the basis of the Christian faith.

> *And if Christ has not been raised, then your faith is useless, and you are still guilty of your sins.* 1 Corinthians 15:17

> *So you see, just as death came into the world through a man, now the resurrection from the dead has begun through another man. Just as everyone dies because we all belong to Adam, everyone who belongs to Christ will be given new life.* 1 Corinthians 15:21-22

> *For sin is the sting that results in death, and the law gives sin its power. But thank God! He gives us victory over sin and death through our Lord Jesus Christ.* 1 Corinthians 15:56-57

> *But God is so rich in mercy, and he loved us so much, that even though we were dead because of our sins, he gave us life when he raised Christ from the dead. (It is only by God's grace that you have been saved!) For he raised us from the dead along with Christ and seated us with him in the heavenly realms because we are united with Christ Jesus.* Ephesians 2:4-6

It's a gift, but you must accept it

It is God's free gift to those who accept it. I emphasized *gift* in the following passages.

> *For the wages of sin is death, but the free __gift__ of God is eternal life through Christ Jesus our Lord.* Romans 6:23

> *God saved you by his grace when you believed. And you can't take credit for this; it is a __gift__ from God. Salvation is not a reward for the good things we have done, so none of us can boast about it.* Ephesians 2:8-9

Once God's gift is accepted, the recipient is referred to as a Christian, or child of God, for all eternity. Contrary to what most folks *believe,* **all humans are not children of God. The Bible states we are all God's creation, but** *only those who are born again are God's children.*

But to all who believed him and accepted him, he gave the right to become children of God. John 1:12

For all who are led by the Spirit of God are children of God.

So you have not received a spirit that makes you fearful slaves. Instead, you received God's Spirit when he adopted you as his own children. Now we call him, "Abba, Father." For his Spirit joins with our spirit to affirm that we are God's children. And since we are his children, we are his heirs. In fact, together with Christ we are heirs of God's glory. But if we are to share his glory, we must also share his suffering. Romans 8:14-17

For you are all children of God through faith in Christ Jesus. Galatians 3:26

But when the right time came, God sent his Son, born of a woman, subject to the law. God sent him to buy freedom for us who were slaves to the law, so that he could adopt us as his very own children. And because we are his children, God has sent the Spirit of his Son into our hearts, prompting us to call out, "Abba, Father." Now you are no longer a slave but God's own child. And since you are his child, God has made you his heir. Galatians 4:4-7

God decided in advance to adopt us into his own family by bringing us to himself through Jesus Christ. This is what he wanted to do, and it gave him great pleasure. Ephesians 1:5

See how very much our Father loves us, for he calls us his children, and that is what we are! But the people who belong to this world don't recognize that we are God's children because they don't know him. Dear friends, we are already God's children, but he has not yet shown us what we will be like when Christ appears. But we do know that we will be like him, for we will see him as he really is. 1 John 3:1-2

The next time someone tells you we are *all* children of God, read them what God has to say about it in the passages above.

You receive salvation at the instant you believe

At the moment of belief, one is saved. Below are two New Testament examples of how people were saved instantly:

Example 1: One day Jesus was in a house in Capernaum. A huge crowd of people had squeezed into the house to listen to him. Four men arrived, carrying a sick friend on a mat. They wanted Jesus to heal him, but could not get into the house. Looking around for another way, they climbed onto the roof and made a hole. They carefully lowered the paralyzed man into the room where Jesus was speaking.

> **Seeing their faith, Jesus said to the man, "Young man, your sins are forgiven." Luke 5:20**

The first thing Jesus did was forgive the man for his sins based strictly on faith. Then Jesus turned to the man and healed him — no strings attached.

Example 2: When Jesus was dying on the Cross, there were two thieves hanging on each side of him. One had faith in Jesus as Messiah, but the other did not. To the thief who had faith, Jesus said:

> **And Jesus replied, "I assure you, today you will be with me in paradise." Luke 23:43**

Jesus did not tell the thief headed for paradise he had to repent of sin, repeat a sinner's prayer, invite him into his life, make him Lord of his life, confess with his mouth, stop sinning, become water baptized, or any of those other rituals many Christians believe must be done to be saved. No soul sleep or purgatory.

It is important to emphasize that no matter how many sins you have committed, how often, or the magnitude of the sins — you were forgiven.

You were made a saint!

If you are a Christian, you were made a saint. Christians are both sinners and saints.

Being a saint does not mean Christians do not sin. All people sin. Because our salvation is absolutely, positively, and unconditionally guaranteed, we Christians can sin more, but we enjoy it less. We enjoy it less because we are convicted by the indwelling of the Holy Spirit.

> _Those who are dominated by the sinful nature think about sinful things, but those who are controlled by the Holy Spirit think about things that please the Spirit._ Romans 8:5

Because I said Christians can sin more, it does not mean I am advocating sin — but truth is truth. We have been *justified* (saved), which is irreversible.

Those who are justified will be conformed to the image of Christ through the process of *sanctification*, which I discuss shortly.

> *Some of you were once like that. But you were cleansed; you were made holy; you were made right with God by calling on the name of the Lord Jesus Christ and by the Spirit of our God.* 1 Corinthians 6:11

The Holy Spirit lives in and through the Christian saint. This does not mean the saint will live a perfect life, nor does it mean Satan will not come furiously after him or her. The Great Apostle Paul was a victim of sin.

> *So the trouble is not with the law, for it is spiritual and good. The trouble is with me, for I am all too human, a slave to sin. I don't really understand myself, for I want to do what is right, but I don't do it. Instead, I do what I hate. But if I know that what I am doing is wrong, this shows that I agree that the law is good. So I am not the one doing wrong; it is sin living in me that does it.*
>
> *And I know that nothing good lives in me, that is, in my sinful nature. I want to do what is right, but I can't. I want to do what is good, but I don't. I don't want to do what is wrong, but I do it anyway. But if I do what I don't want to do, I am not really the one doing wrong; it is sin living in me that does it.*
>
> *I have discovered this principle of life—that when I want to do what is right, I inevitably do what is wrong. I love God's law with all my heart. But there is another power within me that is at war with my mind. This power makes me a slave to the sin that is still within me. Oh, what a miserable person I am! Who will free me from this life that is dominated by sin and death? Thank God! The answer is in Jesus Christ our Lord. So you see how it is: In my mind I really want to obey God's law, but because of my sinful nature I am a slave to sin.* Romans 7:14-25

I do not deserve sainthood! Sometimes I pinch myself to see if I am dreaming. Before being saved, I thought sainthood was only for those people in history designated as saints by the Roman Catholic Church. Ha!

The New Testament word *saint* was translated from the Greek word *hagios*, which means "set apart by (for) God, holy, sacred."

*To the church (assembly) of God which is in Corinth, to those consecrated and purified and made holy in Christ Jesus, [who are] selected and called to be **saints (God's people)**, together with all those who in any place call upon and give honor to the name of our Lord Jesus Christ, both their Lord and ours:*

Grace (favor and spiritual blessing) be to you and [heart] peace from God our Father and the Lord Jesus Christ. 1 Corinthians 1:2-3 (AMP)

*To the **saints (the consecrated people of God)** and believing and faithful brethren in Christ who are at Colossae: Grace (spiritual favor and blessing) to you and [heart] peace from God our Father.* Colossians 1:2 (AMP)

I emphasized the phrases that use the term *saint* in the passages above. Depending on the Bible translation, the term *believer(s)* is used approximately 150 times, *saints* 50 times, and *Christians* only three times. Saints are God's people, but the term *Christian* has become popularized so I use it to describe a believer.

Sinners become saints by being *born again*. God has freely offered the only process for regenerating a sinner into a saint.

God saved you by his grace when you believed. And you can't take credit for this; it is a gift from God. Salvation is not a reward for the good things we have done, so none of us can boast about it. Ephesians 2:8-9

But—"When God our Savior revealed his kindness and love, he saved us, not because of the righteous things we had done, but because of his mercy. He washed away our sins, giving us a new birth and new life through the Holy Spirit. He generously poured out the Spirit upon us through Jesus Christ our Savior. Because of his grace he declared us righteous and gave us confidence that we will inherit eternal life." Titus 3:4-7

All believers are made holy by their faith in Jesus Christ.

I am writing to God's church in Corinth, to you who have been called by God to be his own holy people. He made you holy by means of Christ Jesus, just as he did for all people everywhere who call on the name of our Lord Jesus Christ, their Lord and ours. 1 Corinthians 1:2

Three stages of regeneration

Salvation is also referred to as *regeneration* because the believer is converted from being a non-Christian to a Christian, or regenerated. It is a spiritual regeneration.

There are three stages of regeneration:

1. Justification: that which saves a person. We are made righteous through grace because of the Blood of Christ. Righteousness is imputed by God because of his love for us. It is a gift and is not earned.

2. Sanctification: the growth process of the believer by lessening sinful behavior and living life yielding to guidance from the Holy Spirit.

    *But we are bound to give thanks to God always for you, brethren beloved by the Lord, because God from the beginning chose you for salvation through **sanctification by the Spirit** and belief in the truth, to which He called you by our gospel, for the obtaining of the glory of our Lord Jesus Christ.* 2 Thessalonians 2:13-14 (NKJV)

    The sanctification process begins after a person has been justified (born again), and is not instantaneous, as is justification.

    Not every Christian will act or react exactly the same; consequently, we cannot judge another's salvation. The Holy Spirit functions differently in each of us.

3. Glorification: God's final removal of sinful nature from the saints.

    Rather than our being sinful mortals, we will be totally transformed. Our final glorification is the summit of sanctification.

    Yet what we suffer now is nothing compared to the glory he will reveal to us later. For all creation is waiting eagerly for that future day when God will reveal who his children really are. Against its will, all creation was subjected to God's curse. But with eager hope, the creation looks forward to the day when it will join God's children in glorious freedom from death and decay. For we know that all creation has been groaning as in the pains of childbirth right up to the present time. And we believers also groan, even though we have the Holy Spirit within us as a foretaste of future glory, for we long for our bodies to be released from sin and suffering. We, too, wait with eager hope for the day when God will give us our full rights as his adopted children, including the new bodies he has promised us. We were given this hope when we were saved. (If we already have something, we don't need to hope for it. But if we look forward to something we don't yet have, we must wait patiently and confidently. Romans 8:18-25

At the last trumpet, when Jesus comes, the saints will undergo a fundamental, instant transformation. We saints shall all be glorified instantaneously.

It is the same way with the resurrection of the dead. Our earthly bodies are planted in the ground when we die, but they will be raised to live forever. Our bodies are buried in brokenness, but they will be raised in glory. They are buried in weakness, but they will be raised in strength. They are buried as natural human bodies, but they will be raised as spiritual bodies. For just as there are natural bodies, there are also spiritual bodies.

The Scriptures tell us, "The first man, Adam, became a living person." But the last Adam—that is, Christ—is a life-giving Spirit. What comes first is the natural body, then the spiritual body comes later. Adam, the first man, was made from the dust of the earth, while Christ, the second man, came from heaven. Earthly people are like the earthly man, and heavenly people are like the heavenly man. Just as we are now like the earthly man, we will someday be like the heavenly man.

What I am saying, dear brothers and sisters, is that our physical bodies cannot inherit the Kingdom of God. These dying bodies cannot inherit what will last forever.

But let me reveal to you a wonderful secret. We will not all die, but we will all be transformed! It will happen in a moment, in the blink of an eye, when the last trumpet is blown. For when the trumpet sounds, those who have died will be raised to live forever. And we who are living will also be transformed. For our dying bodies must be transformed into bodies that will never die; our mortal bodies must be transformed into immortal bodies. 1 Corinthians 15:42-53

For we know that when this earthly tent we live in is taken down (that is, when we die and leave this earthly body), we will have a house in heaven, an eternal body made for us by God himself and not by human hands. We grow weary in our present bodies, and we long to put on our heavenly bodies like new clothing. For we will put on heavenly bodies; we will not be spirits without bodies. While we live in these earthly bodies, we groan and sigh, but it's not that we want to die and get rid of these bodies that clothe us. Rather, we want to put on our new bodies so that these dying bodies will be swallowed up by life. God himself has prepared us for this, and as a guarantee he has given us his Holy Spirit. 2 Corinthians 5:1-5

The Doctrine of Glorification is the biblical teaching that we who have been justified and sanctified will be complete in sinlessness. We will experience a state of magnificent eternal joy and purity in the presence of Jesus.

The end of a believer's life is his or her introduction to the essence of our Lord. The final glorification of the Lord's people is not the end — it is the beginning.

> **"The bridge of grace will bear your weight, brother. Thousands of big sinners have gone across that bridge, yea, tens of thousands have gone over it. Some have been the chief of sinners and some have come at the very last of their days but the arch has never yielded beneath their weight. I will go with them trusting to the same support. It will bear me over as it has for them." Charles Haddon Spurgeon (1834-1892)**

<u>**Notes:**</u>

Chapter 15

Salvation Passages

The major theme of the Old and New Testament Bibles involves the Lord Jesus assembling his eternal Kingdom. Below are a few passages I consider more obvious and important. Please peruse these.

From Jesus

Because Jesus is the one who made the ultimate sacrifice, his words must prevail.

"But everyone who denies me here on earth, I will also deny before my Father in heaven." Matthew 10:33, Jesus' words

When Jesus heard this, he told them, "Healthy people don't need a doctor – sick people do. I have come to call not those who think they are righteous, but those who know they are sinners." Mark 2:17

"For even the Son of Man, came not to be served but to serve others, and to give his life as a ransom for many." Mark 10:45, Jesus' words

"Anyone who believes and is baptized will be saved. But anyone who refuses to believe will be condemned." Mark 16:16, Jesus' words

And Jesus said to the woman, "Your faith has saved you; go in peace." Luke 7:50

"For the Son of Man, came to seek and save those who are lost." Luke 19:10, Jesus' words

Jesus replied, "I tell you the truth, unless you are born again, you cannot see the Kingdom of God." John 3:3

"But those who drink the water I give will never be thirsty again. It becomes a fresh, bubbling spring within them, giving them eternal life." John 4:14, Jesus' words

Then Jesus told her, "I Am the Messiah!" John 4:26

"I tell you the truth, those who listen to my message and believe in God who sent me have eternal life. They will never be condemned for their sins, but they have already passed from death into life." John 5:24, Jesus' words

"You search the Scriptures because you think they give you eternal life. But the Scriptures point to me!" John 5:39, Jesus' words

Jesus replied, "I am the bread of life. Whoever comes to me will never be hungry again. Whoever believes in me will never be thirsty. But you haven't believed in me even though you have seen me. However, those the Father has given me will come to me, and I will never reject them. For I have come down from heaven to do the will of God who sent me, not to do my own will. And this is the will of God, that I should not lose even one of all those he has given me, but that I should raise them up at the last day. For it is my Father's will that all who see his Son and believe in him should have eternal life. I will raise them up at the last day." John 6:35-40

"I tell you the truth, anyone who believes has eternal life. Yes, I am the bread of life! Your ancestors ate manna in the wilderness, but they all died. Anyone who eats the bread from heaven, however, will never die. I am the living bread that came down from heaven. Anyone who eats this bread will live forever; and this bread, which I will offer so the world may live, is my flesh." John 6:47-51, Jesus' words

"Yes, I am the gate. Those who come in through me will be saved. They will come and go freely and will find good pastures. The thief's purpose is to steal and kill and destroy. My purpose is to give them a rich and satisfying life." John 10:9-10, Jesus' words

Jesus replied, "I have already told you, and you don't believe me. The proof is the work I do in my Father's name. But you don't believe me because you are not my sheep. My sheep listen to my voice; I know them, and they follow me. I give them eternal life, and they will never perish. No one can snatch them away from me, for my Father has given them to me, and he is more power-ful than anyone else. No one can snatch them from the Father's hand. The Father and I are one." John 10:25-30

Jesus told her, "I am the resurrection and the life. Anyone who believes in me will live, even after dying. Everyone who lives in me and believes in me will never ever die. Do you believe this, Martha?" John 11:25-26

"The time for judging this world has come, when Satan, the ruler of this world, will be cast out. And when I am lifted up from the earth, I will draw everyone to myself." John 12:31-32, Jesus' words

"The world's sin is that it refuses to believe in me." John 16:9, Jesus' words

What the Great Apostle Paul taught regarding salvation

Many consider the Apostle Paul the supreme Christian. Following are a few of Paul's teachings concerning Jesus' free gift.

"Brothers, listen! We are here to proclaim that through this man Jesus there is forgiveness for your sins. Everyone who believes in him is declared right with God—something the law of Moses could never do. Acts 13:38-39

For I am not ashamed of this Good News about Christ. It is the power of God at work, saving everyone who believes – the Jew first and also the Gentile. This Good News tells us how God makes us right in his sight. This is accom-plished from start to finish by faith. As the Scriptures say, "It is through faith that a righteous person has life. Romans 1:16-17

But now God has shown us a way to be made right with him without keeping the requirements of the law, as was promised in the writings of Moses and the prophets long ago. We are made right with God by placing our faith in Jesus Christ. And this is true for everyone who believes, no matter who we are. Romans 3:21-22

Can we boast, then, that we have done anything to be accepted by God? No, because our acquittal is not based on obeying the law. It is based on faith. So we are made right with God through faith and not by obeying the law. Romans 3:27-28

When people work, their wages are not a gift, but something they have earned. But people are counted as righteous, not because of their work, but because of their faith in God who forgives sinners. Romans 4:4-5

If God's promise is only for those who obey the law, then faith is not necessary and the promise is pointless. For the law always brings punishment on those who try to obey it. (The only way to avoid breaking the law is to have no law to break!) Romans 4:14-15

Therefore, since we have been made right in God's sight by faith, we have peace with God because of what Jesus Christ our Lord has done for us. Romans 5:1

So now there is no condemnation for those who belong to Christ Jesus. And because you belong to him, the power of the life-giving Spirit has freed you from the power of sin that leads to death. The law of Moses was unable to save us because of the weakness of our sinful nature. So God did what the law could not do. He sent his own Son in a body like the bodies we sinners have. And in that body God declared an end to sin's control over us by giving his Son as a sacrifice for our sins. He did this so that the just requirement of the law would be fully satisfied for us, who no longer follow our sinful nature but instead follow the Spirit. Romans 8:1-4

What does all this mean? Even though the Gentiles were not trying to follow God's standards, they were made right with God. And it was by faith that this took place. But the people of Israel, who tried so hard to get right with God by keeping the law, never succeeded. Why not? Because they were trying to get right with God by keeping the law instead of by trusting in him. They stumbled over the great rock in their path. God warned them of this in the Scriptures when he said, "I am placing a stone in Jerusalem that makes people stumble, a rock that makes them fall. But anyone who trusts in him will never be disgraced." Romans 9:30-33

For Christ has already accomplished the purpose for which the law was given. As a result, all who believe in him are made right with God. Romans 10:4

For Christ didn't send me to baptize, but to preach the Good News – and not with clever speech, for fear that the cross of Christ would lose its power. The message of the cross is foolish to those who are headed for destruction! But we who are being saved know it is the very power of God. 1 Corinthians 1:17-18

Don't you realize that those who do wrong will not inherit the Kingdom of God? Don't fool yourselves. Those who indulge in sexual sin, or who worship idols, or commit adultery, or are male prostitutes, or practice homosexuality, or are thieves, or greedy people, or drunkards, or are abusive, or cheat people—none of these will inherit the Kingdom of God. Some of you were once like that. But you were cleansed; you were made holy; you were made right with God by calling on the name of the Lord Jesus Christ and by the Spirit of our God. 1 Corinthians 6:9-11*

This means that anyone who belongs to Christ has become a new person. The old life is gone; a new life has begun!

And all of this is a gift from God, who brought us back to himself through Christ. And God has given us this task of reconciling people to him. For God was in Christ, reconciling the world to himself, no longer counting people's sins against them. And he gave us this wonderful message of reconciliation. So we are Christ's ambassadors; God is making his appeal through us. We speak for Christ when we plead, "Come back to God!" For God made Christ, who never sinned, to be the offering for our sin, so that we could be made right with God through Christ. 2 Corinthians 5:17-21*

"You and I are Jews by birth, not 'sinners' like the Gentiles. Yet we know that a person is made right with God by faith in Jesus Christ, not by obeying the law. And we have believed in Christ Jesus, so that we might be made right with God because of our faith in Christ, not because we have obeyed the law. For no one will ever be made right with God by obeying the law." Galatians 2:15-16*

But those who depend on the law to make them right with God are under his curse, for the Scriptures say, "Cursed is everyone who does not observe and obey all the commands that are written in God's Book of the Law." So it is clear that no one can be made right with God by trying to keep the law. For the Scriptures say, "It is through faith that a righteous person has life." This way of faith is very different from the way of law, which says, "It is through obeying the law that a person has life."

But Christ has rescued us from the curse pronounced by the law. When he was hung on the cross, he took upon himself the curse for our wrongdoing. For it is written in the Scriptures, "Cursed is everyone who is hung on a tree." Through Christ Jesus, God has blessed the Gentiles with the same blessing he promised to Abraham, so that we who are believers might receive the promised Holy Spirit through faith. Galatians 3:10-14

But when the right time came, God sent his Son, born of a woman, subject to the law. God sent him to buy freedom for us who were slaves to the law, so that he could adopt us as his very own children. Galatians 4:4-5

And now you Gentiles have also heard the truth, the Good News that God saves you. And when you believed in Christ, he identified you as his own by giving you the Holy Spirit, whom he promised long ago. The Spirit is God's guarantee that he will give us the inheritance he promised and that he has purchased us to be his own people. He did this so we would praise and glorify him. Ephesians 1:13-14

But God is so rich in mercy, and he loved us so much, that even though we were dead because of our sins, he gave us life when he raised Christ from the dead. (It is only by God's grace that you have been saved!) For he raised us from the dead along with Christ and seated us with him in the heavenly realms because we are united with Christ Jesus. So God can point to us in all future ages as examples of the incredible wealth of his grace and kindness toward us, as shown in all he has done for us who are united with Christ Jesus.

God saved you by his grace when you believed. And you can't take credit for this; it is a gift from God. Salvation is not a reward for the good things we have done, so none of us can boast about it. Ephesians 2:4-9

He cancelled the record of the charges against us and took it away by nailing it to Christ's cross. Colossians 2:14

For God chose to save us through our Lord Jesus Christ, not to pour out his anger on us. Christ died for us so that, whether we are dead or alive when he returns, we can live with him forever. 1 Thessalonians 5:9-10

I thank Christ Jesus our Lord, who has given me strength to do his work. He considered me trustworthy and appointed me to serve him, even though I used to blaspheme the name of Christ. In my insolence, I persecuted his people. But God had mercy on me because I did it in ignorance and unbelief. Oh, how generous and gracious our Lord was! He filled me with the faith and love that come from Christ Jesus.

This is a trustworthy saying, and everyone should accept it: "Christ Jesus came into the world to save sinners"—and I am the worst of them all.
1 Timothy 1:12-15

For there is only one God and one Mediator who can reconcile God and humanity–the man Christ Jesus. He gave his life to purchase freedom for everyone. This is the message God gave to the world at just the right time. 1 Timothy 2:5-6

For God saved us and called us to live a holy life. He did this, not because we deserved it, but because that was his plan from before the beginning of time—to show us his grace through Christ Jesus. And now he has made all of this plain to us by the appearing of Christ Jesus, our Savior. He broke the power of death and illuminated the way to life and immortality through the Good News. 2 Timothy 1:9-10

But—"When God our Savior revealed his kindness and love, he saved us, not because of the righteous things we had done, but because of his mercy. He washed away our sins, giving us a new birth and new life through the Holy Spirit. He generously poured out the Spirit upon us through Jesus Christ our Savior. Because of his grace he declared us righteous and gave us confidence that we will inherit eternal life." Titus 3:4-7

For God's will was for us to be made holy by the sacrifice of the body of Jesus Christ, once for all time. Hebrews 10:10

Notes:

Chapter 16

Beware of Galatianism!

It is imperative to familiarize yourself with the term *Galatianism*, it's meaning, and the damage it does to Christendom.

Galatianism is such an underused and unrecognized term that it requires explanation and elaboration. Do not forget this term and its relevancy in Christendom because Galatianism is like a cancer that has permeated the world, killing the chances for millions of nice folks to know Jesus. *Galatianists* (those who promote mixing grace with works) insist good deeds must be added to the gift of grace, which makes God's simple salvation plan confusing and complicated. The mixing of grace with works causes many to believe they are not capable or worthy of being Christians. Works are not necessary for salvation.

> *And if by grace, then is it no more of works: otherwise grace is no more grace. But if it be of works, then it is no more grace: otherwise work is no more work.* Romans 11:6 (KJV)

Insisting works must be added to grace causes many to believe they are not capable of being Christians. Grace plus works triggers an explosion — bang!

> *God saved you by his grace when you believed. And you can't take credit for this; it is a gift from God. Salvation is not a reward for the good things we have done, so none of us can boast about it.* Ephesians 2:8-9

In existence since the beginning of Christian ministry, Galatianism is demonstrated brilliantly by the Great Apostle Paul in the book of *Galatians*. Although many residents of Galatia had received and accepted the simplicity of the *New Covenant* (salvation by faith in Jesus' finished work), self-styled "spiritual men" came on the scene teaching that new Christians needed to add Old Covenant laws to the New Covenant freedom.

The Great Apostle Paul boldly warned those of Galatia about the error of insisting that good deeds must be added to what Jesus had already done. You tell them, Paul!

I am shocked that you are turning away so soon from God, who called you to himself through the loving mercy of Christ. You are following a different way that pretends to be the Good News but is not the Good News at all. You are being fooled by those who deliberately twist the truth concerning Christ. Galatians 1:6-7

When I saw that they were not following the truth of the gospel message, I said to Peter in front of all the others, "Since you, a Jew by birth, have discarded the Jewish laws and are living like a Gentile, why are you now trying to make these Gentiles follow the Jewish traditions? Galatians 2:14

How foolish can you be? After starting your Christian lives in the Spirit, why are you now trying to become perfect by your own human effort? Galatians 3:3

This way of faith is very different from the way of law, which says, "It is through obeying the law that a person has life."

But Christ has rescued us from the curse pronounced by the law. When he was hung on the cross, he took upon himself the curse for our wrongdoing. For it is written in the Scriptures, "Cursed is everyone who is hung on a tree." Through Christ Jesus, God has blessed the Gentiles with the same blessing he promised to Abraham, so that we who are believers might receive the promised Holy Spirit through faith. Galatians 3:12-14

These passages make it crystal clear that Christians are not saved by following outdated laws. Being a law-abiding person will not elevate anyone to the glory awaiting Christians in the next life.

Galatianism is one of the major reasons people are terrified of Jesus. Pathetically, they have heard that getting into Heaven requires faith plus insurmountable work; they feel they could never live up to the strict requirements, and sadly reject the Good News of Jesus' free gift.

The world would be brimming with Christians (people who know Jesus personally) if church leaders would teach the truth of the New Testament rather than instill guilt by teaching laws that were demanded in the Old Testament. Faulty teaching causes immeasurable people to reject the astonishing carpenter named Jesus, who died on a cross to forgive all of mankind for their sins.

Chapter 17

Salvation cannot be Lost

Comprehend this fact: *Once a person is saved, he or she is saved eternally.*

NOTE: Jesus' Blood forgives all sins except the sin of rejecting him as Savior. All of mankind's sins except blaspheming the Holy Spirit (Jesus) were forgiven on the Cross. Whoever rejects Jesus is guilty of blaspheming the Holy Spirit because Jesus is the Holy Spirit.

"But everyone who denies me here on earth, I will also deny before my Father in heaven." Matthew 10:33, Jesus' words

"So I tell you, every sin and blasphemy can be forgiven—except blasphemy against the Holy Spirit, which will never be forgiven. Anyone who speaks against the Son of Man can be forgiven, but anyone who speaks against the Holy Spirit will never be forgiven, either in this world or in the world to come." Matthew 12:31-32, Jesus' words

He that believeth on the Son hath everlasting life: and he that believeth not the Son shall not see life; but the wrath of God abideth on him. John 3:36

"The world's sin is that it refuses to believe in me." John 16:9, Jesus' words

Once saved – always saved

Historically, many clergy have misled, and are still misleading, their flocks by teaching a false doctrine that salvation can be lost because of sinful behavior or by "walking away from Jesus." Nonsense! This erroneous teaching began immediately following Jesus' death and is the work of Satan.

The first Christians (2,000 years ago) became confused by the influence of ignorant "religious" leaders who declared salvation was not a gift — that it must be accompanied by adhering to laws, rules, and deeds. That Satanic teaching continues today.

In Paul's letter to the Galatians, he was explicit that God's New Covenant not be altered.

> *Dear brothers and sisters, I want you to understand that the gospel message I preach is not based on mere human reasoning. I received my message from no human source, and no one taught me. Instead, I received it by direct revelation from Jesus Christ.* Galatians 1:11-12

Many who refer to themselves as Christians (i.e., Mormons and Catholics) insist we must do something to gain salvation, and if gained, can be lost. **This erroneous belief means to regain salvation Jesus would need to be crucified, then rise from the dead again.**

> *If that had been necessary, Christ would have had to die again and again, ever since the world began. But now, once for all time, he has appeared at the end of the age, to remove sin by his own death as a sacrifice.* Hebrews 9:26

Many Christians live guilt-filled lives because they fail to understand the truth about salvation. They constantly wonder if they are doing enough to pay for their own sins. **Guilt is another tool of Satan.**

Ask yourself

Do you honestly think God provided us with a revolving-door salvation plan? Consider this:

> You wake up in the morning saved, but catch a glimpse of an attractive member of the opposite gender on TV while you are dressing. Because lust is a sin, you instantly lose your salvation. In desperation, you fall on your face begging God's forgiveness, hoping, but not knowing, if you have regained your salvation.

> When that confession session is over, you get into your car and head for work. A reckless driver goes through a red light and almost crashes into you, so you

responsively yell and display an obscene gesture. Back again to confessing while begging God's forgiveness, as you worry about losing your salvation.

Throughout the day you experience many thoughts that are not harmonious with being a good Christian. Consequently, when you lay your head on the pillow that night, you are not sure if you would go to Heaven if you die in your sleep. Again, you beg forgiveness. Saved — not saved?

The Lord Jesus did not die on the Cross so you would have to live in agony wondering if you are saved.

> **"When the mask of self-righteousness has been torn from us and we stand stripped of all our accustomed defenses, we are candidates for God's generous grace." Erwin W. Lutzer (born 1941)**

Uncertainty is a pity for both the Christian and for the Jewish Carpenter who willingly sacrificed his life on the Cross for all your sins. The Bible insists it is a *free* gift. (I emphasized words in the following passages.)

> *Can we boast, then, that we have done anything to be accepted by God? No, because our acquittal is **not based on obeying the law**. It is based on faith.* Romans 3:27

> *For the wages of sin is death, but the **free gift** of God is eternal life through Christ Jesus our Lord.* Romans 6:23

> *God saved you by his grace when you believed. And you can't take credit for this; it is a **gift** from God. **Salvation is not a reward for the good things we have done**, so none of us can boast about it.* Ephesians 2:8-9

> *"I give them eternal life, and they will never perish. **<u>No one can snatch them away from me</u>**, for my Father has given them to me, and he is more powerful than anyone else. No one can snatch them from the Father's hand."* John 10:28-29, Jesus' words

> *When people work, their wages are not a gift, but something they have earned. But people are counted as righteous, **not because of their work**, but because of their faith in God who forgives sinners.* Romans 4:4-5

And I am convinced that nothing can ever separate us from God's love. Neither death nor life, neither angels nor demons, neither our fears for today nor our worries about tomorrow—not even the powers of hell can separate us from God's love. No power in the sky above or in the earth below—indeed, **nothing in all creation will ever be able to separate us from the love of God that is revealed in Christ Jesus our Lord.** Romans 8:38-39

In him you also, when you heard the word of truth, the gospel of your salvation, and believed in him, were **sealed with the promised Holy Spirit,** *who is the guarantee of our inheritance until we acquire possession of it, to the praise of his glory.* Ephesians 1:13-14 (ESV)

With the exception of the sin of rejecting Jesus as Savior, all of mankind's sins were nailed to the Cross with Jesus.

When people work, their wages are not a gift, but something they have earned. But people are counted as righteous, not because of their work, but because of their faith in God who forgives sinners. David also spoke of this when he described the happiness of those who are declared righteous without working for it:

"Oh, what joy for those
  whose disobedience is forgiven,
  whose sins are put out of sight.
Yes, what joy for those
  whose record the LORD has cleared of sin." Romans 4:4-8

Miraculously, unlike a person's natural birth, which ends in physical death, salvation is a Spiritual birth that results in eternal life.

For you have been born again, but not to a life that will quickly end. Your new life will last forever because it comes from the eternal, living word of God. 1 Peter 1:23

Martin Luther (1483-1546), a Catholic priest who is given credit for the beginning of Protestantism, made many very intuitive statements. This is my favorite: "Either sin is with you, lying on your shoulders, or it is lying on Christ, the Lamb of God."

Until enlightened, although an exceedingly educated Catholic priest, Luther lived an exhausting guilt-filled life spending many years attempting to forgive himself for his innate sinful nature. He made numerous feeble attempts at living a sinless life, but with no success, causing him overwhelming guilt. In his quest for peace and truth, **Luther searched the Scriptures and finally realized that his guilt and efforts to be perfect had been in vain.** Like being kicked in the head by a butterfly, he finally understood the simplicity of <u>salvation only by grace through faith.</u>

According to the Scriptures, it is impossible to live without sinning.

> *As the Scriptures say,*
> *"No one is righteous—*
> *not even one."* Romans 3:10

> *If we claim we have no sin, we are only fooling ourselves and not living in the truth.* 1 John 1:8

If it were possible to live a sinless life, Jesus Christ died for nothing!

Understand what *repent* means!

NOTE: For a more detailed exegesis of this, please refer to the chapter titled "You need not repent of sin to be saved."

The misconception I had about the biblical term *repent* kept me from learning about Jesus. I was told it meant *stop sinning,* so knowing my carnal nature could never stop sinning, I ran from Jesus. Now, I realize those who were teaching this were unenlightened. This same misconception has undoubtedly scared, and will continue to scare, many from enjoying the freedom from "religion" provided by our Savior. There are many who will never know Jesus because they have been frightened by a phrase that is used incorrectly.

Following is a typical verse that is misinterpreted. Many, at first glance, falsely interpret it to mean *repent of sin.*

> *Then Peter said to them, "Repent, and let every one of you be baptized in the name of Jesus Christ for the remission of sins; and you will receive the gift of the Holy Spirit."* Acts 2:38 (NKJV)

This verse does not say "repent of sin." Yes, the term *repent* is used, but not in the context erroneously taught by those who insist that Christians must stop sinning, turn from sinning, or be sorry for sinning.

It is a mistake to refer to a modern dictionary to find the meaning of a word used 2,000 years ago. *Repent* is derived from the Greek word *metanoia*, which means "a change of mind." *Metanoia* was used frequently by the Apostle Paul to convince the Jews that they must change their minds from depending on the laws to gain favor with God (i.e., the Ten Commandments, plus 603 others) to accepting Jesus as the Messiah. It is one's belief in Jesus that redeems; Jesus was the fulfillment of the law. ***Jesus did what man could not do for himself.***

All sins are equal

Christ's body is not a revolving door exited when we commit what we consider a major sin, because all sins are equal. Sin is sin, and we are all sinners.

> *For the person who keeps all of the laws except one is as guilty as a person who has broken all of God's laws.* James 2:10

Though we are all as guilty as murderers, the power of Jesus' Blood cleansed *all* sins.

> *For God's will was for us to be made holy by the sacrifice of the body of Jesus Christ, once for all time.* Hebrews 10:10

> *All praise to God, the Father of our Lord Jesus Christ. It is by his great mercy that we have been born again, because God raised Jesus Christ from the dead. Now we live with great expectation, and we have a priceless inheritance—an inheritance that is kept in heaven for you, pure and undefiled, beyond the reach of change and decay.* 1 Peter 1:3-4

> *In his kindness God called you to share in his eternal glory by means of Christ Jesus. So after you have suffered a little while, he will restore, support, and strengthen you, and he will place you on a firm foundation. All power to him forever! Amen.* 1 Peter 5:10-11

Repent (change your mind) from believing your obedience to the Old Testament commands will save you. The Holy Spirit indwelling is the only way.

The Apostle Paul struggled with sin

The Apostle Paul was a sinner. Most people feel unworthy of God's love and forgiveness, but even the Apostle Paul, who many believe the paramount Christian, was in bondage to sin. The following words were written by Paul 25 years after the beginning of his ministry clearly revealed he continued to sin — even at the height of his ministry. Yet, Paul remained saved.

> *So the trouble is not with the law, for it is spiritual and good. The trouble is with me, for I am all too human, a slave to sin. I don't really understand myself, for I want to do what is right, but I don't do it. Instead, I do what I hate. But if I know that what I am doing is wrong, this shows that I agree that the law is good. So I am not the one doing wrong; it is sin living in me that does it.*
>
> *And I know that nothing good lives in me, that is, in my sinful nature. I want to do what is right, but I can't. I want to do what is good, but I don't. I don't want to do what is wrong, but I do it anyway. But if I do what I don't want to do, I am not really the one doing wrong; it is sin living in me that does it.*
>
> *I have discovered this principle of life—that when I want to do what is right, I inevitably do what is wrong. I love God's law with all my heart. But there is another power within me that is at war with my mind. This power makes me a slave to the sin that is still within me. Oh, what a miserable person I am! Who will free me from this life that is dominated by sin and death?* Romans 7:14-24

It should comfort you to realize that **we all have weaknesses**, including the Apostle Paul, who many believe to be the greatest Christian ever. Works for me!

Jesus Christ was the answer for Paul's sins

> *Thank God! The answer is in Jesus Christ our Lord. So you see how it is: In my mind I really want to obey God's law, but because of my sinful nature I am a slave to sin.* Romans 7:25

The only antidote for Paul's struggles was Jesus Christ — the medicine for everyone's struggles.

So now there is no condemnation for those who belong to Christ Jesus. And because you belong to him, the power of the life-giving Spirit has freed you from the power of sin that leads to death. The law of Moses was unable to save us because of the weakness of our sinful nature. So God did what the law could not do. He sent his own Son in a body like the bodies we sinners have. And in that body God declared an end to sin's control over us by giving his Son as a sacrifice for our sins. He did this so that the just requirement of the law would be fully satisfied for us, who no longer follow our sinful nature but instead follow the Spirit. **Romans 8:1-4**

Grace is *super, abundant, radical, undeserved, and amazing*

From a Christian perspective, *grace* is what Jesus Christ imparts to humans via his death, burial, and resurrection. It is a gift, but it must be accepted.

Following are three of many Bible passages that make it clear we are saved by grace.

But now God has shown us a way to be made right with him without keeping the requirements of the law, as was promised in the writings of Moses and the prophets long ago. We are made right with God by placing our faith in Jesus Christ. And this is true for everyone who believes, no matter who we are. Romans 3:21-22

And since it is through God's kindness, then it is not by their good works. For in that case, God's grace would not be what it really is—free and undeserved. Romans 11:6

God saved you by his grace when you believed. And you can't take credit for this; it is a gift from God. Salvation is not a reward for the good things we have done, so none of us can boast about it. Ephesians 2:8-9

The Old Testament prepared the world for the forthcoming Savior, Jesus Christ. The entire New Testament is dedicated to teaching the grace of that Savior.

Too much grace?

Meet David Martyn Lloyd-Jones (1899-1981), a Welsh Protestant minister, preacher, and medical doctor who was one of the most influential preachers of the 20th century. Following is his commentary regarding his preaching the Gospel (*Gospel* means Good News):

"If it is true that where sin abounded grace has much more abounded, well then, "shall we continue in sin, that grace may abound yet further?"

First of all, let me make a comment, to me a very important and vital comment. The true preaching of the gospel of salvation by grace alone always leads to the possibility of this charge being brought against it. There is no better test as to whether a man is really preaching the New Testament gospel of salvation than this, that some people might misunderstand it and misinterpret it to mean that it really amounts to this, that because you are saved by grace alone it does not matter at all what you do; you can go on sinning as much as you like because it will redound all the more to the glory of grace. If my preaching and presentation of the gospel of salvation does not expose it to that misunderstanding, then it is not the gospel. Let me show you what I mean.

If a man preaches justification by works, no one would ever raise this question. If a man's preaching is, "If you want to be Christians, and if you want to go to heaven, you must stop committing sins, you must take up good works, and if you do so regularly and constantly, and do not fail to keep on at it, you will make yourselves Christians, you will reconcile yourselves to God and you will go to heaven." Obviously a man who preaches in that strain would never be liable to this misunderstanding. Nobody would say to such a man, "Shall we continue in sin, that grace may abound?" because the man's whole emphasis is just this, that if you go on sinning you are certain to be damned, and only if you stop sinning can you save yourselves. So that misunderstanding could never arise. Nobody has ever brought this charge against the Church of Rome, but it was brought frequently against Martin Luther; indeed that was precisely what the Church of Rome said about the preaching of Martin Luther. They said, "This man who was a priest has changed the doctrine in order to justify his own marriage and his own lust," and so on. "This man," they said, "is an antinomian; and that is heresy." That is the very charge they brought against him. It was also brought George Whitfield two hundred years ago. It is the charge that formal dead Christianity – if there is such a thing – has always brought against this startling, staggering message, that God "justifies the ungodly"…

That is my comment and it is a very important comment for preachers. I would say to all preachers: If your preaching of salvation has not been misunderstood in that way, then you had better examine your sermons again, and you had better make sure that you are really preaching the salvation that is offered in the New Testament to the ungodly, the sinner, to those who are dead in trespasses and sins, to those who are enemies of God. There is this kind of dangerous element about the true presentation of the doctrine of salvation."

Amen to that!

Christians frequently chastise me for emphasizing grace, exclaiming I encourage people to sin. An irate church lady once criticized the late renowned evangelist Dwight L. Moody for the way he preached. His answer to her was, "I like the way I'm doing it better than the way you're not doing it."

Though criticized for proclaiming the truth, I am evangelizing and winning souls to Jesus. Stating I emphasize grace too much is ridiculous. If I taught differently, I would be lying. Unlike many Christians, I am not scaring people from the Savior who died on the Cross to pay for our sins.

Many preachers love to instill fear, although fear is opposite to what the Scriptures teach. Instilling fear by lying doesn't work. It chases would-be Christians from knowing Jesus, which usually results in more sin, including the unpardonable sin of rejecting him. The immoral behavior of a person will not cause their eternal punishment, but rejecting Jesus will. Shame on you preachers who twist the truth!

Rather than scaring people from Jesus by lecturing about Old Testament and/or man-made laws, the Apostle Paul attracted his listeners to the Savior by sharing the reality of abundant grace.

> *God's law was given so that all people could see how sinful they were.* ***But as people sinned more and more, God's wonderful grace became more abundant.*** *So just as sin ruled over all people and brought them to death, now God's wonderful grace rules instead, giving us right standing with God and resulting in eternal life through Jesus Christ our Lord.* Romans 5:20-21 (Emphasis added by me.)

Chastising me for emphasizing grace is simultaneously declaring the Holy Spirit to be incompetent in his guiding each and every Christian to living a God-pleasing life. Grace is a free gift that will not become obsolete or taken away. It is by the miracle of God's loving and abundant grace that we are saved, and it is by God's loving and abundant grace that we cannot lose our salvation. Thank you, Jesus!

Sealed with the promised Holy Spirit

Immediately upon accepting Jesus as his or her Savior, a person is sealed with the promised Holy Spirit. The Holy Spirit does not depart the believer; he does not come and go. Halleluiah!

I emphasized *sealed with the promised Holy Spirit* in Ephesians 1:13-14 below.

"As I began to speak," Peter continued, "the Holy Spirit fell on them, just as he fell on us at the beginning. Then I thought of the Lord's words when he said, 'John baptized with water, but you will be baptized with the Holy Spirit.' And since God gave these Gentiles the same gift he gave us when we believed in the Lord Jesus Christ, who was I to stand in God's way?" Acts 11:15-17

And Christ lives within you, so even though your body will die because of sin, the Spirit gives you life because you have been made right with God. The Spirit of God, who raised Jesus from the dead, lives in you. And just as God raised Christ Jesus from the dead, he will give life to your mortal bodies by this same Spirit living within you. Romans 8:10-11

It is God who enables us, along with you, to stand firm for Christ. He has commissioned us, and he has identified us as his own by placing the Holy Spirit in our hearts as the first installment that guarantees everything he has promised us. 2 Corinthians 1:21-22

*In him you also, when you heard the word of truth, the gospel of your salvation, and believed in him, were **sealed with the promised Holy Spirit**, who is the guarantee of our inheritance until we acquire possession of it, to the praise of his glory.* Ephesians 1:13-14 (ESV)

And do not bring sorrow to God's Holy Spirit by the way you live. Remember, he has identified you as his own, guaranteeing that you will be saved on the day of redemption. Ephesians 4:30

And God has given us his Spirit as proof that we live in him and he in us. 1 John 4:13

Improving behavior

Salvation cannot be lost, but when people become Christians, to show their appreciation for what God provided through Jesus Christ, most attempt to make moral improvements by yielding to the guidance of the Holy Spirit.

The new converts of Galatia struggled with the old laws as opposed to their new freedom in Christ. *Judaizers*, an extreme Jewish faction within the church, taught that Christians must adhere to laws in addition to believing in Christ. The following passage was the Apostle Paul's warning and advice to the new Christians in Galatia, who had struggled with a dual identity.

> *Oh, foolish Galatians! Who has cast an evil spell on you? For the meaning of Jesus Christ's death was made as clear to you as if you had seen a picture of his death on the cross.* **Let me ask you this one question: Did you receive the Holy Spirit by obeying the law of Moses? Of course not! You received the Spirit because you believed the message you heard about Christ. How foolish can you be? After starting your Christian lives in the Spirit, why are you now trying to become perfect by your own human effort?** *Have you experienced so much for nothing? Surely it was not in vain, was it?* Galatians 3:1-4 (Emphasis added by me.)

My point is to put you on the path of listening to the Holy Spirit, rather than feeling guilty because you are not following rules. Discipleship is not about following rules! The Holy Spirit is what gives us the power needed to live the life that God wants for us. We cannot be effective via our own feeble efforts.

The best way for a person to change is to replace the bad behavior with something superior — an *attractive alternative*. Nothing is superior to allowing Jesus' Spirit to be one's personal counselor. Christian reciprocity is allowing Jesus to live through the believer via the Holy Spirit. Our flesh is weak, but Jesus' Spirit is strong. When a Christian allows the Holy Spirit to live through himself or herself, the more moral they become, enjoying immorality less.

A license to sin?

There are Christians who take advantage of grace and use it as a license to sin. Yes, Christians can sin more, but we enjoy it less — because of the indwelling and conviction of the Holy Spirit.

> *But now we have been released from the law, for we died to it and are no longer captive to its power. Now we can serve God, not in the old way of obeying the letter of the law, but in the new way of living in the Spirit.* Romans 7:6

Although as Christians our sins are not counted against us, we must keep in mind the affect our sins have on the Holy Spirit. Emphasis in the following passage is made by me.

> *And **do not bring sorrow to God's Holy Spirit by the way you live**. Remember, he has identified you as his own, guaranteeing that you will be saved on the day of redemption.* Ephesians 4:30

The Holy Spirit does grieve.

The Holy Spirit is your cool personal counselor

It is nonsense to suppose that all Christians must think and act exactly alike. Christians have the Holy Scriptures to guide them, and they are given the Holy Spirit as their personal counselor.

> *"And I will ask the Father, and he will give you another Advocate, who will never leave you. He is the Holy Spirit, who leads into all truth. The world cannot receive him, because it isn't looking for him and doesn't recognize him. But you know him, because he lives with you now and later will be in you."* John 14:16-17, Jesus' words

> *"But when the Father sends the Advocate as my representative—that is, the Holy Spirit— he will teach you everything and will remind you of everything I have told you.*

> *"I am leaving you with a gift—peace of mind and heart. And the peace I give is a gift the world cannot give. So don't be troubled or afraid."* John 14:26-27, Jesus' words

But people who aren't spiritual can't receive these truths from God's Spirit. It all sounds foolish to them and they can't understand it, for only those who are spiritual can understand what the Spirit means. 1 Corinthians 2:14

But you have received the Holy Spirit, and he lives within you, so you don't need anyone to teach you what is true. For the Spirit teaches you everything you need to know, and what he teaches is true—it is not a lie. So just as he has taught you, remain in fellowship with Christ. 1 John 2:27

Sublimate

One of the meanings of *sublimate* is to transfer a harmful thought or act into one of value. It is the transfer of one energy into another. This process can be utilized to grow spiritually.

The Apostle Peter demonstrated the difference between carnal and spiritual thinking when he walked a short distance on the water — then sank. Peter was doing fine until he turned his thoughts from his faith in Jesus to his own carnality. This same transfer of thought from Jesus to ourselves, or the world, is what causes us to sink.

When we find ourselves in moral dilemmas, if we listen intently to the Spirit and respond obediently, we will make the right decision. Conversely, when we listen to the flesh, we sink like a rock.

> *So I say, let the Holy Spirit guide your lives. Then you won't be doing what your sinful nature craves.* Galatians 5:16

Peter failed and so will you. But the more you try, the more you will grow. Practice makes perfect.

> *But the Holy Spirit produces this kind of fruit in our lives: love, joy, peace, patience, kindness, goodness, faithfulness, gentleness, and self-control. There is no law against these things!* Galatians 5:22-23

Learning to behave the way God wants us to behave is a growth process. The more we learn to listen to the Holy Spirit, the more we begin to live beneficial lives — leaving behind our carnality.

There may be periods of slow yet steady growth, and periods of spectacular growth. Whatever the case, accept and submit to it.

When volunteering in a hospital, if you are of the male gender, rather than lusting about the presence of pretty nurses, use that same energy to pray with a patient. It does not always work, but it is worth a try. God understands our weaknesses. If you are of the female gender, use the same technique when drooling over a handsome doctor. That is *sublimation*.

It is guaranteed

If there is only one thing I want from writing this book, it is your having the certainty that your salvation is definite, assured, certified, secure, and guaranteed — paid for by the Blood of Jesus, and sealed with the promised Holy Spirit who lives in you. I emphasized the word *guarantee* in the following passages:

> *The Spirit is God's **guarantee** that he will give us the inheritance he promised and that he has purchased us to be his own people. He did this so we would praise and glorify him.* Ephesians 1:14

> *And do not bring sorrow to God's Holy Spirit by the way you live. Remember, he has identified you as his own, **guaranteeing** that you will be saved on the day of redemption.* Ephesians 4:30

<u>**Notes:**</u>

Chapter 18

Jesus said, "Born Again"

This chapter was created specifically to address a term despised by many. That term is *born again.*

When Christians use *born again* they are referring to the term Jesus used in his conversation with Nicodemus, a Jewish leader who asked Jesus how to receive the Kingdom of God. That conversation, which follows, is the Bible's most important. I made bold the terms *born again*, *Kingdom of God*, and *born of the Spirit* to indicate their importance.

> "There was a man named Nicodemus, a Jewish religious leader who was a Pharisee. After dark one evening, he came to speak with Jesus. "Rabbi," he said, "we all know that God has sent you to teach us. Your miraculous signs are evidence that God is with you."
>
> Jesus replied, "I tell you the truth, unless you are **born again**, you cannot see the **Kingdom of God**."
>
> "What do you mean?" exclaimed Nicodemus. "How can an old man go back into his mother's womb and be born again?"
>
> Jesus replied, "I assure you, no one can enter the **Kingdom of God** without being born of water and the Spirit. Humans can reproduce only human life, but the Holy Spirit gives birth to spiritual life. So don't be surprised when I say, 'You must be **born again**.' The wind blows wherever it wants. Just as you can hear the wind but can't tell where it comes from or where it is going, so you can't explain how people are **born of the Spirit**."
>
> "How are these things possible?" Nicodemus asked.
>
> Jesus replied, "You are a respected Jewish teacher, and yet you don't understand these things? I assure you, we tell you what we know and have seen,

and yet you won't believe our testimony. But if you don't believe me when I tell you about earthly things, how can you possibly believe if I tell you about heavenly things? No one has ever gone to heaven and returned. But the Son of Man has come down from heaven. And as Moses lifted up the bronze snake on a pole in the wilderness, so the Son of Man must be lifted up, so that everyone who believes in him will have eternal life.

"For God so loved the world so much that he gave his one and only Son, so that everyone who believes in him will not perish but have eternal life. God sent his Son into the world not to judge the world, but to save the world through him.

"There is no judgment against anyone who believes in him. But anyone who does not believe in him has already been judged for not believing in God's one and only Son." John 3:1-18

NOTE: Before expounding on Jesus' proclamation that one must be born again, it is essential to clarify a prevalent misunderstanding of water baptism. In the passage above, where it says "water," most Bible scholars agree it is not referring to baptism with water. To read water baptism into this verse because it mentions water is a misinterpretation.

If "born of water" meant water baptism, it would contradict many other Bible passages that make it clear that salvation is by a spiritual birth (spiritual baptism) received only by faith.

(1) The phrase "born of water" may be referring to the water-like fluid released when the amniotic sac breaks prior to a pregnant woman birthing a child.

(2) It may be referring to the cleansing of sins from Jesus' death on the Cross. The term *water* is used frequently in the Old Testament in reference to spiritual cleansing.

(3) My opinion is Jesus was referring to himself as the living water that nourishes the believer and gives eternal life, as the following passages reveal.

He had to go through Samaria on the way. Eventually he came to the Samaritan village of Sychar, near the field that Jacob gave to his son Joseph. Jacob's well was there; and Jesus, tired from the long walk, sat wearily beside the well about noontime. Soon a Samaritan woman came to draw water, and

Jesus said to her, "Please give me a drink." He was alone at the time because his disciples had gone into the village to buy some food.

The woman was surprised, for Jews refuse to have anything to do with Samaritans. She said to Jesus, "You are a Jew, and I am a Samaritan woman. Why are you asking me for a drink?"

Jesus replied, "If you only knew the gift God has for you and who you are speaking to, you would ask me, and I would give you living water."

"But sir, you don't have a rope or a bucket," she said, "and this well is very deep. Where would you get this living water? And besides, do you think you're greater than our ancestor Jacob, who gave us this well? How can you offer better water than he and his sons and his animals enjoyed?"

Jesus replied, "Anyone who drinks this water will soon become thirsty again. But those who drink the water I give will never be thirsty again. It becomes a fresh, bubbling spring within them, giving them eternal life." John 4:4-14

On the last day, the climax of the festival, Jesus stood and shouted to the crowds, "Anyone who is thirsty may come to me! Anyone who believes in me may come and drink! For the Scriptures declare, 'Rivers of living water will flow from his heart.'" (When he said "living water," he was speaking of the Spirit, who would be given to everyone believing in him. But the Spirit had not yet been given, because Jesus had not yet entered into his glory.) John 7:37-39

Many times in the Old Testament, the term *water* is used when referring to spiritual cleansing.

What Jesus was telling Nicodemus

Jesus was declaring that in order to receive the *Kingdom of God* a person must be born of the Holy Spirit (born again). The Kingdom of God includes angels and all persons who have received salvation by being born again (angels do not need to be born again). The Kingdom of God is eternal, as God is eternal, plus it is spiritual — found within all *born again* believers. We enter the Kingdom when we are born again, and we remain in the Kingdom for eternity. It doesn't get more important than that.

The Kingdom is already here, as the passage below reveals.

One day the Pharisees asked Jesus, "When will the Kingdom of God come?"

Jesus replied, "The Kingdom of God can't be detected by visible signs. You won't be able to say, 'Here it is!' or 'It's over there!' For the Kingdom of God is already among you." Luke 17:21-22

We have confident assurance it is so because the Holy Spirit bears witness with our spirits.

For his Spirit joins with our spirit to affirm that we are God's children.
Romans 8:16

> **The phrase born again means "born from above." Jesus is referring to mankind's need for spiritual transformation/regeneration, which is a gift from God via the Holy Spirit to the believer.** This new birth is what gives the believer eternal life.

A person is born again when he or she trusts in the life, death, burial, and resurrection of Jesus for his or her salvation. If you believe in Jesus' finished work on the Cross, you are born again, which is also referred to as *born spiritually, saved, regenerated, converted, justified.* It is inclusive of all people who have received the gift of salvation (eternal life) via their faith in the finished work of Jesus.

Hundreds of millions of individuals have embraced this **belief** and will attest to knowing beyond the shadow of a doubt they have received the Holy Spirit, and have been assured by him they are going to Heaven.

Bad connotation

Sadly, *born again* has been misconstrued primarily because overzealous legalistic Christians have tried to shove it down people's throats rather than kindly and gently explaining its magnificent benefits.

I have discovered that those who holler, "You must be born again," usually do it in a threatening manner, rather than the kindness intended by Jesus. In the minds of many (too many) unsaved persons, the portrayal of a born again Christian is crazy, legalistic, self-righteous, loud-mouthed bigots, etc.

I use *born again* even though the connotation is threatening for many because I believe the time has come for those of us who are born again, and not boisterous, to share our testimonies, demonstrating to the world that we are not crazy, legalistic, self-righteous, judgmental, loud-mouthed bigots. We must represent God in the fashion that he taught.

> *"So now I am giving you a new commandment: Love each other. Just as I have loved you, you should love each other. Your love for one another will prove to the world that you are my disciples."* John 13:34-35

Presenting Jesus' love should be done in a gentle, educational way, and not by threatening Hell, fire, and brimstone to the unsaved.

The proof is in the receiving

Ten days after witnessing Jesus ascension to Heaven, the apostles began to celebrate the Jewish feast of Pentecost, along with Jews from many nations who had come to Jerusalem for this festive occasion.

The day of Pentecost (50 days after Passover, which was when Jesus was crucified), Jesus' followers gathered, when suddenly the sound of a mighty wind filled the house. In amazement, they watched what appeared to be tongues of fire blowing from Heaven and permeating the building. These flames of fire settled on each of them, filling them with the Holy Spirit.

> *Then Peter said to them, "Repent, and let every one of you be baptized in the name of Jesus Christ for the remission of sins; and you shall receive the gift of the Holy Spirit."* Acts 2:38 (KJV)

About 3,000 people became believers that day. Wouldn't you? How about now?

> *Those who believed what Peter said were baptized and added to the church that day—about 3,000 in all.* Acts 2:41

This was the beginning of the Christian Church. You can be part of this Church that will enjoy eternal life by trusting in Jesus' finished work.

> *But to all who believed him and accepted him, he gave the right to become children of God. They are reborn—not with a physical birth resulting from human passion or plan, but a birth that comes from God.* John 1:12-13

But you are not controlled by your sinful nature. You are controlled by the Spirit if you have the Spirit of God living in you. (And remember that those who do not have the Spirit of Christ living in them do not belong to him at all.) Romans 8:9

There is no longer Jew or Gentile, slave or free, male and female. For you are all one in Christ Jesus. Galatians 3:28

Sabbath rest

We Christians know that upon our death we will go directly to the eternal dwelling place of saints (all Christians are saints), not based on anything we do, but because of what Jesus did for us. This fact is so comforting a term has been coined: *Sabbath rest* describes the current peace experienced by the Christian from knowing he or she has been saved eternally. That peace of knowing what Jesus did for us is what motivates Christians to be disciples. *Sabbath rest* should not be confused with resting on Sunday.

God's promise of entering his rest still stands, so we ought to tremble with fear that some of you might fail to experience it. For this good news—that God has prepared this rest—has been announced to us just as it was to them. But it did them no good because they didn't share the faith of those who listened to God. For only we who believe can enter his rest. As for the others, God said,

> *"In my anger I took an oath:*
> *'They will never enter my place of rest,'"*

even though this rest has been ready since he made the world. We know it is ready because of the place in the Scriptures where it mentions the seventh day: "On the seventh day God rested from all his work." But in the other passage God said, "They will never enter my place of rest."

So God's rest is there for people to enter, but those who first heard this good news failed to enter because they disobeyed God. So God set another time for entering his rest, and that time is today. God announced this through David much later in the words already quoted:

> *"Today when you hear his voice,*
> *don't harden your hearts."*

Now if Joshua had succeeded in giving them this rest, God would not have spoken about another day of rest still to come. So there is a special rest still waiting for the people of God. For all who have entered into God's rest have rested from their labors, just as God did after creating the world. So let us do our best to enter that rest. But if we disobey God, as the people of Israel did, we will fall. Hebrews 4:1-11

Sabbath rest quiets a guilty conscience, stills troubling thoughts, and gives hope in desperation. In Christ we find complete rest today and forever. Sabbath rest is what those who understand salvation, and who have been born again, experience when they cease from their own efforts for salvation and depend on the work of Christ.

Then Jesus said, "Come to me, all of you who are weary and carry heavy burdens, and I will give you rest. Take my yoke upon you. Let me teach you, because I am humble and gentle at heart, and you will find rest for your souls. For my yoke is easy to bear, and the burden I give you is light." Matthew 11:28-30

The Apostle Paul shares his weakness with the world as he experienced Sabbath rest.

Each time he said, "My grace is all you need. My power works best in weakness." So now I am glad to boast about my weaknesses, so that the power of Christ can work through me. That's why I take pleasure in my weaknesses, and in the insults, hardships, persecutions, and troubles that I suffer for Christ. For when I am weak, then I am strong. 2 Corinthians 12:9-10

Although God made the offer, you make the decision

God so loved the world that he created a plan that would allow those who accept Jesus Christ as Savior to spend eternity with him. God's plan is so simple that *you* make the final decision regarding your destiny. <u>You can make that decision right now. It has nothing to do with how good you have been or how good you will be.</u> It is contingent on your faith in Jesus Christ as your Savior. Pretty simple, huh? It is going to Hell that takes a lot of work. Make the right choice, and make it now.

The believer's prayer

Although it is a person's faith alone in Jesus' finished work that saves, many Christians repeat a prayer as their acknowledgement. Also, oftentimes people have neglected their Christian life, so they want to begin again. Saying a prayer is not necessary, but

God loves it when we pray. Prayer can be done aloud, silently, publicly, or privately. It is not the intellectual content of the prayer, but its sincerity. Say something like this:

> God,
>
> I believe you came to Earth in the form of a man named Jesus and died on a cross as payment for my sins. Many people saw you come back from being dead, which proved you are God and that you can overcome death. I know you are living in me, which is my assurance I will live eternally with you. I am saying this prayer to reinforce my relationship with you, and I am praying that I will grow in my Christian faith.
>
> Amen.

The Bible says because you are a believer in Jesus' finished work, you were saved the moment you believed. This is also known as *justified, born spiritually, regenerated,* or *born again.*

The seeker's prayer

> God,
>
> I am not yet convinced, but I want to be. If you are for real, and if you came to Earth in the form of a man, I invite your Spirit to live in me and to show me truths as you guide me through my life.
>
> Amen.

I believe if you said the seeker's prayer, God will reveal the truth to you. At the very moment you trust Jesus as the one and only way to dwell with Jesus eternally, you will be saved. Now find a church and purchase an easy-to-read New Testament Bible.

You may know!

If you repeated the believer's prayer, as a believer, you were saved the moment you believed. The prayer was not necessary for your salvation, but it is so cool to be able to communicate directly with Jesus. No intermediary is needed.

If you repeated the seeker's prayer, the Bible says God will give you the gift of faith. Once you have that faith, you too will become a part of Jesus and be able to communicate directly with him. No intermediary will be needed.

Here is another really cool thing. Jesus will instill in you the confidence that you will be with him eternally — no matter what! The Bible states you will **know** you have eternal life. I emphasized the words **you may know** in the following verse:

*I have written this to you who believe in the name of the Son of God, so that **you may know** you have eternal life.* 1 John 5:13

The term *born again* in various translations

The following John 3:3 passages quote Jesus in many New Testament Bible versions.

Although each version may be worded differently, one must agree that Jesus (God incarnate) made it very clear that a person must be *born again, born from above*, or *born anew* (the Greek is purposely ambiguous and can mean *born again, from above*, or *born anew*) to receive the Kingdom of God.

Many people may be offended or frightened by *born again*, but we must face the objections head-on. Apprehension is a sweet victory for Satan.

In the following selected passages I emphasized the words that I am stressing.

1599 Geneva Bible (GNV)

*Jesus answered and said unto him, Verily verily I say unto thee, Except a man be **born again**, he cannot see the kingdom of God.* John 3:3 (GNV)

21st Century King James Version (KJ21)

*Jesus answered and said unto him, "Verily, verily I say unto thee, unless a man be **born again**, he cannot see the Kingdom of God."* John 3:3 (KJ21)

American Standard Version (ASV)

*Jesus answered and said unto him, Verily, verily, I say unto thee, Except one be **born anew**, he cannot see the kingdom of God.* John 3:3 (ASV)

Amplified Bible (AMP)

*Jesus answered him, I assure you, most solemnly I tell you, that unless a person is **born again (anew, from above)**, he cannot ever see (know, be acquainted with, and experience) the kingdom of God.* John 3:3 (AMP)

Common English Bible (CEB)

*Jesus answered, "I assure you, unless someone is **born anew**, it's not possible to see God's kingdom." John 3:3 (CEB)*

Complete Jewish Bible (CJB)

*"Yes, indeed," Yeshua answered him, "I tell you that unless a person is **born again from above**, he cannot see the Kingdom of God." John 3:3 (CJB)*

Douay-Rheims 1899 American Edition (DRA)

*Jesus answered, and said to him: Amen, amen I say to thee, unless a man be **born again**, he cannot see the kingdom of God. John 3:3 (DRA)*

Easy-to-Read Version (ERV)

*Jesus answered, "I assure you, everyone must be born again. Anyone who is not **born again** cannot be in God's kingdom." John 3:3 (ERV)*

English Standard Version (ESV)

*Jesus answered him, "Truly, truly, I say to you, unless one is **born again** he cannot see the kingdom of God." John 3:3 (ESV)*

Expanded Bible (EXB)

*Jesus answered, "•I tell you the truth (Truly, truly I say to you), unless you are **born again (or from above; this may be a play on words, meaning both "again" and "from above")** you cannot be in (experience; see) God's kingdom." John 3:3 (EXB)*

GOD'S WORD Translation (GW)

*Jesus replied to Nicodemus, "I can guarantee this truth: No one can see the kingdom of God without being **born from above**." John 3:3 (GW)*

J.B. Phillips New Testament (PHILLIPS)

*"Believe me," returned Jesus, "a man cannot even see the kingdom of God without being **born again**." John 3:3 (PHILLIPS)*

King James Version (KJV)

*Jesus answered and said unto him, Verily, verily, I say unto thee, Except a man be **born again**, he cannot see the kingdom of God.* John 3:3 (KJV)

The Message (MSG)

*Jesus said, "You're absolutely right. Take it from me: Unless a person is **born from above**, it's not possible to see what I'm pointing to—to God's kingdom."* John 3:3 (MSG)

New American Standard Bible (NASB)

*Jesus answered and said to him, "Truly, truly, I say to you, unless one is **born again** he cannot see the kingdom of God."* John 3:3 (NASB)

New King James Version (NKJV)

*Jesus answered and said to him, "Most assuredly, I say to you, unless one is **born again**, he cannot see the kingdom of God."* John 3:3 (NKJV)

New Living Translation (NLT)

*Jesus replied, "I tell you the truth, unless you are **born again**, you cannot see the Kingdom of God."* John 3:3 (NLT)

New Revised Standard Version (NRSV)

*Jesus answered him, "Very truly, I tell you, no one can see the kingdom of God without being **born from above**."* John 3:3 (NRSV)

New Revised Standard Version Catholic Edition (NRSVCE)

*Jesus answered him, "Very truly, I tell you, no one can see the kingdom of God without being **born from above**."* John 3:3 (NRSVCE)

Orthodox Jewish Bible (OJB)

*In reply, he said to him, Omein, omein, I say to you, unless someone is born anew [**born again, Yn 1:13; Dt 10:16; 30:6; Jer 4:4; Isa 52:1; Ezek 44:7,9**], he is not able to see the Malchut Hashem.* John 3:3 (OJB)

Revised Standard Version (RSV)

*Jesus answered him, "Truly, truly, I say to you, unless one is **born anew**, he cannot see the kingdom of God."* John 3:3 (RSV)

Wycliffe Bible (WYC)

*Jesus answered, and said to him, Truly, truly, I say to thee, but a man be **born again**, he may not see the kingdom of God.* John 3:3 (WYC)

Summation

Born again is used to describe belief in Jesus as one's Savior. *Born again* is also referred to as *born spiritually, saved, regenerated, converted, justified.*

When born again, a person becomes a child of God, which is the absolute assurance that he or she will live eternally with God in Heaven, and then on the New Earth (the New Earth is Heaven on Earth).

> *This means that anyone who belongs to Christ has become a new person. The old life is gone; a new life has begun!* 2 Corinthians 5:17

> *But to all who believed him and accepted him, he gave the right to become children of God. They are reborn—not with a physical birth resulting from human passion or plan, but a birth that comes from God.* John 1:12-13

AMEN!

Chapter 19

Salvation versus Discipleship

There is a distinct difference between *salvation* and *discipleship*. In the chapter **Christian Salvation**, you learned salvation is a free gift to the believer and necessitates only belief in what Jesus did for mankind. Salvation is by *grace* through faith.

Discipleship 101

Discipleship is derived from the Greek word *mathetes*, which means "pupil" or "apprentice." Christian discipleship is the term used to describe the process by which Christians are equipped by the Holy Spirit to grow in the Lord Jesus Christ. This process requires the believer to respond to the Holy Spirit's guidance in everyday life. It is not always easy, but it has rewards.

A person can be a disciple (pupil) of Jesus without being born again. A great example of this would be Mormons, who are members of a very guilt-provoking, legalistic cult that claims to be Christian but fails the test of trustworthiness. Sadly, many Catholics are disciples of Christ, but most have never been exposed to the necessity of being born again.

WARNING: Many folks follow the moral teachings of Jesus but reject him as their only way of obtaining eternal life. They dislike the thought of being born again.

Worldwide, many people attend church, sing in the choir, give money, and try to live moral lives — but neglect the regeneration that accompanies being born again. They recognize Jesus as *a savior*, but not as the only means of salvation. They do not believe he was God incarnate, and they believe they must perform good deeds to go to Heaven. Mormonism is a cult that I will not take

the time to expound on in this book because my purpose is not to criticize Mormons (well, maybe a little), but to warn you that being a disciple is not the same as being saved.

Attempting to write a few pages to effectively and adequately describe Christian discipleship is as ineffectual as trying to write one chapter on how to sail around the world. Because I am an advocate of the KISS principle (Keep It Simple, Stupid), years ago I framed the Prayer of Saint Francis and placed it above my desk. It is very sweet, to the point, and it gives me a daily overview of how I should be living my life.

Probably not written by Saint Francis himself, the poem is attributed to Saint Francis of Assisi and is believed to have first appeared in 1912, printed in a small French magazine. The author could have been the publisher of that magazine, Father Bouquerel, but nobody knows for certain.

THE PRAYER OF SAINT FRANCIS

Lord, make me an instrument of your peace;
Where there is hatred, let me sow love;
Where there is injury, pardon;
Where there is doubt, faith;
Where there is despair, hope;
Where there is darkness, light;
And where there is sadness, joy.

O Divine Master, Grant that I may not seek
To be consoled, as to console;
To be understood, as to understand;
To be loved, as to love;
For it is in giving that we receive;
It is in pardoning that we are pardoned,
And it is in dying that we are born to eternal life.

Amen

Discipleship necessitates cooperation by the believer submitting to the leadership of the Holy Spirit. Discipleship is the process by which Christians grow in the Lord Jesus Christ and are equipped by the Holy Spirit to become more like Christ.

> *He must become greater and greater, and I must become less and less.*
> John 3:30

> WARNING: Emulating Jesus Christ is an admiral endeavor, but please remember that Jesus was God and no living person can attain the greatness of God. I am warning you of this so that you do not get discouraged or feel guilty.

The Bible tells saints to be separate from the world. *Consecrate* means "to set apart or declare sacred; set apart or dedicate to the service of Jesus."

Consecrate also connotes sanctification, which is a critical component in our discipleship.

> *And so, dear brothers and sisters, I plead with you to give your bodies to God because of all he has done for you. Let them be a living and holy sacrifice— the kind he will find acceptable. This is truly the way to worship him. Don't copy the behavior and customs of this world, but let God transform you into a new person by changing the way you think. Then you will learn to know God's will for you, which is good and pleasing and perfect.*

> *Because of the privilege and authority God has given me, I give each of you this warning: Don't think you are better than you really are. Be honest in your evaluation of yourselves, measuring yourselves by the faith God has given us. Just as our bodies have many parts and each part has a special function, so it is with Christ's body. We are many parts of one body, and we all belong to each other.* Romans 12:1-5

> *So put to death the sinful, earthly things lurking within you. Have nothing to do with sexual immorality, impurity, lust, and evil desires. Don't be greedy, for a greedy person is an idolater, worshiping the things of this world. Because of these sins, the anger of God is coming. You used to do these things when your life was still part of this world. But now is the time to get rid of anger, rage, malicious behavior, slander, and dirty language. Don't lie to each other, for you have stripped off your old sinful nature and all its wicked deeds.*

Put on your new nature, and be renewed as you learn to know your Creator and become like him. In this new life, it doesn't matter if you are a Jew or a Gentile, circumcised or uncircumcised, barbaric, uncivilized, slave, or free. Christ is all that matters, and he lives in all of us.

Since God chose you to be the holy people he loves, you must clothe yourselves with tenderhearted mercy, kindness, humility, gentleness, and patience. Make allowance for each other's faults, and forgive anyone who offends you. Remember, the Lord forgave you, so you must forgive others. Above all, clothe yourselves with love, which binds us all together in perfect harmony. And let the peace that comes from Christ rule in your hearts. For as members of one body you are called to live in peace. And always be thankful.

Let the message about Christ, in all its richness, fill your lives. Teach and counsel each other with all the wisdom he gives. Sing psalms and hymns and spiritual songs to God with thankful hearts. And whatever you do or say, do it as a representative of the Lord Jesus, giving thanks through him to God the Father. Colossians 3:5-17

As saints, our lives should be a living sacrifice to Jesus.

Put Jesus first

Then, calling the crowd to join his disciples, he said, "If any of you wants to be my follower, you must turn from your selfish ways, take up your cross, and follow me. Mark 8:34

The Cross is a representation of the transition from spiritual death to spiritual life.

Here is Jesus' commandment to us:

Jesus replied, "'You must love the Lord your God with all your heart, all your soul, and all your mind.' This is the first and greatest commandment. A second is equally important: 'Love your neighbor as yourself.' The entire law and all the demands of the prophets are based on these two commandments." Matthew 22:37-40

It is important to notice that Jesus didn't say we must like one another. Love and like are two different emotions.

Jesus loved the world so much that he died on a cross to pay for our sins. He took our punishment because he loved us. Now he wants us to love him (he is God) and love one another.

When we serve others we are serving God

Jesus called his followers to be servants of others. Jesus was humble enough to set the example.

> *But Jesus called them together and said, "You know that the rulers in this world lord it over their people, and officials flaunt their authority over those under them. But among you it will be different. Whoever wants to be a leader among you must be your servant, and whoever wants to be first among you must become your slave. For even the Son of Man came not to be served but to serve others and to give his life as a ransom for many."* Matthew 20:25-28

To show others what genuine service involves, he performed one of the most humbling examples by washing his disciples' feet.

> *So he got up from the table, took off his robe, wrapped a towel around his waist, and poured water into a basin. Then he began to wash the disciples' feet, drying them with the towel he had around him.* John 13:4-5

> *After washing their feet, he put on his robe again and sat down and asked, "Do you understand what I was doing? You call me 'Teacher' and 'Lord,' and you are right, because that's what I am. And since I, your Lord and Teacher, have washed your feet, you ought to wash each other's feet. I have given you an example to follow. Do as I have done to you. I tell you the truth, slaves are not greater than their master. Nor is the messenger more important than the one who sends the message. Now that you know these things, God will bless you for doing them."* John 13:12-17

If God (Jesus) is humble enough to wash others' feet, you can and should humble yourself to serve others. An example of how to serve others:

> *Share each other's burdens, and in this way obey the law of Christ. If you think you are too important to help someone, you are only fooling yourself. You are not that important.* Galatians 6:2-3

We all love stuff, but it is just stuff. Not only do the following verses provide us with a suggestion on how we can find more peace while on earth, but they also remind us there are rewards in God's Kingdom.

> *"Sell your possessions and give to those in need. This will store up treasure for you in heaven! And the purses of heaven never get old or develop holes. Your treasure will be safe; no thief can steal it and no moth can destroy it. Wherever your treasure is, there the desires of your heart will also be."* Luke 12:33-34, Jesus' words

The following passage is Jesus' assurance that acts of kindness will have rewards:

> *Then he turned to his host. "When you put on a luncheon or a banquet," he said, "don't invite your friends, brothers, relatives, and rich neighbors. For they will invite you back, and that will be your only reward. Instead, invite the poor, the crippled, the lame, and the blind. Then at the resurrection of the righteous, God will reward you for inviting those who could not repay you."* Luke 14:12-14

Be meek in your giving, says Jesus:

> *"Watch out! Don't do your good deeds publicly, to be admired by others, for you will lose the reward from your Father in heaven. When you give to someone in need, don't do as the hypocrites do—blowing trumpets in the synagogues and streets to call attention to their acts of charity! I tell you the truth, they have received all the reward they will ever get. But when you give to someone in need, don't let your left hand know what your right hand is doing. Give your gifts in private, and your Father, who sees everything, will reward you."* Matthew 6:1-4, Jesus' words

Discipleship should be the fruit of thankfulness, not the yoke of guilt

Do you feel like you want to do something in return to say thanks for what Jesus did? Discipleship is the way.

Paul tells us how to live a new life in Jesus.

> *So don't let anyone condemn you for what you eat or drink, or for not celebrating certain holy days or new moon ceremonies or Sabbaths. For these rules are only shadows of the reality yet to come. And Christ himself is that*

reality. Don't let anyone condemn you by insisting on pious self-denial or the worship of angels, saying they have had visions about these things. Their sinful minds have made them proud, and they are not connected to Christ, the head of the body. For he holds the whole body together with its joints and ligaments, and it grows as God nourishes it.

You have died with Christ, and he has set you free from the spiritual powers of this world. So why do you keep on following the rules of the world, such as, "Don't handle! Don't taste! Don't touch!"? Such rules are mere human teachings about things that deteriorate as we use them. These rules may seem wise because they require strong devotion, pious self-denial, and severe bodily discipline. But they provide no help in conquering a person's evil desires. Colossians 2:16-23

Paul continues:

Since you have been raised to new life with Christ, set your sights on the realities of heaven, where Christ sits in the place of honor at God's right hand. Think about the things of heaven, not the things of earth. For you died to this life, and your real life is hidden with Christ in God. And when Christ, who is your life, is revealed to the whole world, you will share in all his glory.

So put to death the sinful, earthly things lurking within you. Have nothing to do with sexual immorality, impurity, lust, and evil desires. Don't be greedy, for a greedy person is an idolater, worshiping the things of this world. Because of these sins, the anger of God is coming. You used to do these things when your life was still part of this world. But now is the time to get rid of anger, rage, malicious behavior, slander, and dirty language. Don't lie to each other, for you have stripped off your old sinful nature and all its wicked deeds. Put on your new nature, and be renewed as you learn to know your Creator and become like him. In this new life, it doesn't matter if you are a Jew or a Gentile, circumcised or uncircumcised, barbaric, uncivilized, slave, or free. Christ is all that matters, and he lives in all of us.

Since God chose you to be the holy people he loves, you must clothe yourselves with tenderhearted mercy, kindness, humility, gentleness, and patience. Make allowance for each other's faults, and forgive anyone who offends you. Remember, the Lord forgave you, so you must forgive others. Above all, clothe yourselves with love, which binds us all together in perfect harmony. And let the peace that comes from Christ rule in your hearts. For as members of one body you are called to live in peace. And always be thankful.

Let the message about Christ, in all its richness, fill your lives. Teach and counsel each other with all the wisdom he gives. Sing psalms and hymns and spiritual songs to God with thankful hearts. And whatever you do or say, do it as a representative of the Lord Jesus, giving thanks through him to God the Father. Colossians 3:1-17

First and foremost: Listen to and obey the Holy Spirit.

And do not bring sorrow to God's Holy Spirit by the way you live. Remember, he has identified you as his own, guaranteeing that you will be saved on the day of redemption.
Ephesians 4:30

Chapter 20

Die to the Law and Live by the Spirit

This chapter advances discipleship to another level.

A little about the Old Testament laws

Beginning with Adam and Eve, mankind has been of a sinful nature. Before the death of Jesus Christ, God gave the Israelites laws regarding moral behavior. God gave these laws so people would have a guide by which to live, and a standard by which they might recognize God's purity and their sinfulness. There are 613 such laws, or commandments (including the Ten Commandments), stated in the Old Testament, but these laws were fulfilled by Jesus' death on the Cross.

> *For Christ has already accomplished the purpose for which the law was given. As a result, all who believe in him are made right with God.* Romans 10:4

> *Before the way of faith in Christ was available to us, we were placed under guard by the law. We were kept in protective custody, so to speak, until the way of faith was revealed.*

> *Let me put it another way. The law was our guardian until Christ came; it protected us until we could be made right with God through faith. And now that the way of faith has come, we no longer need the law as our guardian.* Galatians 3:23-25

> **He did this by ending the system of law with its commandments and regulations. He made peace between Jews and Gentiles by creating in himself one new people from the two groups. Ephesians 2:15**

The Ten Commandments were not, and are not, laws for Gentiles.

Warning

Remember, because of human weakness, God made a New Covenant, which is obtained simply by the recipient accepting the life, death, and resurrection of Jesus Christ as the only method by which he or she can be hailed into God's abode as his child. Be warned that *church leaders may be guilty of adding Old Testament laws, practices, customs, and traditions to their teachings.* Christians have been unchained from the Old Testament law! Ascertain if you are receiving truth from your teachers.

> *Let God's curse fall on anyone, including us or even an angel from heaven, who preaches a different kind of Good News than the one we preached to you. I say again what we have said before: If anyone preaches any other Good News than the one you welcomed, let that person be cursed.* Galatians 1:8-9

> *So Christ has truly set us free. Now make sure that you stay free, and don't get tied up again in slavery to the law.* Galatians 5:1

You must study your Bible to discern truth. Do not put all of your faith in another mortal, but depend on the Word of God and guidance from Holy Spirit.

The avoidance of sin is accomplished out of love for Jesus and love for others. Love is to be our motivation.

As a teenager, I was very ornery, but my parents provided extreme love and understanding. They both worked to provide my older sister, Tami, and me with all of those material things teenagers desire. Yes, I pushed the envelope, but in appreciation for their love, I tempered my ornery behavior because I loved and respected them. This same principle applies to my love for Jesus and his finished work on the Cross for mavericks like me. My flesh is weak, but my spirit is stronger. Thank you, Jesus!

When we recognize the value of Jesus' sacrifice on our behalf, our response should be to follow his example in expressing love to others. Our motivation for overcoming misbehavior is love, not a desire to obey commandments. We attempt to obey the Law of Love because we love Jesus.

You must die to the Law

Oh, how important this is.

> *"For God loved the world so much that he gave his one and only Son, so that everyone who believes in him will not perish but have eternal life. God sent*

his Son into the world not to judge the world, but to save the world through him." John 3:16-17, Jesus' words

Brothers, listen! We are here to proclaim that through this man Jesus there is forgiveness for your sins. Everyone who believes in him is declared right with God—something the law of Moses could never do. Acts 13:38-39

Obviously, the law applies to those to whom it was given, for its purpose is to keep people from having excuses, and to show that the entire world is guilty before God. For no one can ever be made right with God by doing what the law commands. The law simply shows us how sinful we are. Romans 3:19-22

For God presented Jesus as the sacrifice for sin. People are made right with God when they believe that Jesus sacrificed his life, shedding his blood. This sacrifice shows that God was being fair when he held back and did not punish those who sinned in times past, for he was looking ahead and including them in what he would do in this present time. God did this to demonstrate his righteousness, for he himself is fair and just, and he declares sinners to be right in his sight when they believe in Jesus. Romans 3:25-26

Can we boast, then, that we have done anything to be accepted by God? No, because our acquittal is not based on obeying the law. It is based on faith. So we are made right with God through faith and not by obeying the law. Romans 3:27-28

If God's promise is only for those who obey the law, then faith is not necessary and the promise is pointless. For the law always brings punishment on those who try to obey it. (The only way to avoid breaking the law is to have no law to break!) Romans 4:14-15

God's law was given so that all people could see how sinful they were. But as people sinned more and more, God's wonderful grace became more abundant. So just as sin ruled over all people and brought them to death, now God's wonderful grace rules instead, giving us right standing with God and resulting in eternal life through Jesus Christ our Lord. Romans 5:20-21

Sin is no longer your master, for you no longer live under the requirements of the law. Instead, you live under the freedom of God's grace. Romans 6:14

But now we have been released from the law, for we died to it and are no longer captive to its power. Now we can serve God, not in the old way

of obeying the letter of the law, but in the new way of living in the Spirit.
Romans 7:6

*So now there is no condemnation for those who belong to Christ Jesus. And
because you belong to him, the power of the life-giving Spirit has freed you
from the power of sin that leads to death. The law of Moses was unable to
save us because of the weakness of our sinful nature. So God did what the
law could not do. He sent his own Son in a body like the bodies we sinners
have. And in that body God declared an end to sin's control over us by giving
his Son as a sacrifice for our sins. He did this so that the just requirement of
the law would be fully satisfied for us, who no longer follow our sinful nature
but instead follow the Spirit.* Romans 8:1-4

*What does all this mean? Even though the Gentiles were not trying to follow
God's standards, they were made right with God. And it was by faith that
this took place. But the people of Israel, who tried so hard to get right with
God by keeping the law, never succeeded. Why not? Because they were trying
to get right with God by keeping the law instead of by trusting in him. They
stumbled over the great rock in their path. God warned them of this in the
Scriptures when he said,*

> *"I am placing a stone in Jerusalem that makes people stumble,*
>   *a rock that makes them fall.*
> *But anyone who trusts in him*
>   *will never be disgraced."* Romans 9:30-33

*When I was with the Jews, I lived like a Jew to bring the Jews to Christ. When
I was with those who follow the Jewish law, I too lived under that law. Even
though I am not subject to the law, I did this so I could bring to Christ those
who are under the law.* 1 Corinthians 9:20

*The old way, with laws etched in stone, led to death, though it began with
such glory that the people of Israel could not bear to look at Moses' face. For
his face shone with the glory of God, even though the brightness was already
fading away. Shouldn't we expect far greater glory under the new way, now
that the Holy Spirit is giving life? If the old way, which brings condemnation,
was glorious, how much more glorious is the new way, which makes us right
with God!* 2 Corinthians 3:7-9

*"You and I are Jews by birth, not 'sinners' like the Gentiles. Yet we know that
a person is made right with God by faith in Jesus Christ, not by obeying the*

law. And we have believed in Christ Jesus, so that we might be made right with God because of our faith in Christ, not because we have obeyed the law. For no one will ever be made right with God by obeying the law."

But suppose we seek to be made right with God through faith in Christ and then we are found guilty because we have abandoned the law. Would that mean Christ has led us into sin? Absolutely not! Rather, I am a sinner if I rebuild the old system of law I already tore down. For when I tried to keep the law, it condemned me. So I died to the law—I stopped trying to meet all its requirements—so that I might live for God. My old self has been crucified with Christ. It is no longer I who live, but Christ lives in me. So I live in this earthly body by trusting in the Son of God, who loved me and gave himself for me. I do not treat the grace of God as meaningless. For if keeping the law could make us right with God, then there was no need for Christ to die." Galatians 2:15-21

But those who depend on the law to make them right with God are under his curse, for the Scriptures say, "Cursed is everyone who does not observe and obey all the commands that are written in God's Book of the Law." So it is clear that no one can be made right with God by trying to keep the law. For the Scriptures say, "It is through faith that a righteous person has life." This way of faith is very different from the way of law, which says, "It is through obeying the law that a person has life."

But Christ has rescued us from the curse pronounced by the law. When he was hung on the cross, he took upon himself the curse for our wrongdoing. For it is written in the Scriptures, "Cursed is everyone who is hung on a tree." Through Christ Jesus, God has blessed the Gentiles with the same blessing he promised to Abraham, so that we who are believers might receive the promised Holy Spirit through faith. Galatians 3:10-14

But when the right time came, God sent his Son, born of a woman, subject to the law. God sent him to buy freedom for us who were slaves to the law, so that he could adopt us as his very own children. Galatians 4:4-5

For if you are trying to make yourselves right with God by keeping the law, you have been cut off from Christ! You have fallen away from God's grace. Galatians 5:18

God saved you by his grace when you believed. And you can't take credit for this; it is a gift from God. Salvation is not a reward for the good things we have done, so none of us can boast about it. Ephesians 2:8-9

Do not get involved in foolish discussions about spiritual pedigrees or in quarrels and fights about obedience to Jewish laws. These things are useless and a waste of time. Titus 3:9

You must live by the Spirit

Rather than trying to remember more than 600 individual commandments in the Old Testament law, Christians should simply focus on loving the Lord Jesus and loving others.

Jesus replied, "'You must love the Lord your God with all your heart, all your soul, and all your mind.' This is the first and greatest commandment. A second is equally important: 'Love your neighbor as yourself.' The entire law and all the demands of the prophets are based on these two commandments." Matthew 22:37-40

Some believe, because we have been freed from Old Testament law, we will use this as an excuse to sin. The Apostle Paul addresses this very issue in Romans Chapter 6:

Well then, should we keep on sinning so that God can show us more and more of his wonderful grace? Of course not! Since we have died to sin, how can we continue to live in it? Or have you forgotten that when we were joined with Christ Jesus in baptism, we joined him in his death? For we died and were buried with Christ by baptism. And just as Christ was raised from the dead by the glorious power of the Father, now we also may live new lives.

Since we have been united with him in his death, we will also be raised to life as he was. We know that our old sinful selves were crucified with Christ so that sin might lose its power in our lives. We are no longer slaves to sin. For when we died with Christ we were set free from the power of sin. And since we died with Christ, we know we will also live with him. We are sure of this because Christ was raised from the dead, and he will never die again. Death no longer has any power over him. When he died, he died once to break the power of sin. But now that he lives, he lives for the glory of God. So you also should consider yourselves to be dead to the power of sin and alive to God through Christ Jesus. Romans 6:1-11

Paul's prayer for spiritual growth:

When I think of all this, I fall to my knees and pray to the Father, the Creator of everything in heaven and on earth. I pray that from his glorious, unlimited resources he will empower you with inner strength through his Spirit. Then Christ will make his home in your hearts as you trust in him. Your roots will grow down into God's love and keep you strong. And may you have the power to understand, as all God's people should, how wide, how long, how high, and how deep his love is. May you experience the love of Christ, though it is too great to understand fully. Then you will be made complete with all the fullness of life and power that comes from God.

Now all glory to God, who is able, through his mighty power at work within us, to accomplish infinitely more than we might ask or think. Glory to him in the church and in Christ Jesus through all generations forever and ever! Amen. **Ephesians 3:14-21**

Notes:

Chapter 21

What a Homosexual Must Do to get to Heaven

The main thing is to keep the main thing the main thing.

This chapter will be very explicit regarding what a person (homosexual or not) must do to receive eternal life. That is the main thing.

Because numerous counterfeit prerequisites permeate Christendom, I will address those first. A homosexual is **not** required to:

1. Repent of sin. (*Repent of sin* is a manmade phrase, not biblical. *Repent* means "change of mind." To receive eternal life in the place Jesus has prepared for Christians, a person must *repent* of the notion of working his or her way there, and accept Jesus as Savior.) NOBODY HAS EVER RECEIVED THE FREE GIFT OF ETERNAL LIFE BY REPENTING OF SIN!
2. Make Jesus Lord of your life. Like it or not, Jesus, as God, is already Lord of all lives. (But to receive the free gift of salvation you must "trust" Jesus as your Savior, at which time you will be baptized by the Holy Spirit, who will be your counselor. *Don't be drunk with wine, because it will ruin your life. Instead, be filled with the Holy Spirit.* Ephesians 5:18)
3. Confess with your mouth that Jesus is Lord. (This was a one-time instruction from Paul to a certain group of Jews.)
4. Give your life to the Lord. (This is a phrase that is used, but it doesn't save. A person is saved by his or her faith.)
5. Be sorry for sinning. (Only a fool would not be sorry for sinning, but sorrow does not save. Only faith in Jesus saves.)
6. Ask forgiveness for sins. (All sins were forgiven on the Cross.)
7. Stop sinning. (Nobody can quit sinning.)
8. Invite Jesus into your heart. (Not necessary, but it demonstrates faith.)
9. Go forward in an alter call. (Although going forward demonstrates faith.)
10. Become water baptized. (Water baptism is an outward expression of an inward confession.)

11. Say a prayer. (Saying a prayer shows sincerity, but it is not the prayer that saves. We are saved by our faith.)
12. Obey Jesus' two commands. (He did say to obey his commands if you love him.)
13. Do good deeds. (Good deeds are discipleship. Be a disciple.)
14. Attend or join a church. (Jesus likes to see people in church.)
15. Give money to a church. (Monetary contributions are good deeds, but not necessary.)
16. Participate in Communion. (Communion is done in remembrance, but it doesn't save.)
17. Confess sins. (He already knows everyone's sins and they were all forgiven at the Cross.)
18. Repeat Hail Marys. (Nonsense!)
19. Light candles. (Pretty, but an unnecessary ritual.)
20. Perform rituals. (Make sure your rituals aren't pagan.)
21. Receive Last Rites. (More nonsense!)
    ...and the list goes on and on.

Know what you believe and why you believe it! If a person believes that any of the actions listed above must be added to Jesus' finished work, he or she is adding works to faith. To be saved, a person must believe and trust in Jesus as Savior. It is a gift to those who believe.

> *And if by grace, then is it no more of works: otherwise grace is no more grace. But if it be of works, then it is no more grace: otherwise work is no more work.* Romans 11:6 (KJV)

> *God saved you by his grace when you believed. And you can't take credit for this; it is a gift from God. Salvation is not a reward for the good things we have done, so none of us can boast about it.* Ephesians 2:8-9

Christians are saved by *super, abundant, radical, undeserved, amazing, grace* through faith. It is not how much faith a person has, or how he or she behaves — it is faith that saves. It's a gift — it's a gift — it's a gift!

> *Let God's curse fall on anyone, including us or even an angel from heaven, who preaches a different kind of Good News than the one we preached to you. I say again what we have said before: If anyone preaches any other Good News than the one you welcomed, let that person be cursed.* Galatians 1:8-9

According to God's standard of perfection, a person cannot do anything to make himself or herself blameless.

Being gay will not send someone to Hell, but rejecting Jesus as Savior will. Ask yourself this question: If I were to die this very moment, would I go to Heaven? If the answer is no, or if you are unsure, then it is time for you to be baptized and sealed with the promised Holy Spirit.

The believer's prayer

Although it is a person's faith alone in Jesus' finished work that saves, many Christians repeat a prayer as their acknowledgement. Also, oftentimes people have neglected their Christian life, so they want to begin again. Saying a prayer is not necessary, but God loves it when we pray. Prayer can be done aloud, silently, publicly, or privately. It is not the intellectual content of the prayer, but its sincerity. Say something like this:

> God,
>
> I believe you came to Earth in the form of a man named Jesus and died on a cross as payment for my sins. Many people saw you come back from being dead, which proved you are God and that you can overcome death. I know you are living in me, which is my assurance I will live eternally with you. I am saying this prayer to reinforce my relationship with you, and I am praying that I will grow in my Christian faith.
>
> Amen.

The Bible says because you are a believer in Jesus' finished work, you were saved the moment you believed. This is also known as *justified, born spiritually, regenerated,* or *born again.*

The seeker's prayer

> God,
>
> I am not yet convinced, but I want to be. If you are for real, and if you came to Earth in the form of a man, I invite your Spirit to live in me and to show me truths as you guide me through my life.
>
> Amen.

I believe if you said the seeker's prayer, God will reveal the truth to you. At the very moment you trust Jesus as your only way to be saved from eternal punishment, you will be saved. Now find a church and purchase an easy-to-read New Testament Bible.

SECTION FOUR

Know what you believe, and why you believe it!

Notes:

Chapter 22

Avoid Legalism and Legalists

*L*egalism is a non-biblical, guilt-provoking, severe Christian stance that demands adherence to laws to be saved and/or to remain saved. It is usually imposed by folks who do not smile.

Legalists are those arrogant, uneducated, miserable Christians who embrace legalism. They typically scare people from Jesus by their assemblage of non-biblical *shall-not's*. I do not have the authority to judge the salvation of legalists, but if they are depending on keeping laws rather than trusting in Jesus' finished work for eternal life, they may not be saved.

>>>>**Legalism is a policy opposed to uncontaminated grace, beginning immediately following the formation of the early Christian Church.**<<<<

The Book of Galatians, which is the Monroe Doctrine of Christianity, competently illustrates freedom from the Law. Paul pronounces this:

> *I am shocked that you are turning away so soon from God, who called you to himself through the loving mercy of Christ. You are following a different way that pretends to be the Good News but is not the Good News at all. You are being fooled by those who deliberately twist the truth concerning Christ.*

> *Let God's curse fall on anyone, including us or even an angel from heaven, who preaches a different kind of Good News than the one we preached to you. I say again what we have said before: If anyone preaches any other Good News than the one you welcomed, let that person be cursed.* Galatians 1:6-9

Legalistic Christians demand that to be saved and/or to remain saved the individual must adhere to strict rules that prohibit such activities as playing musical instruments, watching movies, dancing, taking a chance on a lottery ticket, watching a horserace, enjoying wealth, use of tobacco, enjoying alcoholic beverages, having fun on Sundays, etc.

A few passages make it appear that someone may be saved by his or her works, or that he or she may backslide from salvation, but if one studies the entire Word of God, they will realize it clearly states that salvation is by faith alone. In my book *JESUS CHRIST Is the EASY and ONLY Way to HEAVEN*, I explained and clarified the passages that are interpreted incorrectly.

We all like to think that "good people" will somehow be exempted from eternal damnation, but the Bible says there is no one good and that all our righteous acts are like "filthy rags."

> *But no, all have turned away;*
> *   all have become corrupt.*
> *No one does good,*
> *   not a single one!* Psalm 14:3

> *We are all infected and impure with sin.*
> *   When we display our righteous deeds,*
> *   they are nothing but filthy rags.*
> *Like autumn leaves, we wither and fall,*
> *   and our sins sweep us away like the wind.* Isaiah 64:6

The question is: Are Christians bound to laws?

Jesus' death on the Cross gave Christians boundless freedom, but freedom has consequences if abused. Carnal desires may have penalties.

- ✓ Playing musical instruments is not harmful, but some of the music of today is Satanic — be careful.
- ✓ Movies are entertaining, if we select those that don't promote immoral behavior.
- ✓ Dancing is cool if not done on a pole.
- ✓ Buying a lottery ticket is not a sin unless it leads to addictive gambling. Many argue that gambling is trying to get something for nothing. So what? Salvation is getting something for nothing.
- ✓ Racing horses is no more sinful than playing football. In fact, there is much more gambling involved in football than horseracing.
- ✓ Wealth is not sinful, unless it is gained or used immorally.
- ✓ Smoking causes cancer and heart disease.

✓ Jesus' first miracle was turning water into wine at a party. It was wine! Do not get drunk.

✓ Rest on Sundays? Sundays were made for man to participate in endeavors that are emotionally fulfilling. Jesus said so.

Legalists promote legalism as being virtuous, but it fails to accomplish God's purposes because it presents Christianity as a stern religion rather than a comforting faith in the Savior who set us free from religion.

> **So Christ has truly set us free. Now make sure that you stay free, and don't get tied up again in slavery to the law. Galatians 5:1**

Beware: It was the religious folks who crucified Jesus, and religious folks will try to crucify you. Religious Christians love to figuratively crucify other Christians.

> *You may think you can condemn such people, but you are just as bad, and you have no excuse! When you say they are wicked and should be punished, you are condemning yourself, for you who judge others do these very same things.* Romans 2:1

Legalists are famous for judging others. Legalistic Christians will attempt to put someone into religious bondage by looking for another's faults while not recognizing their own. This is a major problem in Christendom.

> *"And why worry about a speck in your friend's eye when you have a log in your own?"* Matthew 7:3, Jesus' words

God loves the imperfect

Many of God's favorites were very imperfect people and, though carnal, they had faith. The following are a few examples of some very imperfect people whom God loved dearly:

- **Abraham sacrificed Sarah's safety to save his own neck.**
- **David, although Godly, had an adulterous affair and was a murderer.**
- **Jacob was cunning and deceptive.**

- Moses was a murderer.
- Noah got drunk.
- Peter denied Jesus three times and periodically lost his faith.
- Rahab was a prostitute.
- Samson was a womanizer.
- Thomas was a doubter.
- Paul struggled with sin.

Each of these individuals had two distinct things in common: imperfection and faith in God. Instead of hiding human weaknesses, the Bible records them faithfully to show there are no perfect humans. If we could be saved by following laws, then Jesus Christ's death was in vain.

> *For God was in Christ, reconciling the world to himself, no longer counting people's sins against them. And he gave us this wonderful message of reconciliation.* 2 Corinthians 5:19

The entire New Testament warns against legalism. I could list dozens of passages stating this, but for the sake of brevity, I have listed just a few.

> *For the law was given through Moses, but God's unfailing love and faithfulness came through Jesus Christ.* John 1:17

> *Brothers, listen! We are here to proclaim that through this man Jesus there is forgiveness for your sins. Everyone who believes in him is declared right with God—something the law of Moses could never do.* Acts 13:38-39

> *Can we boast, then, that we have done anything to be accepted by God? No, because our acquittal is not based on obeying the law. It is based on faith. So we are made right with God through faith and not by obeying the law.* Romans 3:27-28

> *Let me put it another way. The law was our guardian until Christ came; it protected us until we could be made right with God through faith. And now that the way of faith has come, we no longer need the law as our guardian.* Galatians 3:24-25

You have died with Christ, and he has set you free from the spiritual powers of this world. So why do you keep on following the rules of the world, such as, "Don't handle! Don't taste! Don't touch!"? Such rules are mere human teachings about things that deteriorate as we use them. These rules may seem wise because they require strong devotion, pious self-denial, and severe bodily discipline. But they provide no help in conquering a person's evil desires. Colossians 2:20-23

We must die to the law and live by the Spirit

The Holy Spirit is our counselor. He convicts us of what is good and bad behavior for us individually. He teaches us truth and guides us into righteousness. He comforts us in the difficult times, and gives us peace. He also generously gives us liberties.

But when the Father sends the Advocate as my representative—that is, the Holy Spirit—he will teach you everything and will remind you of everything I have told you.

"I am leaving you with a gift—peace of mind and heart. And the peace I give is a gift the world cannot give. So don't be troubled or afraid. John 14:26-27

But when you are directed by the Spirit, you are not under obligation to the law of Moses. Galatians 5:18

When I think of all this, I fall to my knees and pray to the Father, the Creator of everything in heaven and on earth. I pray that from his glorious, unlimited resources he will empower you with inner strength through his Spirit. Then Christ will make his home in your hearts as you trust in him. Your roots will grow down into God's love and keep you strong. And may you have the power to understand, as all God's people should, how wide, how long, how high, and how deep his love is. May you experience the love of Christ, though it is too great to understand fully. Then you will be made complete with all the fullness of life and power that comes from God.

Now all glory to God, who is able, through his mighty power at work within us, to accomplish infinitely more than we might ask or think. Glory to him in the church and in Christ Jesus through all generations forever and ever! Amen. Ephesians 3:14-21

For when we brought you the Good News, it was not only with words but also with power, for the Holy Spirit gave you full assurance that what we said was true. And you know of our concern for you from the way we lived when we were with you. So you received the message with joy from the Holy Spirit in spite of the severe suffering it brought you. In this way, you imitated both us and the Lord. 1 Thessalonians 1:5-6

But the Holy Spirit produces this kind of fruit in our lives: love, joy, peace, patience, kindness, goodness, faithfulness, gentleness, and self-control. There is no law against these things! Galatians 5:22-23

Freedom has consequences

Don't be stupid and allow your freedom to hurt you or others.

You say, "I am allowed to do anything"—but not everything is good for you. And even though "I am allowed to do anything," I must not become a slave to anything. 1 Corinthians 6:12

You say, "I am allowed to do anything"—but not everything is good for you. You say, "I am allowed to do anything"—but not everything is beneficial. 1 Corinthians 10:23

Many unlearned Christians are fearful that if they do not live by Jewish laws, plus many so-called Christian laws, it will lead to immoral behavior. Not if we live by the Spirit!

The Holy Spirit is very good at what he does! He does not make us into robots, yet is very persistent in convicting us individually. Unlike "religions" that establish rules collectively for all followers, Christianity is a trust in which the individual has a personal connection with Jesus.

Jesus desires his born again disciples (one can be a disciple and not be born again) to be moral, but morality is not something that is manmade. It is spiritual via fidelity with Jesus. Playing musical instruments, watching movies, dancing, taking a chance on a lottery ticket, watching a horserace, enjoying wealth, using tobacco, enjoying alcoholic beverages, having fun on Sundays, etc., may be naughty for some, but not for others. That which is moral or immoral for the individual Christian will be revealed via Holy Spirit conviction.

All Christians will stand before the Judgment Seat of Christ (The Judgment Seat of Christ is not for salvation because upon our death Christians go immediately to the place Jesus prepared for us) for our individual rewards.

> *For no one can lay any foundation other than the one we already have—Jesus Christ.*
>
> *Anyone who builds on that foundation may use a variety of materials—gold, silver, jewels, wood, hay, or straw. But on the judgment day, fire will reveal what kind of work each builder has done. The fire will show if a person's work has any value. If the work survives, that builder will receive a reward. But if the work is burned up, the builder will suffer great loss. **The builder will be saved, but like someone barely escaping through a wall of flames.*** 1 Corinthians 3:11-15

I love the last verse, which I emphasized: "The builder will be saved, but like someone barely escaping through a wall of flames." This proves beyond the shadow of doubt that unfruitful Christians will be in Heaven, but just by their chinny-chin-chin. This verse proves it is our faith that saves us — even if barely.

> *So why do you condemn another believer? Why do you look down on another believer? Remember, we will all stand before the judgment seat of God. For the Scriptures say,*
>
>> *"'As surely as I live,' says the Lord,*
>> *'every knee will bend to me,*
>> *and every tongue will confess and give praise to God.'"*
>
> *Yes, each of us will give a personal account to God. So let's stop condemning each other. Decide instead to live in such a way that you will not cause another believer to stumble and fall.* Romans 14:10-13

Notes:

Chapter 23

Two Judgments (know these)

Satan has circulated two false beliefs regarding life after death:

(1) God will allow entrance if the person has been a good person. This is not true because the Bible says none are good.

(2) The deceased will stand before God, who will ask why he or she should be permitted into Heaven. If that person declares he or she has accepted Jesus as Savior, permission will be granted. This is not true because the Bible says the deceased person goes directly to Heaven or Hell based on acceptance or rejection of Jesus as Savior — while he or she was alive.

A person's destination is decided before the person dies — by that person.

Christians go directly to Heaven if their names were written in the Lamb's Book of Life. One does not have to tell God he or she was saved — he already knew that when he put that person's name in the Book.

The unsaved go directly to Hell because their names were not written in the Lamb's Book of Life. It is absent from the Book because they rejected Jesus as Savior.

The *Biblical fact* is there are two judgments after death

1. The Judgment Seat of Christ (aka, Christ's Judgment and/or Bema Seat) is for those who have been saved by grace through faith. This judgment is to determine the heavenly rewards for those who have trusted Jesus as Savior. There will be no judgment for sin at this seat because the Christian's sin is remembered no more. This judgment is to determine the rewards for the good deeds (discipleship) by the Christian after they are saved.

> *For we must all stand before Christ to be judged. We will each receive whatever we deserve for the good or evil we have done in this earthly body.*
> 2 Corinthians 5:10

For those who have accepted Jesus as his or her Savior, the following applies:

> *So we are always confident, even though we know that as long as we live in these bodies we are not at home with the Lord. For we live by believing and not by seeing. Yes, we are fully confident, and we would rather be away from these earthly bodies, for then we will be at home with the Lord.*
> 2 Corinthians 5:6-8

As seen in the above text, the moment we are absent from our bodies, we are present with the Lord. Only a small minority of Christians believe we will go into soul sleep until the final resurrection. The overwhelming majority of Christians believe that Jesus' words to the thief on the Cross affirm we immediately ascend to Heaven upon our death.

> *And Jesus replied, "I assure you, today you will be with me in paradise."*
> Luke 23:43

2. The Great White Throne Judgment is for those who have rejected Christ as Savior, and who are going to Hell regardless of their life's good works. They may be very fine, moral people who have tried to work their way to Heaven rather than trusting in Jesus. At the time of an individual's death, if that person has not trusted Jesus Christ as Savior, he or she will receive eternal punishment, as explained in the next passage. Do not gamble by using works as your wager.

> *And I saw a great white throne and the one sitting on it. The earth and sky fled from his presence, but they found no place to hide. I saw the dead, both great and small, standing before God's throne. And the books were opened, including the Book of Life. And the dead were judged according to what they had done, as recorded in the books. The sea gave up its dead, and death and the grave gave up their dead. And all were judged according to their deeds. Then death and the grave were thrown into the lake of fire. This lake of fire is the second death. And anyone whose name was not found recorded in the Book of Life was thrown into the lake of fire.*
> Revelation 20:11-15

Chapter 24

No Condemnation

If you have read this book from the very beginning, you are aware there is no condemnation for Christians. Because many people skip around when reading a textbook like this, I thought it would be a good idea to have a brief chapter that reassures
Jesus' finished work imparts *no condemnation*. *No condemnation* is defined as
"judged and found innocent."

All humans are born into the physical family of Adam, which results in our being
sinners by birth. Christians, as recipients of the Holy Spirit, receive the gift of righteousness simply by believing and accepting.

I emphasized the terms ***condemnation*** and ***righteousness*** in the following verse:

> *Yes, Adam's one sin brings* **condemnation** *for everyone, but Christ's one act*
> *of* **righteousness** *brings a right relationship with God and new life for every-*
> *one.* Romans 5:18

Many Christians can be very condemning of believers and non-believers who do not
imitate them. One of the most important passages that jumped from the Bible and
grabbed me when I began to study the New Testament was Romans 8:1, which is also
one of the most quoted passages by Christians. Here, Paul tells the Romans (and us)
there is no condemnation for Christians. Oh, what a relief that was!

Following are passages from several different Bible translations. I have emphasized
the term(s) and/or phrases that verify there is *no condemnation*, as well as the words
that are key to our being free of condemnation.

> *So now there is* **no condemnation** *for* **those who belong to Christ Jesus**.
> Romans 8:1(NLT)

> *Therefore, there is **no longer any condemnation** awaiting **those who are in union with the Messiah Yeshua.** Romans 8:1 (CJB)*

> *Now then there is **no condemnation** to **them that are in Christ Jesus, which walk not after the flesh, but after the Spirit.** Romans 8:1 (GNV)*

> *There is therefore now **no condemnation** to **them which are in Christ Jesus, who walk not after the flesh, but after the Spirit.** Romans 8:1 (KJV)*

> *There is therefore now **no condemnation** to **them which are in Christ Jesus, who walk not after the flesh, but after the Spirit.** Romans 8:1 (NASB)*

> *Therefore, [there is] now **no condemnation** (no adjudging guilty of wrong) for **those who are in Christ Jesus, who live [and] walk not after the dictates of the flesh, but after the dictates of the Spirit.** Romans 8:1 (AMP)*

> Therefore, now there is **no *gezar din* (verdict) of *ashem* (guilty), no *harsha'ah* (condemnation as guilty)** for those in Moshiach Yehoshua (cf. Ro 5:18). Romans 8:1 (OJB)

Because believers are in Christ and Christ in them, we have the joy of being counted as righteous, simply because Christ is righteous. ***When God looks at the Christian, he does not see the sinful human, but the person who has been robed with the righteousness of Christ.***

A Christian's union with Christ Jesus results in our having God's wisdom, being acceptable to God, and being pure because of our sins that were washed in the Blood of Jesus. ***Christ is the source of a Christian's righteousness, by Jesus' Spirit who lives in him or her.***

> *This Good News tells us how God makes us right in his sight. This is accomplished from start to finish by faith. As the Scriptures say, "It is through faith that a righteous person has life." Romans 1:17*

> *But now God has shown us a way to be made right with him without keeping the requirements of the law, as was promised in the writings of Moses and the prophets long ago. We are made right with God by placing our faith in Jesus Christ. And this is true for everyone who believes, no matter who we are. Romans 3:21-22*

For the Scriptures tell us, "Abraham believed God, and God counted him as righteous because of his faith."

When people work, their wages are not a gift, but something they have earned. But people are counted as righteous, not because of their work, but because of their faith in God who forgives sinners. David also spoke of this when he described the happiness of those who are declared righteous without working for it:

> *"Oh, what joy for those*
> *whose disobedience is forgiven,*
> *whose sins are put out of sight.*
> *Yes, what joy for those*
> *whose record the Lord has cleared of sin."* Romans 4:3-8

For God made Christ, who never sinned, to be the offering for our sin, so that we could be made right with God through Christ. 2 Corinthians 5:21

No more condemnation abolishes guilt

Christians who live in guilt by not forgiving themselves for their sinful nature are condemning themselves unnecessarily. As Christians, we must comprehend and appreciate the fact that our justification (forgiveness) is found in Jesus' finished work on the Cross, and not our good deeds.

> *God saved you by his grace when you believed. And you can't take credit for this; it is a gift from God. Salvation is not a reward for the good things we have done, so none of us can boast about it.* Ephesians 2:8-9

Notes:

Chapter 25

The Ten Commandments were only for the Israelites

God had many behavioral covenants with mankind, beginning with Adam. Because of the weakness of humans, they all failed. The Mosaic Covenant (named that because it was given to Moses to give to the people) consisted of what we call *The Ten Commandments*. Throughout this book, I reiterated that the Ten Commandments were only for the Israelites, but because so many today believe these were commandments given to all of mankind for all time, this important topic deserves its own chapter.

The Glorious New Covenant is for all

*The old way, with laws etched in stone, led to death, though it began with such glory that the people of Israel could not bear to look at Moses' face. For his face shone with the glory of God, even though the brightness was already fading away. Shouldn't we expect far greater glory under the new way, now that the Holy Spirit is giving life? **If the old way, which brings condemnation, was glorious, how much more glorious is the new way, which makes us right with God!** In fact, that first glory was not glorious at all compared with the overwhelming glory of the new way. So if the old way, which has been replaced, was glorious, how much more glorious is the new, which remains forever!*

*Since this new way gives us such confidence, we can be very bold. We are not like Moses, who put a veil over his face so the people of Israel would not see the glory, even though it was destined to fade away. **But the people's minds were hardened, and to this day whenever the old covenant is being read, the same veil covers their minds so they cannot understand the truth. And this veil can be removed only by believing in Christ.** Yes, even today when they read Moses' writings, their hearts are covered with that veil, and they do not understand.*

*But whenever someone turns to the Lord, the veil is taken away. **For the Lord is the Spirit, and wherever the Spirit of the Lord is, there is freedom.** So all of us who have had that veil removed can see and reflect the glory of the Lord. And the Lord—who is the Spirit—makes us more and more like him as **we are changed into his glorious image.** 2 Corinthians 3:7-18 (Emphasis added by me.)*

The Old Covenant was for the Israelites only

The Gentiles were not, and are not subject to laws.

*When the **Gentiles** sin, they will be destroyed, even though **they never had God's written law.** And the Jews, who do have God's law, will be judged by that law when they fail to obey it. Romans 2:12 (Emphasis added by me.)*

I have been talking to people for more than three decades regarding Christian salvation and I still cannot believe how many people tell me they think they will go to Heaven because they *try to live according to the Ten Commandments*. This is a false understanding of the Bible.

It is understandable why people are deceived regarding the Jewish laws because there are many public buildings that have the Ten Commandments etched in marble or stone, and we hear folks mention these Israelite commands almost daily. Our legal system is based on them, as is our moral system. For the record: I am a proponent of removing the Ten Commandments from buildings and replacing them with John 3:16-18.

"For God loved the world so much that he gave his one and only Son, so that everyone who believes in him will not perish but have eternal life. God sent his Son into the world not to judge the world, but to save the world through him.

There is no judgment against anyone who believes in him. But anyone who does not believe in him has already been judged for not believing in God's one and only Son." John 3:16-18, Jesus' words

The Ten Commandments are laws that God gave to the nation of Israel shortly after their exodus from Egypt. The Ten Commandments are essentially a summary of the 613 commandments contained in the Old Testament law. Given only to the Israelites, there is no mention anywhere in the Bible they were given to the Gentile.

Why, then, was the law given? It was given alongside the promise to show people their sins. But the law was designed to last only until the coming of the child who was promised. God gave his law through angels to Moses, who was the mediator between God and the people. Galatians 3:19

Many people erroneously consider the Ten Commandments as a set of rules that, if obeyed, will assure admission into Heaven. The purpose of the Ten Commandments was to convince the Israelites it was impossible to follow these laws, thus preparing them for the coming Messiah who would save mankind by fulfilling the law.

"Don't misunderstand why I have come. I did not come to abolish the law of Moses or the writings of the prophets. No, I came to accomplish their purpose. I tell you the truth, until heaven and earth disappear, not even the smallest detail of God's law will disappear until its purpose is achieved." Matthew 5:17-18, Jesus' words

Some interpret the passage above to mean that Jesus did not "abolish" the law, so it must still be binding. ***Christ did not insinuate the binding nature of these laws would be in effect forever, because such a view would contradict everything taught by the New Testament.*** Therefore, we cannot allow one word — *abolish* — to give new meaning to the entire Bible. Jesus did not come to Earth for the purpose of opposing the law — his goal was not to abolish it, but to fulfill it.

Law and grace don't mix

Many, if not most, people incorrectly believe Christians must mix commandments (works) with grace to be saved. This erroneous belief makes God's simple plan confusing and complicated. This mixing of grace and works is referred to as ***Galatianism***.

Galatianism is such an underused and unrecognized term that it requires explanation and elaboration. Do not forget this term and its relevancy in Christendom, because Galatianism is like a cancer that has permeated the world, killing the chances for millions of nice folks to know Jesus. *Galatianists* (those who promote mixing grace with works) insist good deeds must be added to the gift of grace, which makes God's simple salvation plan confusing and complicated. The mixing of grace with works causes many to believe they are not capable or worthy of being Christians. Works are not necessary for salvation.

And if by grace, then is it no more of works: otherwise grace is no more grace. But if it be of works, then it is no more grace: otherwise work is no more work. Romans 11:6 (KJV)

> **"Insisting works must be added to grace causes many to believe they are not capable of being Christians. Grace plus works triggers an explosion — bang!" Tim Finley (born – 1946)**

In existence since the beginning of the Christian Church, Galatianism is demonstrated best in the book of Galatians. Although many residents of Galatia had received and accepted the simplicity of the New Covenant, self-styled "spiritual men" came on the scene teaching that new Christians needed to add Old Covenant laws to the New Covenant freedom. The Great Apostle Paul boldly warned those of Galatia about the error of insisting that good deeds must be added to what Jesus had already done in order to obtain eternal life.

I am shocked that you are turning away so soon from God, who called you to himself through the loving mercy of Christ. You are following a different way that pretends to be the Good News but is not the Good News at all. You are being fooled by those who deliberately twist the truth concerning Christ. **Galatians 1:6-7**

When I saw that they were not following the truth of the gospel message, I said to Peter in front of all the others, "Since you, a Jew by birth, have discarded the Jewish laws and are living like a Gentile, why are you now trying to make these Gentiles follow the Jewish traditions? **Galatians 2:14**

How foolish can you be? After starting your Christian lives in the Spirit, why are you now trying to become perfect by your own human effort? **Galatians 3:3**

This way of faith is very different from the way of law, which says, "It is through obeying the law that a person has life."

But Christ has rescued us from the curse pronounced by the law. When he was hung on the cross, he took upon himself the curse for our wrongdoing. For it is written in the Scriptures, "Cursed is everyone who is hung on a tree." Through Christ Jesus, God has blessed the Gentiles with the same blessing he promised to Abraham, so that we who are believers might receive the promised Holy Spirit through faith. **Galatians 3:12-14**

Before the way of faith in Christ was available to us, we were placed under guard by the law. We were kept in protective custody, so to speak, until the way of faith was revealed.

Let me put it another way. The law was our guardian until Christ came; it protected us until we could be made right with God through faith. And now that the way of faith has come, we no longer need the law as our guardian. **Galatians 3:23-25**

Those passages make it crystal clear Christians are not saved by adhering to laws fulfilled by Jesus.

The system of law and commandments ended for all.

He did this by ending the system of law with its commandments and regulations. He made peace between Jews and Gentiles by creating in himself one new people from the two groups. **Ephesians 2:15**

Warning

Because of human weakness, God made a New Covenant, which is simply your accepting the life, death, and resurrection of Jesus Christ as the only way to become one of Jesus' saints.

Please be warned that your church leaders may be guilty of adding laws, practices, customs, and traditions to their teachings that are not from the New Testament. It is your responsibility to ascertain if you are receiving the truth.

So Christ has truly set us free. Now make sure that you stay free, and don't get tied up again in slavery to the law. Galatians 5:1

Notes:

You must study your Bible to ascertain truth. Do not put all of your faith in another mortal, but depend on the Word of God and guidance from the Holy Spirit.

Chapter 26

Faith without Works is Not Dead – per se

There are two schools of thought in Christendom that clash. Those schools can be a huge divider of Christians.

Following decades of diligently examining the Holy Scriptures, I knowledgeably endorse #1, and am eager to debate those who erroneously choose #2.

(1) **Salvation by grace through faith — no good deeds necessary.** The entire Old and New Testaments reveal and revere the Savior Jesus, who saves by grace through faith all who accept his finished work on the Cross. There are hundreds of passages that substantiate this, but following are two of the most quoted New Testament passages:

> *And if by grace, then is it no more of works: otherwise grace is no more grace. But if it be of works, then it is no more grace: otherwise work is no more work.* Romans 11:6 (KJV)

> *God saved you by his grace when you believed. And you can't take credit for this; it is a gift from God. Salvation is not a reward for the good things we have done, so none of us can boast about it.* Ephesians 2:8-9

(2) **Salvation by grace through faith plus good deeds.** Following is the lonely, but most quoted verse used to defend this erroneous pretense.

> *So you see, faith by itself isn't enough. Unless it produces good deeds, it is dead and useless.* James 2:17

The verse above, from the Book of James, has caused much controversy in Christendom between those who advocate *salvation by grace through faith* (like me), and those who are not as learned as I. These good deeds-based (works-based) fanatics latch on the word *dead* and won't let go. "Dead, dead, dead" — they say. **"Bull, bull, bull" — I say!**

James 2:17 is one of those passages loaded in the guns of legalistic Christians, who fire it at everyone not living to the satisfactions of the huntsmen. "Bang, bang, I gotcha" — they broadcast.

The brief Book of James was very perplexing to me as a new and unlearned Christian because parts of it seemed to contradict the grace melody in the entire New Testament. Furthermore, I couldn't understand why James didn't speak much about his brother, Jesus. It seemed more like a letter written to Jews about how to live by the outdated law. I was so pleased with Paul's teaching about my not having to work my way to Heaven that when I read James' book with seemingly legalistic mandates, I choked.

At that time I neglected to realize James only wrote one book of the New Testament, while the Great Apostle Paul is credited with 13 of the 27 New Testament books, not including Hebrews, which is thought to have also been written by Paul. Discovering Paul wrote 32 percent of the text of the New Testament gave me an enhanced assessment of Paul's purpose. Although size does not make a difference, I believe that Paul's expansive ministry, as compared to the limited extent of James' ministry, gives us a clue as to which is comprehensive. James was writing primarily to Jewish Christians who may have been taking advantage of grace. Some scholars believe James was putting a legalistic twist on his writing because he was not happy with Paul's emphasis on grace. Even if this was the case, apparently the Holy Spirit saw fit to have it appear in his Bible. Perhaps just to make us think.

Although James was writing to Jewish Christians, and Paul was writing to many sects of folks, those same writings are applicable today if interpreted correctly. Correct interpretation is essential.

In 9th grade biology, before we dissected a frog, we had to know it was a frog. Before making the first cut, it was imperative that we understood the intricacies of what we were going to examine. That same approach must be taken when establishing something as important as doctrine. Know what you are about to dissect, why you are dissecting it, and be informed enough to make an accurate assessment of what you discover.

I have been studying the Bible for more than thirty years, so please respect my opinion when I tell you not to use just one or two passages to establish doctrine if they differ with multiple other passages. Sound doctrine cannot be established using one passage if dozens of other, more clear passages conflict. We determine meaning by carefully comparing all verses and passages throughout the entire Bible, and not by cherry-picking a verse here and there. The Bible must be studied, not just read. In the Doctrine of Salvation, the Bible is very explicit that Jesus' shed Blood finalized the forgiveness of all sin. No works are necessary.

In the New Testament, approximately 150 passages deal with the doctrine of salvation; 115 of these declare that we must believe and 35 declare that we must have faith, which is a synonym for believing. By believing, one places trust in Jesus Christ's finished work on the Cross. Therefore, Scripture is misinterpreted if one confuses believing with anything that adds to belief.

Singling out James 2:17 distorts the *salvation by grace through faith* doctrine. It is a desperate attempt used by inexperienced and/or unkind Christians to impose stipulations on Jesus' free gift.

> *"For God loved the world so much that he gave his one and only Son, so that **everyone who believes in him** will not perish but have eternal life. God sent his Son into the world not to judge the world, but to save the world through him.*
>
> *There is no judgment against anyone who **believes** in him. But anyone who does not **believe** in him has already been judged for not believing in God's one and only Son."* John 3:16-18, Jesus' words (Emphasis added by me.)

Christians not learned in the interpretation of Scripture may innocently become victims of one lone verse (James 2:17), scaring them into believing they must work, work, work to get to Heaven; if they do not, their faith is dead. Dead faith does not mean *no faith*. I can assure you there have been times in my life that my faith was dead because I had become spiritually lazy and lethargic, but I still retained my faith. ***Dead faith is faith, just like a dead fish is still a fish.***

If James is suggesting our salvation is contingent upon good deeds, he is contradicting the entire GOOD NEWS of the New Testament. So we must look deeper and study more diligently.

The Book of James

Many Christians have been confused and deprived of the absolute assurance of their salvation by the misinterpretation of the Book of James. Attempting to add works for salvation is inconsistent with the entire Good News of the New Testament. James made many valid moral suggestions to his readers, but his inferring good deeds must be added to belief can damage the entire New Testament message by demanding works must be added to Jesus' gift — unless we know to whom the Book of James was written, and why.

To whom and why

The epistle of James is a letter written to Jewish Christians who were scattered throughout the Mediterranean area because of persecution. They were probably afraid to demonstrate their faith for fear of persecution, just as many Christians today fear persecution. They were not allowing their lights to shine so that man could know they were saved.

> *"You are the light of the world—like a city on a hilltop that cannot be hidden. No one lights a lamp and then puts it under a basket. Instead, a lamp is placed on a stand, where it gives light to everyone in the house. In the same way, let your good deeds shine out for all to see, so that everyone will praise your heavenly Father."* Matthew 5:14-16, Jesus' words

James is rebuking them basically by insisting they show their faith.

Because James was writing to saved people, as a knowledgeable teacher he could not have been suggesting works were mandatory for salvation, so we must presume he was teaching how to be sanctified. *Justification* **(salvation) is a one-time, instantaneous, irrevocable free gift, but** *sanctification* **is the believer's growth process by lessening sinful behavior and yielding one's life to the guidance of the Holy Spirit. This adaptation takes place after a person has been justified (saved), but is not instantaneous, as is justification. Sanctification is the result of the saved person's efforts combined with the counseling of the Holy Spirit. It is the growth process of a Christian, also referred to as discipleship.**

The world-renowned scholar Martin Luther (1483-1546) detested the Book of James, referring to it as "the epistle of straw," probably because certain parts seemed to contradict Paul's teachings of salvation by grace only through faith. Most scholars believe James was merely emphasizing good deeds to illustrate one's thankfulness for salvation by grace.

> *But we are bound to give thanks to God always for you, brethren beloved by the Lord, because God from the beginning chose you for salvation through* **sanctification by the Spirit** *and belief in the truth, to which He called*

you by our gospel, for the obtaining of the glory of our Lord Jesus Christ. 2 Thessalonians 2:13-14 (NKJV)

James is not saying we are saved eternally by works, but if one's faith does not produce good deeds, it is an unfruitful faith. The question is not loss of salvation, which is impossible, but loss of rewards both here and in eternity.

James also realizes there are consequences to living a sinful life, and while performing good deeds we are too busy to partake in unhealthy, immoral behavior. We are being saved from the consequences of sinful behavior.

Usually, but not always

The salvation experience by faith in Jesus Christ usually results in good deeds, but not always. Jesus, in his kindness and generosity, allows for those with faith alone to be saved.

> *For no one can lay any foundation other than the one we already have— Jesus Christ.*
>
> *Anyone who builds on that foundation may use a variety of materials—gold, silver, jewels, wood, hay, or straw. But on the judgment day, fire will reveal what kind of work each builder has done. The fire will show if a person's work has any value. If the work survives, that builder will receive a reward. But if the work is burned up, the builder will suffer great loss.* **The builder will be saved, but like someone barely escaping through a wall of flames.** 1 Corinthians 3:11-15 (Emphasis added by me.)

I love the last verse. This proves it is our faith that saves us — even if barely.

Don't be misled by someone who teaches to be saved, you must:

1. Repent of sin. (*Repent of sin* is a manmade phrase, not biblical. *Repent* means "change of mind." To receive eternal life in the place Jesus has prepared for Christians, a person must *repent* of the notion of working his or her way there, and accept Jesus as Savior.) NOBODY HAS EVER RECEIVED THE FREE GIFT OF ETERNAL LIFE BY REPENTING OF SIN!
2. Make Jesus Lord of your life. Like it or not, Jesus, as God, is already Lord of all lives. (But to receive the free gift of salvation you must "trust" Jesus as your Savior, at which time you will be baptized by the Holy Spirit, who will be your

counselor. *Don't be drunk with wine, because it will ruin your life. Instead, be filled with the Holy Spirit.* Ephesians 5:18)

3. Confess with your mouth that Jesus is Lord. (This was a one-time instruction from Paul to a certain group of Jews.)
4. Give your life to the Lord. (This is a phrase that is used, but it doesn't save. A person is saved by his or her faith.)
5. Be sorry for sinning. (Only a fool would not be sorry for sinning, but sorrow does not save. Only faith in Jesus saves.)
6. Ask forgiveness for sins. (All sins were forgiven on the Cross.)
7. Stop sinning. (Nobody can quit sinning.)
8. Invite Jesus into your heart. (Not necessary, but it demonstrates faith.)
9. Go forward in an alter call. (Although going forward demonstrates faith.)
10. Become water baptized. (Water baptism is an outward expression of an inward confession.)
11. Say a prayer. (Saying a prayer shows sincerity, but it is not the prayer that saves. We are saved by our faith.)
12. Obey Jesus' two commands. (He did say to obey his commands if you love him.)
13. Do good deeds. (Good deeds are discipleship. Be a disciple.)
14. Attend or join a church. (Jesus likes to see people in church.)
15. Give money to a church. (Monetary contributions are good deeds, but not necessary.)
16. Participate in Communion. (Communion is done in remembrance, but it doesn't save.)
17. Confess sins. (He already knows everyone's sins and they were all forgiven at the Cross.)
18. Repeat Hail Marys. (Nonsense!)
19. Light candles. (Pretty, but an unnecessary ritual.)
20. Perform rituals. (Make sure your rituals aren't pagan.)
21. Receive Last Rites. (More nonsense!)
    ...and the list goes on and on.

Know what you believe and why you believe it! If a person believes that any of the actions listed above must be added to Jesus' finished work, he or she is adding works to faith. To be saved, a person must believe and trust in Jesus as Savior. It is a gift to those who believe.

> *And if by grace, then is it no more of works: otherwise grace is no more grace. But if it be of works, then it is no more grace: otherwise work is no more work.*
> Romans 11:6 (KJV)

God saved you by his grace when you believed. And you can't take credit for this; it is a gift from God. Salvation is not a reward for the good things we have done, so none of us can boast about it. Ephesians 2:8-9

Christians are saved by *super, abundant, radical, undeserved, amazing, grace* through faith. It is not how much faith a person has, or how he or she behaves — it is faith that saves. It's a gift — it's a gift — it's a gift!

Let God's curse fall on anyone, including us or even an angel from heaven, who preaches a different kind of Good News than the one we preached to you. I say again what we have said before: If anyone preaches any other Good News than the one you welcomed, let that person be cursed. Galatians 1:8-9

According to God's standard of perfection, a person cannot do anything to make himself or herself blameless.

A few religions, including some that label themselves as Christian, still have priests who continue to stand before the altar day after day performing religious sacrifices in the hope of getting sins forgiven. This monotonous act is not only futile, but also blasphemous. Those who participate in this ritual are claiming that the Blood of Jesus was insufficient in cleansing sins once and for all.

Unlike those other high priests, he does not need to offer sacrifices every day. They did this for their own sins first and then for the sins of the people. But Jesus did this once for all when he offered himself as the sacrifice for the people's sins. The law appointed high priests who were limited by human weakness. But after the law was given, God appointed his Son with an oath, and his Son has been made the perfect High Priest forever. Hebrews 7:27-28

To summarize

James 2:17 cannot argue against salvation by faith alone and win. To be theologically correct, it must be interpreted: Faith should be demonstrated by good works. That makes sense.

For we are God's masterpiece. He has created us anew in Christ Jesus, so we can do the good things he planned for us long ago. Ephesians 2:10

James's point is that we demonstrate our faith by our discipleship.

"You are the light of the world—like a city on a hilltop that cannot be hidden. No one lights a lamp and then puts it under a basket. Instead, a lamp is placed on a stand, where it gives light to everyone in the house. In the same way, let your good deeds shine out for all to see, so that everyone will praise your heavenly Father." Matthew 5:14-16, Jesus' words

Ask yourself this question: Am I doing good works to be saved, or am I doing them because I am saved?

Chapter 27

You Need Not Confess to be Forgiven

Understand 1 John 1:9!

But if we confess our sins to him, he is faithful and just to forgive us our sins and to cleanse us from all wickedness. 1 John 1:9

<u>TRUTH</u>

I work hard to ascertain the Bible truth and am a fanatic about explaining what I discover.

> *Work hard so you can present yourself to God and receive his approval. Be a good worker, one who does not need to be ashamed and who correctly explains the word of truth. 2 Timothy 2:15 (Emphasis added by me.)*

When establishing doctrine, it is a major mistake to use just one lone passage, such as 1 John 1:9, without studying other verses and passages that pertain to the doctrinal topic. Doctrine cannot be established using one passage if dozens of other passages are inconsistent with it. We determine meaning by carefully comparing verses and passages to other verses and passages throughout the Bible regarding the topic or doctrine we are studying, and not by cherry-picking a verse here and there. The Bible must be studied, not just read.

If we compare the lone 1 John 1:9 verse to the entire New Testament, we have an inconsistency because the Bible is very explicit that Jesus' shed Blood finalized the forgiveness of all sin, so confession for forgiveness is an exercise in futility.

Many Christians continually confess their sins, hoping God will forgive them. This insult to Christ's Blood can probably be blamed on the misinterpretation of one isolated Bible verse that has influenced millions of people to believe they must constantly <u>re-crucify Christ</u> over and over by seeking God's forgiveness each time they sin.

1 John 1:9 is the only New Testament verse in which confession and forgiveness are mentioned simultaneously. Obviously, this verse is not applicable to those who have already been saved. Asking forgiveness is not necessary for the saved individual.

The New Testament makes it clear that Christ's death on the Cross paid for all sins once and for all.

If someone cuddles this lone verse to establish the Doctrine of Forgiveness, it can be disastrous. Tragically, many church leaders have never studied the correct meaning of 1 John 1:9, which can be catastrophic because the Christian never delights in *Sabbath rest* because he or she is too busy confessing.

Knowledgeable Christians know that upon their death they will go directly to Heaven, not based on anything they do, but what Jesus did for them. This fact is so comforting that a term has been coined: *Sabbath rest* describes the current peace experienced by the Christian from knowing he or she has been saved eternally. That peace of knowing what Jesus did for us is what motivates Christians to be disciples. *Sabbath rest* should not be confused with resting on Sunday.

> *God's promise of entering his rest still stands, so we ought to tremble with fear that some of you might fail to experience it. For this good news—that God has prepared this rest—has been announced to us just as it was to them. But it did them no good because they didn't share the faith of those who listened to God. For only we who believe can enter his rest. As for the others, God said,*
>
> > *"In my anger I took an oath:*
> > *'They will never enter my place of rest,'"*
>
> *even though this rest has been ready since he made the world. We know it is ready because of the place in the Scriptures where it mentions the seventh day: "On the seventh day God rested from all his work." But in the other passage God said, "They will never enter my place of rest."*
>
> *So God's rest is there for people to enter, but those who first heard this good news failed to enter because they disobeyed God. So God set another time for entering his rest, and that time is today. God announced this through David much later in the words already quoted:*

"Today when you hear his voice,
don't harden your hearts."

Now if Joshua had succeeded in giving them this rest, God would not have
spoken about another day of rest still to come. So there is a special rest still
waiting for the people of God. For all who have entered into God's rest have
rested from their labors, just as God did after creating the world. So let us do
our best to enter that rest. But if we disobey God, as the people of Israel did,
we will fall. Hebrews 4:1-11

Sabbath rest quiets a guilty conscience, stills troubling thoughts, and gives hope in desperation. In Christ we find complete rest today and forever. Sabbath rest is what those who understand salvation, and who have accepted Jesus as Savior, experience when they cease from their own efforts for salvation and depend on the work of Christ.

> **A blood-bought child of God cannot experience peace if he or she is continually forced to remember and then confess sins for forgiveness, when his or her sins have already been forgiven by Jesus' shed Blood. It is conflicting for a Christian to believe his or her sins were forgiven, but think they must also confess each sin to be forgiven. That conflict is the prescription for horrendous anxieties. Jesus did not allow himself to be criticized, rejected, brutalized, spat on, and crucified so his children would anguish attempting to remember all of their sins, as 1 John 1:9 suggests.**

The problem in using this one lone verse

To understand the truthful implication of the isolated verse 1 John 1:9, we must understand to whom it was written.

The letters in the New Testament were written to Christian leaders who would read them to many people with varying and inconsistent beliefs. They were read to Christian believers, Jews, idol worshipers, atheists, agnostics, and those with other beliefs. John, when writing this letter, knew immoral non-believers would be present, so he articulated we are all sinners in need of forgiveness. **The Christians and Jews knew they were forgiven sinners; therefore, John clearly was not addressing them.**

John's letter was not written to all people for all time! Among others, a particular group John was addressing were the *Gnostics*, a sect still in existence (i.e., Christian Scientists). Gnosticism is a belief system that describes the physical world as evil and the spiritual world as good. They believe that Jesus only "appeared" as a fleshly being, but in fact, he was not a man of flesh, he was totally Spiritual. Because of their emphasis on the spiritual world, many continue to teach that moral rules are only for those who cannot see beyond the physical level of life, although not all Gnostics believe exactly alike.

It is obvious from the beginning of the book of 1 John its author was trying to convince listeners that Jesus was God incarnate — that Jesus was of flesh — and that Jesus' Blood cleansed us from every sin.

John also said if they thought they had no sin, they were wrong. His stating they must confess their sins meant they must be aware they were sinners, *and must recognize their need for the Savior Jesus to be forgiven.*

> **Once a person has been saved, there is no further need to confess or ask forgiveness.**

Hey, Catholics, John did not say one must confess sins to another human for forgiveness. Yes, Christians are given the authority and responsibility to tell others he or she has been forgiven as the result of Jesus' crucifixion. But, it is referred to as *sharing one's testimony — or witnessing* — not confessing to a priest.

From cover to cover, the New Testament emphasizes that our sins were forgiven once and for all on the Cross. There are no strings attached!

> *I am shocked that you are turning away so soon from God, who called you to himself through the loving mercy of Christ. You are following a different way that pretends to be the Good News but is not the Good News at all. You are being fooled by those who deliberately twist the truth concerning Christ.*
>
> *Let God's curse fall on anyone, including us or even an angel from heaven, who preaches a different kind of Good News than the one we preached to you.* Galatians 1:6-8

In the New Testament, approximately 150 passages deal with the doctrine of salvation; 115 of these declare that we must believe, and 35 declare that we must have faith, which is a synonym for believing. By believing, one places his trust in Jesus Christ's finished work on the Cross. Scripture is misinterpreted if one confuses believing with anything that adds to belief.

Confess is used again, but not to receive forgiveness

Romans 10:9-13

> *If you confess with your mouth that Jesus is Lord and believe in your heart that God raised him from the dead, you will be saved. For it is by believing in your heart that you are made right with God, and it is by confessing with your mouth that you are saved. As the Scriptures tell us, "Anyone who trusts in him will never be disgraced." Jew and Gentile are the same in this respect. They have the same Lord, who gives generously to all who call on him. For "Everyone who calls on the name of the Lord will be saved."* Romans 10:9-13 (Emphasis added by me.)

During the time when the Christian Church was being established, most Jews rejected Jesus as their Messiah. If an individual publically acknowledged Jesus as the Messiah, the result would probably be persecution and death. Too many people get hung up on Paul's use of the word *mouth*, when the entire salvation (justification) message throughout the Scriptures is that we must *believe* to be saved. Paul is the world's greatest advocate of salvation by faith alone. He only uses the word mouth once. Oral confession is not the process of salvation; it is one of the many evidences of salvation. Obviously, there is a psychological satisfaction received when we make an oral statement. Most people, when born again, are very excited; hence, verbal about their new life in Jesus.

A person does not have to make an oral proclamation to believe something. The entire Bible from Genesis thru Revelation shouts that a person is saved by his or her faith.

Romans 10:9-13 is not establishing public confession as mandatory for accepting Jesus as the Messiah. One must **believe** in his or her heart, which is synonymous with believing in one's brain. The heart and brain are spiritually connected. (Refer to the next chapter for this phenomenal revelation.)

James 5:16

> *Confess your sins to each other and pray for each other so that you may be healed. The earnest prayer of a righteous person has great power and produces wonderful results.* James 5:16

This passage uses the term *confess* but it is not used in the context of salvation. Confession to one another is good for peace of mind. As Christians, when we share our burdens and shortcomings, we gain strength and wisdom.

If we have sinned against a brother or sister in Christ, we should confess to them and ask for forgiveness, but this is in no way coupled to our eternal destiny, which is a free gift based on faith alone.

Chapter 28

You Need Not Invite Jesus into your Heart to be Saved

Nowhere in the Bible does it say a person is saved by inviting Jesus into his or her heart. It does not say: "Ask Jesus into your heart," or anything similar. That is another of many manmade assertions. Inviting Jesus into one's heart sounds sweet, warm, and fuzzy, but it is not how to be saved.

The Bible clearly states we are saved by our faith and not by anything we say or do.

> God saved you by his grace **when you believed**. And you can't take credit for this; **it is a gift** from God. Salvation is not a reward for the good things we have done, so none of us can boast about it. Ephesians 2:8-9 (Emphasis added by me.)

In the world of Christianity you will often hear the phrase, "Invite Jesus Christ into your heart," as the method by which an individual receives salvation. This phrase is used frequently by evangelists implying this invitation is a prerequisite for being saved. This is technically not true because it is not something we do for God that saves us, but our belief in what Jesus did for us. I used the word *technically* because it is not the invitation that makes a person a Christian, but the faith that precedes the invitation. The person making the invitation usually has the faith first, resulting in the invitation being made. In reality, they were saved the moment they believed, and not when they made the invitation.

If a person is a doubter who wants to believe, and he or she asks Jesus to present himself, he will. At the moment the doubter receives the truth and accepts it, he or she will be immediately saved.

For instance, when I accepted Jesus as my Savior, I really had no idea what I was doing. I was told if I became born again I would receive the free gift of eternal life — so I prayed to God to be born again. I was not sure what being born again involved, yet immediately I knew I was born spiritually when God whispered to me that all of my past, present, and future sins had been forgiven on the Cross, and he assured my eternal destiny in the dwelling place of saints (I became a saint and it wasn't anything I did, but what he did for me).

I did not say a "sinner's prayer" or even acknowledge my faith, but I requested the faith, which I received the very moment I prayed *The Seekers Prayer*. I did not invite Jesus into my heart, or say I was sorry for my sins, or anything other than I wanted to go to Heaven when I died.

My being technical may be *too* technical for some, but I believe it imperative. The truth will free many from the bondage of false teachings that frighten numerous folks from our loving Savior.

Because God knows all, if you seek Jesus, he will respond.

> *"If you look for me wholeheartedly, you will find me."* Jeremiah 29:13, Jesus' words before the incarnation

> *"Keep on asking, and you will receive what you ask for. Keep on seeking, and you will find. Keep on knocking, and the door will be opened to you. For everyone who asks, receives. Everyone who seeks, finds. And to everyone who knocks, the door will be opened."* Matthew 7:7-8, Jesus' words

Why do people say, "Invite Jesus into your heart?"

It is probably said because it is a sweet-sounding phrase handed down from generation to generation. If people are told a tale long enough, people will begin to believe it. It sounds so believable and endearing that few have taken the time to research its truthfulness. Inviting Jesus into one's heart is sort of like a Valentine invitation to Jesus.

Furthermore, it probably started because the term *heart* is used frequently throughout the Bible. In *Strong's Exhaustive Concordance of the Bible*, which is a listing of primary words contained in the King James Version of the Bible, the *brain* is never mentioned, whereas *heart* is cited more than 800 times. Cool!

Why *heart* was used instead of *brain*

The Bible was written 2,000 years ago, but science is just catching up.

Hey Doc, if the heart is purely an organ used to pump blood throughout the body, then why wasn't the term *brain* used in the Scriptures? Does our *heart* make rational, intelligent decisions? Here is the answer:

> According to scientists' recent discoveries, our hearts play just as important a part in our evaluations and appropriate actions as our brains. In fact, maybe more.

When author and scientist Paul Pearsall was lecturing to an international group of psychologists, psychiatrists, and social workers in Houston, TX, he talked about his belief in the central role of the heart in both physical and spiritual life.

Another physician came to the microphone to share her story, sobbing as she spoke:

> I have a patient, an eight-year-old little girl who received the heart of a murdered 10-year-old girl. Her mother brought her to me when she started screaming at night about her dreams of the man who had murdered her donor. She said her daughter knows who it was. After several sessions, I just could not deny the reality of what this child was telling me. Her mother and I finally decided to call the police and, using the descriptions from the little girl, they found the murderer. He was easily convicted with the evidence my patient provided. The time, the weapon, the place, the clothes he wore, what the little girl he killed had said to him — everything the little heart transplant recipient reported was completely accurate.

Dr. Don Colbert, M.D., presents an interesting theory from his very fascinating book, titled, *Deadly Emotions.*

> Even before the brain of a fetus forms, a tiny heart begins to beat. Scientists don't know what makes it begin its long journey of beating for seventy, eighty, or more years. Medical practitioners use the word "autorhythmic" to describe how a heart begins beating all by itself.

> While the source of the heart's beating is found within the heart itself, researchers believe the brain controls the timing of each beat. Even so, a heart does not need to be "hardwired" to the brain to continue a steady, rhythmical beating. When a surgeon is harvesting a heart for transplantation, he severs the nerves running to the deceased person's brain. He then places the heart into another person's chest and restores the beat. Surgeons do not know how to reconnect the nerves of the newly installed heart to the brain, so a

connection between the two organs is lost, at least temporarily. Nevertheless, the new heart that is jump-started continues to beat, beat, beat.

How can this be? In recent years neuroscientists have discovered that the heart has it's own independent nervous system. At least forty thousand nerve cells (neurons) exist in a human heart. That's the same amount found in various subcortical (beneath the cerebral cortex) centers of the brain. In other words, the heart is more than a mere biological pump. These abundant nerve cells give it a thinking, feeling capability.

The heart's "brain" and the nervous system relay messages back and forth to the brain in the skull, creating a two-way communication between these two organs. In the 1970's physiologists John and Beatrice Lacey of the Fels Research Institute found a flaw in current popular thinking about the brain. The popular approach was to assume that the brain made all of the body's decisions. The Lacey's research indicated otherwise.

Specifically, these researchers found that while the brain may send instructions to the heart through the nervous system, the heart doesn't automatically obey.

Instead, the heart seems to respond at times as if it is "considering" the information that it has received. Sometimes when the brain sends an arousal signal to the body in response to external stimuli, the heart speeds up, as might be expected. On other occasions, however, the heart slows down while all other organs are aroused as expected.

The selectivity of the heart's response suggested to the Laceys that the heart does not mechanically respond to the brain's signals. Rather, the heart seems to have an opinion of its own, which it communicates back to the brain.

What was even more interesting in the Laceys' research was the fact that the messages that the heart sent to the brain seemed to be ones that the brain not only understood but obeyed. In effect, heart and brain hold an intelligent dialogue. At times the heart submits to the brain, and on occasions the brain seems to submit to the heart. The messages from the heart appear to be capable of affecting an individual's behavior.

The ultimate "real you" is a composite of what your heart tells your brain, your brain tells your heart, and your will decides to believe, say, and do. (Pages 141 and 142)

The Bible never fails us

Heart, when used in the Bible, refers to the Christian's personal characteristics. It refers to one's mind, soul, spirit, and entire emotional nature in understanding — both good and bad. The heart is the organ said to have the ability to reason, question, meditate, motivate, and think. These mental processes are normally associated with the brain, and not the heart.

How is your heart? Jesus can soften it. Having a soft heart does not mean one has a weak mind! When a Christian's heart is softened, his or her character is simultaneously strengthened.

Notes:

Chapter 29

You Need Not Say a Prayer to be Saved

work hard to ascertain the word of truth and am a fanatic about explaining what I discover.

> *Work hard so you can present yourself to God and receive his approval. Be a good worker, one who does not need to be ashamed and who **correctly explains the word of truth**. 2 Timothy 2:15 (Emphasis added by me.)*

Say a prayer?

I constantly hear Christians stating that, to be saved, one must make an audible confession of faith, usually by reciting a prayer. This false teaching usually comes from one lone passage:

> *If you confess with your mouth that Jesus is Lord and believe in your heart that God raised him from the dead, you will be saved. For it is by believing in your heart that you are made right with God, and it is by confessing with your mouth that you are saved. Romans 10:9-10*

Romans 10:9-10 is a passage frequently used by many well-meaning Christians desiring to lead someone to salvation. There is absolutely nothing wrong with an audible confession of faith; however, a person is **not** saved by repeating words. **Nowhere in the Bible does it record a person being saved by repeating a prayer. Salvation is a gift received by believing — not by saying or doing something.**

Jesus saves and heals via faith in him. **The Bible does not say one must:**

1. Repent of sin. (*Repent of sin* is a manmade phrase, not biblical. *Repent* means "change of mind." To receive eternal life in the place Jesus has prepared for Christians, a person must *repent* of the notion of working his or her way there, and accept Jesus as Savior.) NOBODY HAS EVER RECEIVED THE FREE GIFT OF ETERNAL LIFE BY REPENTING OF SIN!

2. Make Jesus Lord of your life. Like it or not, Jesus, as God, is already Lord of all lives. (But to receive the free gift of salvation you must "trust" Jesus as your Savior, at which time you will be baptized by the Holy Spirit, who will be your counselor. *Don't be drunk with wine, because it will ruin your life. Instead, be filled with the Holy Spirit.* Ephesians 5:18)

3. Confess with your mouth that Jesus is Lord. (This was a one-time instruction from Paul to a certain group of Jews.)

4. Give your life to the Lord. (This is a phrase that is used, but it doesn't save. A person is saved by his or her faith.)

5. Be sorry for sinning. (Only a fool would not be sorry for sinning, but sorrow does not save. Only faith in Jesus saves.)

6. Ask forgiveness for sins. (All sins were forgiven on the Cross.)

7. Stop sinning. (Nobody can quit sinning.)

8. Invite Jesus into your heart. (Not necessary, but it demonstrates faith.)

9. Go forward in an alter call. (Although going forward demonstrates faith.)

10. Become water baptized. (Water baptism is an outward expression of an inward confession.)

11. Say a prayer. (Saying a prayer shows sincerity, but it is not the prayer that saves. We are saved by our faith.)

12. Obey Jesus' two commands. (He did say to obey his commands if you love him.)

13. Do good deeds. (Good deeds are discipleship. Be a disciple.)

14. Attend or join a church. (Jesus likes to see people in church)

15. Give money to a church. (Monetary contributions are good deeds, but not necessary.)

16. Participate in Communion. (Communion is done in remembrance, but it doesn't save.)

17. Confess sins. (He already knows everyone's sins and they were all forgiven at the Cross.)

18. Repeat Hail Marys. (Nonsense!)

19. Light candles. (Pretty, but an unnecessary ritual.)

20. Perform rituals. (Make sure your rituals aren't pagan.)

21. Receive Last Rites. (More nonsense!)
    ...and the list goes on and on.

Know what you believe and why you believe it! If a person believes that any of the actions listed above must be added to Jesus' finished work, he or she is adding works to faith. To be saved, a person must believe and trust in Jesus as Savior. It is a gift to those who believe.

And if by grace, then is it no more of works: otherwise grace is no more grace. But if it be of works, then it is no more grace: otherwise work is no more work. Romans 11:6 (KJV)

God saved you by his grace when you believed. And you can't take credit for this; it is a gift from God. Salvation is not a reward for the good things we have done, so none of us can boast about it. Ephesians 2:8-9

Christians are saved by *super, abundant, radical, undeserved, amazing, grace* through faith. It is not how much faith a person has, or how he or she behaves — it is faith that saves. It's a gift — it's a gift — it's a gift!

Let God's curse fall on anyone, including us or even an angel from heaven, who preaches a different kind of Good News than the one we preached to you. I say again what we have said before: If anyone preaches any other Good News than the one you welcomed, let that person be cursed. Galatians 1:8-9

According to God's standard of perfection, a person cannot do anything to make himself or herself blameless — including saying a prayer.

Notes:

Chapter 30

You Need Not Ask Forgiveness to be Saved

From childhood we are told to ask forgiveness every time we do wrong. Consequently, it seems natural for us to continually ask the Lord Jesus' forgiveness. Asking forgiveness is common courtesy, but it does not make sense to constantly ask forgiveness once you have been forgiven. All your sins, inequities, and transgressions were forgiven on the Cross.

Pre-Jesus, God's forgiveness required an animal's blood sacrifice. The Old Testament animal blood sacrifices only atoned (compensated) for sin partially and for a short time, hence the need to repeat the sacrifices yearly. Forgiveness was a continuous procedure.

Christ shed his own Blood once for all time, making future sacrifices unnecessary. This is what Jesus meant by his dying words on the Cross: "It is finished" (John 19:30). Never again would the blood of bulls and goats cleanse men from their sin. *Only by accepting Jesus' blood, shed on the Cross for the remission of sins, can we stand before God covered in the righteousness of Christ.* Wow!

> *For God made Christ, who never sinned, to be the offering for our sin, so that we could be made right with God through Christ.* 2 Corinthians 5:21

The above verse confidently declares we are made right with God through Christ. This confirms there is nothing we can do except receive Jesus' free gift of forgiveness. Jesus became sin for us, which resulted in *God's wrath cast on Jesus for the sake of the world. God did this through Jesus so we may become righteous. **Asking God to forgive is asking Jesus to bleed again.***

If a person needed to ask forgiveness for every sin, but forgot just one, then he or she would have to spend eternity in Hell for that omission. Whoops!

The place Jesus prepared for his saints is for perfect people (saints), and we Christians were perfected only by Christ's Blood. Rather than ask forgiveness, just say, "THANK

YOU, JESUS." I thank Jesus about a dozen times a day for his forgiveness. The only way I know I have righteousness is by my faith because my days are contrary to righteousness. My sins were imputed on Jesus.

God has forgotten your sins

> *For God was in Christ, reconciling the world to himself, no longer counting people's sins against them. And he gave us this wonderful message of reconciliation.* 2 Corinthians 5:19

The verse above says, "no longer counting people's sins against them." God is no longer counting your sins, so do not insult him by continually asking forgiveness. You have been forgiven once and forever.

> *We are made right with God by placing our faith in Jesus Christ. And this is true for everyone who believes, no matter who we are.* Romans 3:22

> *So we praise God for the glorious grace he has poured out on us who belong to his dear Son. He is so rich in kindness and grace that he purchased our freedom with the blood of his Son and forgave our sins.* Ephesians 1:6-7

> *You were dead because of your sins and because your sinful nature was not yet cut away. Then God made you alive with Christ, for he forgave all our sins. He canceled the record of the charges against us and took it away by nailing it to the cross.* Colossians 2:13-14

> *He himself is the sacrifice that atones for our sins—and not only our sins but the sins of all the world.* 1 John 2:2

Do not be hardheaded. There is no need to ask Jesus to die on the Cross again, and again, and again. The issue of asking forgiveness was completed at the Cross.

Not semantics

If you think there is no difference between asking forgiveness and thanking Jesus for his forgiveness, you are wrong! Only when you get into the habit of constantly thanking Jesus rather than continually asking forgiveness will you begin to feel the complete peace and freedom that accompanies Christianity.

You will never fully understand the power of the Blood until you fully feel the enormity and finality of God's forgiveness.

Jesus knew that his mission was now finished, and to fulfill Scripture he said, "I am thirsty." A jar of sour wine was sitting there, so they soaked a sponge in it, put it on a hyssop branch, and held it up to his lips. When Jesus had tasted it, he said, "It is finished!" Then he bowed his head and released his spirit. John 19:28-30

It is finished! Jesus said it, and I believe it.

You should have no guilt

"Brothers, listen! We are here to proclaim that through this man Jesus there is forgiveness for your sins. Everyone who believes in him is declared right with God—something the law of Moses could never do. Acts 13:38-39

God's grace is greater than your sins

God has acquitted you. You will have regrets about the immorality in your life, but knowing you have been completely exonerated will set you free from all guilt — but only after you completely comprehend GRACE.

Guilt is a tool Satan utilized to take your eyes off Jesus. Scripture says there is no condemnation to those who are in Christ Jesus. God does not condemn you; subsequently you certainly should not condemn yourself.

Bask in God's forgiveness

If you are saved, but the victim of Satan's lie that you can lose your salvation, I ask you: Which and whose sins did Jesus' shed Blood not forgive? Answer: Jesus death on the Cross was propitiation for all sin except that of rejecting him.

It is difficult to imagine you have been forgiven for everything you have done, everything you are doing, and everything you will do. *When you grasp this phenomenal concept, you will be so amazed you will bask in God's GRACE.* Then you will do three things: (1) You will become a disciple of Christ. (2) You will be able to forgive yourself. (3) You will be able to forgive others.

Sabbath rest

We Christians know that upon our death we will go directly to Heaven, not based on anything we do, but what Jesus did for us. This fact is so comforting a term has been coined: *Sabbath rest* describes current and eternal rest in Christ experienced by the Christian. *Sabbath rest* should not be confused with resting on Sunday.

> *God's promise of entering his rest still stands, so we ought to tremble with fear that some of you might fail to experience it. For this good news—that God has prepared this rest—has been announced to us just as it was to them. But it did them no good because they didn't share the faith of those who listened to God. For only we who believe can enter his rest. As for the others, God said,*
>
> > *"In my anger I took an oath:*
> > *'They will never enter my place of rest,'"*
>
> *even though this rest has been ready since he made the world. We know it is ready because of the place in the Scriptures where it mentions the seventh day: "On the seventh day God rested from all his work." But in the other passage God said, "They will never enter my place of rest."*
>
> *So God's rest is there for people to enter, but those who first heard this good news failed to enter because they disobeyed God. So God set another time for entering his rest, and that time is today. God announced this through David much later in the words already quoted:*
>
> > *"Today when you hear his voice,*
> > *don't harden your hearts."*
>
> *Now if Joshua had succeeded in giving them this rest, God would not have spoken about another day of rest still to come. So there is a special rest still waiting for the people of God. For all who have entered into God's rest have rested from their labors, just as God did after creating the world. So let us do our best to enter that rest. But if we disobey God, as the people of Israel did, we will fall.* Hebrews 4:1-11

Sabbath rest quiets a guilty conscience, stills troubling thoughts, and gives hope in desperation. In Christ we receive complete rest today and forever. Sabbath rest is what those who understand salvation and who have accepted Jesus as Savior experience when they cease from their own efforts for salvation and depend on the work of Christ.

> *Then Jesus said, "Come to me, all of you who are weary and carry heavy burdens, and I will give you rest. Take my yoke upon you. Let me teach you, because I am humble and gentle at heart, and you will find rest for your souls. For my yoke is easy to bear, and the burden I give you is light."*
> Matthew 11:28-30

The Apostle Paul shares his weakness with the world as he experienced Sabbath rest.

> *Each time he said, "My grace is all you need. My power works best in weakness." So now I am glad to boast about my weaknesses, so that the power of Christ can work through me. That's why I take pleasure in my weaknesses, and in the insults, hardships, persecutions, and troubles that I suffer for Christ. For when I am weak, then I am strong.* 2 Corinthians 12:9-10

Now, shout it from the rooftops

Now that you know the truth, the whole truth, and nothing but the truth, it is time to share this *Good News.*

In addition to the Apostles, Jesus sent 72 disciples to deliver the Good News (He may have sent more but only 72 are recorded in the Bible). It does not take a rocket scientist to ascertain that Jesus wants the Good News to be shared.

> *The Lord now chose seventy-two other disciples and sent them ahead in pairs to all the towns and places he planned to visit. These were his instructions to them: "The harvest is great, but the workers are few. So pray to the Lord who is in charge of the harvest; ask him to send more workers into his fields. Now go, and remember that I am sending you out as lambs among wolves.*
> Luke 10:1-3

Christians are ambassadors

> *For God was in Christ, reconciling the world to himself, no longer counting people's sins against them. And he gave us this wonderful message of*

reconciliation. So we are Christ's ambassadors; God is making his appeal through us. We speak for Christ when we plead, "Come back to God!" For God made Christ, who never sinned, to be the offering for our sin, so that we could be made right with God through Christ. 2 Corinthians 5:19-21

The Great Commission

The following passage is our mandate and opportunity to share the Good News of salvation by grace through faith:

> *"Therefore, go and make disciples of all the nations, baptizing them in the name of the Father and the Son and the Holy Spirit. Teach these new disciples to obey all the commands I have given you. And be sure of this: I am with you always, even to the end of the age."* Matthew 28:19-20, Jesus' words

> **"God's plan for enlarging His kingdom is so simple — one person telling another about the Savior. Yet we're busy and full of excuses. Just remember, someone's eternal destiny is at stake. The joy you'll have when you meet that person in heaven will far exceed any discomfort you felt in sharing the gospel." Charles Stanley (born 1932)**

Shake the dust from your feet:

> *"Whenever you enter a city or village, search for a worthy person and stay in his home until you leave town. When you enter the home, give it your blessing. If it turns out to be a worthy home, let your blessing stand; if it is not, take back the blessing. If any household or town refuses to welcome you or listen to your message, shake its dust from your feet as you leave."* Matthew 10:11-14, Jesus' words

Although the above passage refers to instructions Jesus gave to the apostles when they were sent to minister to Jewish communities, Jesus' advice is applicable to individuals who are ministers of salvation. When witnessing, don't nag or scare folks into accepting Jesus as their savior. If they refuse to hear the Good News, perhaps you should move on.

NOTES: If you are an evangelist, please do not make the HUGE mistake, made by many, of telling someone they must <u>repent of sin</u> to be saved from eternal damnation. That is NOT BIBLICAL.

In this chapter, I probably presented more substantiation than is necessary to convince most, but I am extremely passionate about ensuring that everyone thoroughly understands the truth.

Chapter 31

You Need Not Repent of Sin to be Saved

This chapter is all-encompassing tackling this **repent of sin hogwash**, which is one of those many erroneous salvation stipulations that have been repeated for so long that people believe it. I will not rest until I educate as many as possible about this colossal error in teaching. *Repent of sin* is not biblical. To reiterate, repent of sin is not biblical.

Please help me Jesus

Distraught from hearing Christians misuse the phrase *repent of sin* regarding the Doctrine of Salvation, I am painstakingly writing this very in-depth chapter to set the record straight. I work hard to ascertain truth and am a fanatic about explaining what I discover.

> *Work hard so you can present yourself to God and receive his approval. Be a good worker, one who does not need to be ashamed and who **correctly explains the word of truth**.* 2 Timothy 2:15 (Emphasis added by me.)

The misuse of *repent of sin* has caused a massive misunderstanding among both believers and non-believers. Satan, the author of confusion (I Corinthians 14:33), has delighted in the exploitation of this non-biblical phrase.

Constantly hearing the phrase *repent of sin to be saved* for many years before I was saved caused me to reject Jesus as my Savior. I was deceptively told *repent of sin* meant I had to stop sinning, turn from sin, or be sorry for my sins in order to be saved.

I knew I couldn't stop sinning, nor did I think I could turn from my sins (whatever that means). I was sorry for many of my sins, but not as sorry as perhaps I should have been. I enjoyed many of my sins, as do most folks. In other words, I was not desperate enough to become a religious nut, or a goody two-shoes.

Until age 34, I rejected Jesus because the Good News message was repeatedly accompanied by the phrase *repent of sin*, which I now know is not a prerequisite for salvation — *nor is it biblically correct.*

The Good News is we are saved by *super, abundant, radical, undeserved, amazing, grace* through faith, not by repenting of sin. ***Nobody has ever been saved by repenting of sin!***

> *God saved you by his grace when you believed. And you can't take credit for this; it is a gift from God. Salvation is not a reward for the good things we have done, so none of us can boast about it.* Ephesians 2:8-9

The passage above does **NOT** say:

1. Repent of sin. (*Repent of sin* is a manmade phrase, not biblical. *Repent* means "change of mind." To receive eternal life in the place Jesus has prepared for Christians, a person must *repent* of the notion of working his or her way there, and accept Jesus as Savior.) NOBODY HAS EVER RECEIVED THE FREE GIFT OF ETERNAL LIFE BY REPENTING OF SIN!
2. Make Jesus Lord of your life. Like it or not, Jesus, as God, is already Lord of all lives. (But to receive the free gift of salvation you must "trust" Jesus as your Savior, at which time you will be baptized by the Holy Spirit, who will be your counselor. *Don't be drunk with wine, because it will ruin your life. Instead, be filled with the Holy Spirit.* Ephesians 5:18)
3. Confess with your mouth that Jesus is Lord. (This was a one-time instruction from Paul to a certain group of Jews.)
4. Give your life to the Lord. (This is a phrase that is used, but it doesn't save. A person is saved by his or her faith.)
5. Be sorry for sinning. (Only a fool would not be sorry for sinning, but sorrow does not save. Only faith in Jesus saves.)
6. Ask forgiveness for sins. (All sins were forgiven on the Cross.)
7. Stop sinning. (Nobody can quit sinning.)
8. Invite Jesus into your heart. (Not necessary, but it demonstrates faith.)
9. Go forward in an alter call. (Although going forward demonstrates faith.)
10. Become water baptized. (Water baptism is an outward expression of an inward confession.)

11. Say a prayer. (Saying a prayer shows sincerity, but it is not the prayer that saves. We are saved by our faith.)
12. Obey Jesus' two commands. (He did say to obey his commands if you love him.)
13. Do good deeds. (Good deeds are discipleship. Be a disciple.)
14. Attend or join a church. (Jesus likes to see people in church)
15. Give money to a church. (Monetary contributions are good deeds, but not necessary.)
16. Participate in Communion. (Communion is done in remembrance, but it doesn't save.)
17. Confess sins. (He already knows everyone's sins and they were all forgiven at the Cross.)
18. Repeat Hail Marys. (Nonsense!)
19. Light candles. (Pretty, but an unnecessary ritual.)
20. Perform rituals. (Make sure your rituals aren't pagan.)
21. Receive Last Rites. (More nonsense!)
      …and the list goes on and on.

Know what you believe and why you believe it! If a person believes that any of the actions listed above must be added to Jesus' finished work, he or she is adding works to faith. To be saved, a person must believe and trust in Jesus as Savior. It is a gift to those who believe.

> *And if by grace, then is it no more of works: otherwise grace is no more grace. But if it be of works, then it is no more grace: otherwise work is no more work.* Romans 11:6 (KJV)

> *God saved you by his grace when you believed. And you can't take credit for this; it is a gift from God. Salvation is not a reward for the good things we have done, so none of us can boast about it.* Ephesians 2:8-9

Christians are saved by *super, abundant, radical, undeserved, amazing, grace* through faith. It is not how much faith a person has, or how he or she behaves — it is faith that saves. It's a gift — it's a gift — it's a gift!

> *Let God's curse fall on anyone, including us or even an angel from heaven, who preaches a different kind of Good News than the one we preached to you. I say again what we have said before: If anyone preaches any other Good News than the one you welcomed, let that person be cursed.* Galatians 1:8-9

The problem

The problem is not using the terms *repent* or *repentance*. The problem is people using them incorrectly.

Through the centuries, *repent* evolved to mean something far different than when it was spoken by John the Baptist, the Apostle Paul, the Apostle John, and Jesus Christ.

> **The world-famous preacher Charles Haddon Spurgeon (1834-1892) made the statement: "Brethren, we shall not adjust our Bible to the age, but the age to the Bible."**

We have all heard many famous preachers say, "If you want to be saved, repent of your sins."

If turning from your sins means to stop sinning, then people can only be saved if they stop sinning. Nobody has ever stopped sinning, unless they are dead or in a coma.

If repentance means turning from sin, and turning from sin means to stop sinning, then a person must live a sinless life in order to be saved. If living a sinless life could save, all mankind would go to Hell, because there are no unflawed people.

Many who would like to be saved believe it is impossible because they have been taught incorrectly. For centuries, ignorant teachers have convinced innocent people of a non-existent prerequisite.

We should have sorrow for our sin, but sorrow is not repentance. Sorrow is sorrow. Sorrow for our sins is not what saves us. What saves us is trusting in Jesus' finished work on the Cross.

If we could stop sinning, Jesus died for nothing. Read and reread the following verse until you completely understand it.

> *I do not treat the grace of God as meaningless. For if keeping the law could make us right with God, then there was no need for Christ to die.*
> **Galatians 2:21**

Correct Bible interpretation

To completely understand the Bible, you need to learn Hebrew, Aramaic, and Greek. Mistakes are made if one attempts to use a modern English dictionary to define many of the Hebrew, Greek, and Aramaic words, or terms, used 2,000 years ago — especially when the original manuscripts are no longer in existence.

Although *repent* appears in the Bible, including stating that God repented, it is misunderstood in most instances. *Repenting of sin* is not a requirement for salvation. ***Repenting of believing that you can earn your way to Heaven is.***

Repent, as it relates to Christ, means to change our minds about living by laws, being good to receive forgiveness, or anything else that we might do for Jesus to be saved. It may also mean repenting (changing one's mind) from believing in other gods, or repenting (changing one's mind) from being an atheist or agnostic. It does not mean to be sorry for, turn from, or stop sinning. When a doubter places faith in Jesus as having taken his or her place on the Cross and having taken the penalty for his or her sins, <u>*that* is repenting (changing their minds) from disbelief to belief.</u>

Tragically, many Bible publishers have incorrectly used the term *repent* in a way that is confusing to the reader. When Paul was warning folks to repent, he was directing them to abandon their polytheistic and idolatrous pagan notions. The Jesus movement was new to people, most who had many gods and many beliefs. Paul was warning folks to **change their minds** (repent) from worshiping false idols to accepting Jesus as the Messiah.

The following paragraph is so important that I am begging you to commit it to memory.

> *Repentance* is the translation of the Greek word *metanoia*. The literal meaning of *metanoia* is "a change of mind." *Meta* means "change." *Noia* means "mind." *Meta-noia* means "a change of mind." Therefore, repentance (*metanoia*) is a change of mind.

In the New Testament, the term *repent* was usually used to warn the Jews that to gain favor with God they must *change their minds* from depending on the Jewish laws (i.e., the Ten Commandments) to accepting Jesus as the Messiah.

> **For they don't understand God's way of making people right with himself. Refusing to accept God's way, they cling to their**

own way of getting right with God by trying to keep the law. For Christ has already accomplished the purpose for which the law was given. As a result, all who believe in him are made right with God. **Romans 10:3-4**

Acts 2:38

Acts 2:38 is a typical example of how *repent* is sometimes mistranslated and/or misunderstood.

The Book of Acts was authored by Luke, a physician and co-worker with Paul in his missionary work, and was written to a man named Theophilus, as was the Book of Luke. Both Luke and Acts were written in refined Koine Greek. Although Luke's letters were written to Theophilus, most biblical scholars accept them as an address to all believers for all time.

Acts describes how the Church began and grew. The Church began with the outpouring of the promised Holy Spirit, which inspired evangelism. The Good News of the New Covenant began in Jerusalem and spread to Rome. It first went to the Jews; most rejected it, insisting Jesus was not the Messiah.

Acts 2:38 quotes Peter, who preached an authoritative message encouraging fellow Jews and residents of Jerusalem to "repent" (change their minds) from clinging to their Jewish heritage of laws and to accept the grace of Jesus the Messiah.

It is important to observe that only the New Living Translation (NLT) uses the phrase "repent of sin" in Acts 2:38. Although I frequently use the NLT, in this particular instance the NLT translated erroneously. Furthermore, not all versions use the term *repent*, as you will see. For the serious Bible student to obtain the most accurate interpretation of the Bible, we must study, study, and study. When studying the Doctrine of Salvation, the term *repent* necessitates thorough analysis.

I inventoried many Acts 2:38 verses from many English translations of the Bible. I emphasized the term(s) used by Peter so you may begin to have a clear knowledge of what each version says.

21st Century King James Version (KJ21)

Then Peter said unto them, "__Repent__ and be baptized, every one of you, in the name of Jesus Christ for the remission of sins; and ye shall receive the gift of the Holy Ghost." Acts 2:38 (KJ21)

American Standard Version (ASV)

*And Peter said unto them, **Repent ye**, and be baptized every one of you in the name of Jesus Christ unto the remission of your sins; and ye shall receive the gift of the Holy Spirit.* Acts 2:38 (ASV)

Amplified Bible (AMP)

*And Peter answered them, **Repent (change your views and purpose to accept the will of God in your inner selves instead of rejecting it)** and be baptized, every one of you, in the name of Jesus Christ for the forgiveness of and release from your sins; and you shall receive the gift of the Holy Spirit.* Acts 2:38 (AMP)

Common English Bible (CEB)

*Peter replied, "**Change your hearts and lives.** Each of you must be baptized in the name of Jesus Christ for the forgiveness of your sins. Then you will receive the gift of the Holy Spirit."* Acts 2:38 (CEB)

Contemporary English Version (CEV)

*Peter said, "**Turn back to God!** Be baptized in the name of Jesus Christ, so that your sins will be forgiven. Then you will be given the Holy Spirit."* Acts 2:38 (CEV)

Darby Translation (DARBY)

*And Peter said to them, **Repent**, and be baptized, each one of you, in the name of Jesus Christ, for remission of sins, and ye will receive the gift of the Holy Spirit.* Acts 2:38 (DARBY)

Douay-Rheims 1899 American Edition (DRA)

*But Peter said to them: **Do penance**, and be baptized every one of you in the name of Jesus Christ, for the remission of your sins: and you shall receive the gift of the Holy Ghost.* Acts 2:38 (DRA)

Easy-to-Read Version (ERV)

*Peter said to them, "**Change your hearts and lives** and be baptized, each one of you, in the name of Jesus Christ. Then God will forgive your sins, and you will receive the gift of the Holy Spirit."* Acts 2:38 (ERV)

English Standard Version (ESV)

*And Peter said to them, "**Repent** and be baptized every one of you in the name of Jesus Christ for the forgiveness of your sins, and you will receive the gift of the Holy Spirit."* Acts 2:38 (ESV)

GOD'S WORD Translation (GW)

*Peter answered them, "**All of you must turn to God and change the way you think and act**, and each of you must be baptized in the name of Jesus Christ so that your sins will be forgiven. Then you will receive the Holy Spirit as a gift."* Acts 2:38 (GW)

Holman Christian Standard Bible (HCSB)

*"**Repent**," Peter said to them, "and be baptized, each of you, in the name of Jesus Christ for the forgiveness of your sins, and you will receive the gift of the Holy Spirit."* Acts 2:38 (HCSB)

King James Version (KJV)

*Then Peter said unto them, **Repent**, and be baptized every one of you in the name of Jesus Christ for the remission of sins, and ye shall receive the gift of the Holy Ghost.* Acts 2:38 (KJV)

New American Standard Bible (NASB)

*Peter said to them, "**Repent**, and each of you be baptized in the name of Jesus Christ for the forgiveness of your sins; and you will receive the gift of the Holy Spirit."* Acts 2:38 (NASB)

New International Version (NIV)

*Peter replied, "**Repent** and be baptized, every one of you, in the name of Jesus Christ for the forgiveness of your sins. And you will receive the gift of the Holy Spirit."* Acts 2:38 (NIV)

New King James Version (NKJV)

*Then Peter said to them, "**Repent**, and let every one of you be baptized in the name of Jesus Christ for the remission of sins; and you shall receive the gift of the Holy Spirit." Acts 2:38 (NKJV)*

New Living Translation (NLT)

*Peter replied, "Each of you must **repent of your sins** and turn to God, and be baptized in the name of Jesus Christ for the forgiveness of your sins. Then you will receive the gift of the Holy Spirit." Acts 2:38 (NLT)*

New Revised Standard Version (NRSV)

*Peter said to them, "**Repent**, and be baptized every one of you in the name of Jesus Christ so that your sins may be forgiven; and you will receive the gift of the Holy Spirit." Acts 2:38 (NRSV)*

New Revised Standard Version Catholic Edition (NRSVCE)

*Peter said to them, "**Repent**, and be baptized every one of you in the name of Jesus Christ so that your sins may be forgiven; and you will receive the gift of the Holy Spirit." Acts 2:38 (NRSVCE)*

Worldwide English (New Testament) (WE)

*'**Stop your wrong ways and turn back to God**,' answered Peter. 'And then everyone of you can be baptised in the name of Jesus Christ. Your wrong ways will be forgiven you, and you will receive the Holy Spirit.' Acts 2:38 (WE)*

Wycliffe Bible (WYC)

*And Peter said to them, **Do ye penance [Penance, he said, do ye]**, and each of you be baptized in the name of Jesus Christ, into remission of your sins; and ye shall take the gift of the Holy Ghost. Acts 2:38 (WYC)*

Young's Literal Translation (YLT)

...and Peter said unto them, '__Reform__, and be baptized each of you on the name of Jesus Christ, to remission of sins, and ye shall receive the gift of the Holy Spirit,...' Acts 2:38 (YLT)

Two of the passages above say one should do *penance*. Penance is a sacrament of the Roman Catholic Church used as a form of discipline or punishment imposed on someone to demonstrate sorrow for his or her sins. The Catholics refer to this as *doing penance*. The penitent first confesses his or her sin(s) to a priest. The penitent is then given instructions on what to do in order to atone for his or her sin(s). Penance usually takes the form of praying specific prayers repeatedly, fasting, or some other form of payment. Penance is not biblical, although it appears in a few Bibles. Nowhere does Scripture teach that deeds make restitution for sin. Martin Luther discovered this the hard way.

> **"If ever a monk could get to heaven through monastic discipline, I was that monk. And yet my conscience would not give me certainty, but I always doubted and said, 'You didn't do that right. You weren't contrite enough. You left that out of your confession.' The more I tried to remedy an uncertain, weak, and troubled conscience with human traditions, the more I daily found it more uncertain, weaker, and more troubled."**
> **Martin Luther (1483-1546)**

Interestingly, in the passages above, several words or phrases are not verbatim from one version to another. "Hmmm," you say, "If the Bible is the infallible Word of God, why wouldn't all of the versions be the same?"

Great question, but difficult to answer without making it appear that someone goofed. Who goofed? I will try to answer that to the best of my ability, but it is complicated.

> The answer is: If we could read the Bible from the original manuscripts, in the original languages, they would be identical. The original manuscripts are no longer in existence, and because we don't all speak ancient Hebrew, Aramaic, and Koine Greek, we must settle for what someone else tells us their words mean. Those someone's are the Bible translators and publishers.

Bibles are copyrighted. Publishing Bibles is a for-profit business. Bible publishers are interested in making a profit. To be copyrighted they must make their Bibles different from other publishers.

Our having numerous English Bible translations is both good and bad. It is good because the Word of God is available in many translations for the purpose of comparison and readability. It is bad because having so many different translations can cause confusion due to varying interpretations. The confusion causes disharmony because it divides Christians.

Bible translations are inspired by the Holy Spirit, but subject to human error. Keep that in mind before getting into a disagreement.

All Bible translations are fallible, but *scholars believe the contents of today's New Testaments are truthful if studied faithfully and diligently.* This must be done by comparing the various translations and studying the writings of scholars, with assistance from the Holy Spirit. There are human errors; however, only a fraction of these have serious consequences, such as *repent of sin.*

Important opinions of scholars

Following are seven opinions of scholars regarding their interpretations of the terms *repent* and *repentance*. I was so impressed with the opinions that I italicized and made bold what I believe are the most important points.

1. The word Metanoia is in every instance translated repentance. The word means a change of mind. ***The common practice of reading into this word the thought of sorrow or heart anguish is responsible for much confusion in the field of Soteriology ...*** This definition of this word as it is used in the New Testament is fundamental. Little or no progress can be made in a right induction of the Word of God on this theme, unless the true and accurate meaning of the word is discovered and defended throughout. Chafer, Lewis Sperry. *Systematic Theology*, Vol. III (p. 372). (Emphasis added by me.)

2. Often the idea of believing is expressed by the word, repent (Acts 2:38; 3:19; 5:31; 8:22; 11:18; 17:30; 20:21; 26:20) ... The word means to change one's mind, and by its usage in the Book of Acts it means to change one's mind about Jesus of Nazareth being the Messiah. ***This involves***

no longer thinking of Him as merely the carpenter's son of Nazareth, an imposter, but now receiving Him as both Lord (Jehovah) and Messiah. Thus, repentance as preached by the apostles was not a prerequisite to nor a consequence of salvation, but was actually the act of faith in Jesus which brought salvation to the one who repented. Ryrie, Charles. *Biblical Theology of the New Testament* (p. 116, 117). (Emphasis added by me.)

3. *What place has repentance in salvation? Should we tell people to repent of their sins to be saved? The Gospel of John is the Holy Spirit's Gospel Tract, written that men might believe that Jesus is the Christ, the Son of God; and that believing they might have life through His name (20:31). And it does not mention the word 'repentance.' But that is only because repentance is a necessary part of saving faith. Strictly speaking, the repentance means a 'change of mind'. It is by no means the same thing as sorrow (II Corinthians 7:10).* Since it is not possible to an unbeliever to become a believer without changing his mind, it is therefore unnecessary to say anything about it. The only thing for a man to do in order to be saved is to believe on the Lord Jesus Christ: and to believe on Him is the same thing as receiving Him (John 1:11-13). Pettingill, William. *Bible Questions Answered* (p. 215-216). (Emphasis added by me.)

4. *But in order to clarify the subject, it may be well to observe carefully what repentance is not, and then to notice briefly what it is. First, then repentance is not to be confounded with penitence... penitence is simply sorrow for sin... Nowhere is man exhorted to feel a certain amount of sorrow for his sins in order to come to Christ. Second, penance is not repentance. Penance is the effort in some way to atone for the wrong done...* In the third place, let us remember that reformation is not repentance... Need I add that repentance then is not to be considered synonymous with joining a church or taking up one's religious duties, as people say. It is not doing anything. ...the Greek word, metanoia, which is translated "repentance" in our English Bibles, literally means a change of mind. Ironside, Harry. *Except Ye Repent* (p. 12-15). (Emphasis added by me.)

5. When thinking of the word repent or repentance, there are at least two general ideas that are not repentance. *Repentance does not mean to be sorry for some wrong I have done...* Some may think repentance

is promising to do good. I do not want to seem to be too harsh, but how much good is it going to do for anyone to promise to do good? ...Repentance is primarily a judgment about myself. ***The expression is often used which has an awkward translation into English is 'repenting of our sins'. Actually this is not a sound idea.*** The reason it is so awkward to say is that man does not 'repent his sins' nor does he 'repent of his sins', he repents himself. Repentance is judgment upon myself whereby I admit that I am not good... Repentance is a very important matter. Because it is not until I am willing to acknowledge before God that I am nothing in myself that I will believe the Gospel. Gutzke, Manford. *Plain Talk About Christian Words* (p. 122, 123). (Emphasis added by me.)

6. ***It is our purpose to discuss the Scriptural doctrine of repentance. It is important because so many minds have been confused concerning the simplicity of salvation by the perversion of the Scriptural teaching of this important doctrine... The doctrine has suffered tremendously from an erroneous concept held by most men, for when the word 'repent' is used, it brings to mind of the average individual the thought of sorrow for sin... And this sorrow for sin is usually called 'repentance'. But there could be nothing further from the concept of the Word of God than the idea that repentance means sorrow for sins. From the Word of God we discover that the word translated 'repent' means 'a change of mind'... Now, such as change of mind as the Scripture enjoins when it speaks of repentance may produce a sorrow for sin, but it will be the result after one has seen his sin in the light of holiness of God and has changed his attitude toward it.*** Pentecost, J. Dwight. *Things Which Become Sound Doctrine* (p. 61, 62). (Emphasis added by me.)

7. ***Repentance, as it relates to Christ, means to change our minds about Him, who He is and what He's done to provide forgiveness, and deliverance from our sins. When we place faith in Jesus as having taken our place personally on the cross and borne the penalty due our sins, then we're automatically repenting, because we couldn't accept Him in this way without having had to change our minds in some way concerning Him.*** Lindsey, Hal. *The Liberation of Planet Earth* (p. 133). (Emphasis added by me.)

Notice I emphasized the entire quote in numbers 6 and 7.

Furthermore

The Gospel of John, the only evangelical book of the canonical gospels (Matthew, Mark, Luke, John), mentions the word *believe* or *believed* approximately 100 times, without mentioning *repent* once.

Another example of using *repent* can be found in Acts 17:30. I did not list passages from the numerous translations and how they differ. Please take my word for it — they do. The various translations use differing terms to explain Paul's message, including *repent*. This passage communicates Paul's concern for those who are worshiping false gods, and for Jews depending on the Jewish laws (i.e., the Ten Commandments) to gain favor with the God of Abraham, Isaac, and Jacob. *Repent* is used to advise a change of mind.

Conclusion

Although *repent* appears in the Bible, it is misunderstood in most instances. *Repenting of sin is not a requirement for salvation. Repenting of believing that you can earn your way to the glorious place that awaits you in the next life is*. We are saved by God's grace — not by our good works!

> *And if by grace, then is it no more of works: otherwise grace is no more grace. But if it be of works, then it is no more grace: otherwise work is no more work.* Romans 11:6 (KJV)

> *God saved you by his grace when you believed. And you can't take credit for this; it is a gift from God. Salvation is not a reward for the good things we have done, so none of us can boast about it.* Ephesians 2:8-9

However, we are saved so we can do good works!

> *For we are God's masterpiece. He has created us anew in Christ Jesus, so we can do the good things he planned for us long ago.* Ephesians 2:10

Chapter 32

You Need Not be Water Baptized to be Saved

Water baptism has never been what saves. When people hear *baptism*, they immediately associate it with <u>water baptism</u>. This has caused mass confusion concerning the various baptism doctrines.

The notion of water baptism usually comes from the following narrative:

> There was a man named Nicodemus, a Jewish religious leader who was a Pharisee. After dark one evening, he came to speak with Jesus. "Rabbi," he said, "we all know that God has sent you to teach us. Your miraculous signs are evidence that God is with you."
>
> Jesus replied, "I tell you the truth, unless you are born again, you cannot see the Kingdom of God."
>
> "What do you mean?" exclaimed Nicodemus. "How can an old man go back into his mother's womb and be born again?"
>
> Jesus replied, "I assure you, no one can enter the Kingdom of God without being **<u>born of water</u>** and the Spirit. Humans can reproduce only human life, but the Holy Spirit gives birth to spiritual life. So don't be surprised when I say, 'You must be born again.' The wind blows wherever it wants. Just as you can hear the wind but can't tell where it comes from or where it is going, so you can't explain how people are born of the Spirit." John 3:1-8 (Emphasis added by me.)

It is a natural mistake to assume that because it says **born of water,** it is insinuating water baptism. What does *born of water* mean?

Our minds play tricks on us and this is a typical trick. Most Bible scholars agree *born of water* is not referring to baptism with water. To unconsciously read *water baptism* into this verse because it mentions water is a misinterpretation. If Jesus meant one must be *water baptized* to enter the Kingdom of God, it would contradict the entire theme of the New Testament, which makes it clear we are saved only by faith in Jesus finished work on the Cross — not by being dunked in water.

Possible meanings

(1) The phrase *born of water* may be referring to the water-like fluid released when the amniotic sac breaks prior to a pregnant woman birthing a child.

(2) It may be referring to the cleansing of sins we received from Jesus' death on the Cross. The term *water* is used frequently in the Old Testament in reference to spiritual cleansing.

(3) My opinion (and I am always right) is that Jesus was referring to himself as the living water that nourishes the believer and gives eternal life, as the following passages reveal:

He had to go through Samaria on the way. Eventually he came to the Samaritan village of Sychar, near the field that Jacob gave to his son Joseph. Jacob's well was there; and Jesus, tired from the long walk, sat wearily beside the well about noontime. Soon a Samaritan woman came to draw water, and Jesus said to her, "Please give me a drink." He was alone at the time because his disciples had gone into the village to buy some food.

The woman was surprised, for Jews refuse to have anything to do with Samaritans. She said to Jesus, "You are a Jew, and I am a Samaritan woman. Why are you asking me for a drink?"

Jesus replied, "If you only knew the gift God has for you and who you are speaking to, you would ask me, and I would give you living water."

"But sir, you don't have a rope or a bucket," she said, "and this well is very deep. Where would you get this living water? And besides, do you think you're greater than our ancestor Jacob, who gave us this well? How can you offer better water than he and his sons and his animals enjoyed?"

Jesus replied, "Anyone who drinks this water will soon become thirsty again. But those who drink the water I give will never be thirsty again. It becomes a fresh, bubbling spring within them, giving them eternal life."
John 4:4-14 (Emphasis added by me.)

*On the last day, the climax of the festival, **Jesus stood and shouted to the crowds, "Anyone who is thirsty may come to me! Anyone who believes in me may come and drink! For the Scriptures declare, 'Rivers of living water will flow from his heart.'"** (When he said "living water," he was speaking of the Spirit, who would be given to everyone believing in him. But the Spirit had not yet been given, because Jesus had not yet entered into his glory.)* John 7:37-39 (Emphasis added by me.)

The living water is the truth that Jesus is the Messiah who guarantees everlasting life to all who drink (meaning they partake in the nourishment of the Holy Spirit). ***The nourishment of the Holy Spirit quenches one's soul.***

Study, study, study

When establishing doctrine, it is a major mistake to use just one lone passage without studying other verses and passages that pertain to the topic. Doctrine cannot be established using one passage if dozens of other passages are inconsistent with its interpretation. We determine meaning by carefully comparing verses and passages to other verses and passages throughout the Bible regarding the topic or doctrine we are studying. The Bible must be studied, not just read.

Baptize generally means "to immerse." The immersion can be with many substances. There are several baptisms taught in the Bible, but the two that determine one's eternal destination are the *Holy Spirit baptism* and the *baptism of fire* — not water baptism.

To demonstrate that baptism does not always refer to water baptism, following are four baptisms taught in the Bible that are **not** related to water. I emphasized the words that verify my point.

(1) Baptism of the Holy Spirit

*"I baptize you with water to show that your hearts and lives have changed. But there is one coming after me who is greater than I am, whose sandals I am not good enough to carry. He will baptize you with the **Holy Spirit** and fire."* Matthew 3:11 (NCV) (Emphasis added by me.)

(2) Baptism of fire (Hell)

"I baptize you with water to show that your hearts and lives have changed. But there is one coming after me who is greater than I am, whose sandals I am

*not good enough to carry. He will baptize you with the Holy Spirit and **fire**."* Matthew 3:11 (NCV) (Emphasis added by me.)

(3) Baptism of death

*But Jesus answered and said, Ye know not what ye ask. Are ye able to drink of the cup that I shall drink of, and to be **baptized with the baptism that I am baptized with**? They say unto him, We are able.* Matthew 20:22 (KJV) (Emphasis added by me.)

(4) Baptism of suffering

*"I have come to set the world on fire, and I wish it were already burning! I have a terrible **baptism of suffering** ahead of me, and I am under a heavy burden until it is accomplished."* Luke 12:49-50, Jesus words (Emphasis added by me.)

(5) Baptism of Moses

*In the cloud and in the sea, all of them were **baptized as followers of Moses**.* 1 Corinthians 10:2 (Emphasis added by me.)

The two baptisms that relate to Heaven or Hell

The two baptisms that determine eternal destination are the *Holy Spirit baptism* and the *baptism of fire*. Those who are baptized in the promised Holy Spirit go to Heaven, but those who are baptized with fire go to Hell. John the Baptist prepared the way for Jesus:

*"I baptize you with water to show that your hearts and lives have changed. But there is one coming after me who is greater than I am, whose sandals I am not good enough to carry. He will baptize you with the Holy Spirit and fire. **He will come ready to clean the grain, separating the good grain from the chaff. He will put the good part of the grain into his barn, but he will burn the chaff with a fire that cannot be put out."** Matthew 3:11-12 (NCV, Emphasis added by me.)

Jesus Christ baptizes all living believers with the Holy Spirit the moment that they believe. Jesus Christ will baptize all non-believers with fire when they are immersed in the everlasting Lake of Fire, the eternal Hell. A believer will never experience the baptism of fire, and a non-believer will never experience the baptism of the Holy Spirit.

"There is no judgment against anyone who believes in him. But anyone who does not believe in him has already been judged for not believing in God's one and only Son." John 3:18, Jesus' words

And God will provide rest for you who are being persecuted and also for us when the Lord Jesus appears from heaven. He will come with his mighty angels, in flaming fire, bringing judgment on those who don't know God and on those who refuse to obey the Good News of our Lord Jesus. They will be punished with eternal destruction, forever separated from the Lord and from his glorious power. When he comes on that day, he will receive glory from his holy people—praise from all who believe. And this includes you, for you believed what we told you about him. 2 Thessalonians 1:7-10

I was baptized by the Holy Spirit in 1980, which guaranteed my eternal life in the glorious place Christ prepared for me, but not water baptized until 2004. I had intended to do so, but for one reason or another, I procrastinated.

Why Jesus was baptized

At first glance, it seems Jesus baptism had no purpose. John's water baptizing was primarily for Jews as spiritual cleansing, and in preparation for the coming Messiah. Because Jesus was the Messiah, he did not need to be water baptized.

"I baptize you with water to show that your hearts and lives have changed. But there is one coming after me who is greater than I am, whose sandals I am not good enough to carry. He will baptize you with the Holy Spirit and fire." Matthew 3:11 (NCV)

When Jesus requested that he (Jesus) be water baptized, John hesitated. Jesus insisted.

But Jesus said, "It should be done, for we must carry out all that God requires." So John agreed to baptize him. Matthew 3:15

There are no Bible passages that precisely explain why Jesus insisted he be water baptized, but there are various speculations from scholars.

- Jesus was about to begin his ministry, and he probably thought it appropriate to be recognized.

- Jesus may have been demonstrating humility by identifying with mankind. Jesus, as God, the Creator of all things, came to Earth in the form of a human so folks could identify with him. Very cool.

- Jesus asking John to water baptize him undoubtedly displayed his approval of John's mission, producing credibility to John's ministering the coming of the Jewish Messiah.

- I believe the most important reason was that Jesus' baptism verified for future generations the perfect picture of the triune nature of God.

  After his baptism, as Jesus came up out of the water, the heavens were opened and he saw the Spirit of God descending like a dove and settling on him. And a voice from heaven said, "This is my dearly loved Son, who brings me great joy." Matthew 3:16-17

  This must have been, and still is, very impressive. It represents the work of the Father, Son, and Holy Spirit in the salvation of those who believe.

It is inconsequential to us why Jesus chose to be baptized, so let's not be unnecessarily concerned.

Water baptism began as a Jewish ritual

Water baptism was originally a symbolic purification in early Jewish tradition (before Christ). When a Gentile converted to Judaism, they were water baptized and circumcised, according to Jewish tradition.

God told Abraham (the father of Judaism, Christianity, and Islam) to circumcise himself, his household and his slaves as an everlasting covenant in their flesh.

  Then God said to Abraham, "Your responsibility is to obey the terms of the covenant. You and all your descendants have this continual responsibility. This is the covenant that you and your descendants must keep: Each male among you must be circumcised. You must cut off the flesh of your foreskin as a sign of the covenant between me and you. From generation to generation, every male child must be circumcised on the eighth day after his birth. This applies not only to members of your family but also to the servants born in your household and the foreign-born servants whom you have purchased. All must be circumcised. Your bodies will bear the mark of my everlasting covenant. Any male who fails to be circumcised will be cut off from the covenant family for breaking the covenant." Genesis 17:9-14

Water was used to symbolize cleansing and consecration — very much a Jewish concept. Because of this, when John the Baptist came on the scene, the Jews of his day saw nothing pagan or wrong in his demand that people be symbolically cleansed of their sins in the Jordan River.

John's message was adhering to what historic prophets had declared. He preached God's future judgment, warning that Israel must be spiritually renewed because the coming of the Messiah was at hand.

Holy Spirit baptism

Holy Spirit baptism is an entirely different ballgame.

> *Then Peter said to them, "**Repent** and let every one of you be baptized in the name of Jesus Christ for the remission of sins; and you shall receive the **gift of the Holy Spirit**."* Acts 2:38 (NKJV – Emphasis added by me.)

The term *repent* in the verse above means to change one's mind from believing he or she can merit Heaven by following laws to accepting Jesus as his or her only means of salvation. Notice it also states that the Holy Spirit is a gift.

> *Some of us are Jews, some are Gentiles, some are slaves, and some are free. But we have all been baptized into one body by one Spirit, and we all share the same Spirit.* 1 Corinthians 12:13

The result of Holy Spirit baptism is that the believer becomes a part of Jesus Christ's body, and simultaneously the Holy Spirit indwells the new believer, making that person a Christian. One does not become a Christian by being dunked in water. In Acts 10:47, Peter asked:

> *"Can anyone object to their being baptized, now that they have received the Holy Spirit just as we did?"*

In this passage, the people were clearly saved and received the Holy Spirit before being water baptized.

It is also very important to appreciate that the Great Apostle Paul recognized this, when he made this statement:

> *For Christ didn't send me to baptize, but to preach the Good News—and not with clever speech, for fear that the cross of Christ would lose its power.* 1 Corinthians 1:17

Though Paul did baptize some, it is clear from his statement that he did not consider water baptism necessary for salvation.

Infant baptism

Infant baptism is a ceremony never practiced in the New Testament early church, so it is very conflicting to fundamental Christian doctrine. Salvation is by one method only: *mature* belief in the life, death, and resurrection of the Lord Jesus Christ. Infants do not have the capacity for that *mature* faith. Infant baptism is a fuzzy, sweet ceremony, but it does not save a soul.

Constantine wasn't real bright

I hope you will get a kick out of the following story:

In approximately 313 AD, the Roman Emperor Constantine had a vision of a fiery red cross. On the cross was written, "By this thou shalt conquer." Constantine's interpretation was that he should give up paganism and become a Christian. He called a council and the first hierarchy of the early Christian Church was formed. This hierarchy was the beginning of the Roman Catholic Church.

Because water baptism had been a historic ceremony, Constantine, not having been water baptized yet, was in a dilemma because he was under the false impression it was water baptism, not Holy Spirit baptism that saved. He thought, "If I am saved from my sins by water baptism, what is to become of my sins that I may commit after I am baptized?" He decided to postpone water baptism until immediately before his death.

Chapter 33

You Need Not Go to Church to be Saved

Attending church will not save anyone from eternal Hell, unless the church is successful in leading someone to justification by faith in Jesus.

A church serves several purposes. It is a place to:

- worship God
- learn about the indwelling of the Holy Spirit
- be taught the Word of God by fellow believers
- fellowship with other believers
- welcome non-believers who will become justified by faith in Jesus
- demonstrate the love of God to the community
- obtain spiritual food

There are several reasons Christians and non-Christians are reluctant to attend a church. They:

- are lazy
- are mad at God
- are agnostics (I don't believe in atheists)
- think churches spend too much time begging for money
- don't like organized religion
- feel guilty for past, present, and future sins
- think churches are full of hypocrites
- have more attractive alternatives (i.e., sleeping, beach, TV, etc.)

No church is perfect. I found one once, but as soon as they accepted me as a member it was no longer perfect. In the process of trying to find the right church for me, I did a little church hopping, which is why I appreciate the following fictitious account:

> Once upon a time, there was a fellow who was lost at sea but who found refuge on a deserted island. Twenty-five years later, he was rescued. The rescuers

noticed three buildings side by side. They asked him why he had built three buildings, to which he replied, "The one in the middle is where I live, the one on the left is my church, and the one on the right is the church I used to attend."

Ha! Ha!

Nobody can say with authority whether changing churches is right or wrong. It depends on circumstances.

The Bible encourages us to have fellowship with one another

All the believers devoted themselves to the apostles' teaching, and to fellowship, and to sharing in meals (including the Lord's Supper), and to prayer.
Acts 2:42

And let us not neglect our meeting together, as some people do, but encourage one another, especially now that the day of his return is drawing near.
Hebrews 10:25

These passages encourage Christians to congregate, but church attendance is not mandatory for eternal life in the eternal dwelling place of saints (in Heaven, and then on the New Earth). Many good people attend church regularly hoping this will contribute to their salvation. Church attendance reaps rewards, but it won't save.

No perfect churches

There are no perfect churches because they all consist of flawed folks like me. Fortunately, there are churches that teach more biblical truth than others. Christians must be careful choosing the church to which they become affiliated, because not all churches teach the truth, the whole truth, and nothing but the truth. For the purpose of increasing attendance, there is a trend to teach what people want to hear, rather than truth.

Another problem is many pastors fail to interpret the Scriptures correctly. They may be outstanding orators, charismatic leaders, and good businessmen, but if they have not been trained in a reliable Bible school, they may be teaching faulty doctrine.

Be careful of cults, religions, and denominations that sound appealing but whose authenticity fails when put to the Bible test. The leaders sell the sizzle rather than the steak, which brings in the masses, but errors in Christian truth. Be very careful.

Finding a church in which you are comfortable is important, but there are critical criteria the church should meet.

Essential Church doctrine

The most important concern when choosing a church is to be certain their doctrine is Biblical.

> **"Not knowing the doctrines of the Bible, the child of God will be, even when sincere, 'tossed to and fro, and carried about with every wind of doctrine, by the slight of men, and cunning craftiness, whereby they lie in wait to deceive'; the many well-meaning believers who are drawn into modern cults and heresies being sufficient proof. On the other hand, the divine purpose is that the servant of Christ shall be fully equipped to 'preach the word; be instant in season, out of season; reprove, rebuke, exhort with all longsuffering and doctrine.'"**
> **Lewis Sperry Chafer (1871-1952)**

The original church

The original (New Testament) church had a central governing body of apostles and elders in Jerusalem. This body was possibly modeled after the 70-member Jewish Sanhedrin, whose primary task was the preservation of doctrine and practice. Apostles, chosen by God and recognized by a body of believers, established the early churches. Paul and other apostles ordained presbyters (elders) to preside over the church in each city or region.

Do not use the following as criteria for choosing your church

- ➢ Where your parents went (your family could have been wrong)
- ➢ Close to where you live
- ➢ You like their music
- ➢ They have nice potlucks
- ➢ To obtain business contacts
- ➢ You can dress casually
- ➢ You can show off your fancy clothes
- ➢ They do not talk about sin
- ➢ They do not talk about Hell

The primary purpose of any church should be to teach attendees how to get to Heaven. Unfortunately, many folks have been taught that works must be added to grace, so be patient and gentle. Deprogramming may be futile, but for the sake of the individual it should be attempted, but with love.

> *Let your conversation be gracious and attractive so that you will have the right response for everyone.* Colossians 4:6

Another purpose of a church should be to teach the attendee how to obtain God's rewards by being a disciple of Christ. Discipleship takes a lifetime of learning and doing.

Ask!

You must ask your pastor, or the church secretary, for a copy of the doctrine. Do not be embarrassed or timid about this because that is their job, and if you drop anything in the offering, you are paying their wages. You are entitled and expected to know your church's doctrine. It is also in their best interest for you to know in the beginning what they believe and teach, so someday you do not realize you made the wrong choice and leave. No church wants revolving-door members.

Chapter 34

Fall out of Fellowship with Jesus?

"**F**all out of fellowship with Jesus" is a statement that makes my blood boil because it is used by Christians attempting to control other Christians by using guilt. Guilt is a tool of Satan.

To ascertain if a believer can fall out of fellowship with Jesus, we must first define the word *fellowship*. *Fellowship* is easy to define when used to describe our personal relationships with one another. We think of fellowships as people sharing similar interests, ideals, or experiences in a congenial atmosphere and on equal terms.

The magnitude of our fellowship with Jesus is beyond our comprehension because of our limited capacity to understand the magnificent nature of God. God, in a man named Jesus, subjected himself to horrific pain, suffering, and death for all mankind. He did this knowing everything we would do throughout our lives, to express his *agape* love. The Greek word *agape*, when describing Jesus' love for mankind, is unlike our English word *love*, which is used to refer to romantic feelings, friendship, or brotherly affection. **Agape love is unique because it describes the fact that Jesus does not just love — Jesus *is* love.**

Jesus' love was displayed on the Cross, where he died for unworthy people — we are all unworthy. *His love is not a love that has stipulations based upon our earthly performance.* He does not love us a bunch one moment, then just a little the next. Jesus' love for Christians is unconditional and eternal.

For years after I was saved, I heard Christians warn one another they had better walk the straight and narrow or they would fall out of fellowship with Jesus. That sounded humanly logical, so I never doubted or questioned it. *Miserably, as a new Christian, I wondered daily, sometimes hourly, if I was still in fellowship with Jesus because of my imperfections. I had less peace than before I was saved because before I was saved I knew I was out of fellowship with him. As a new Christian, I didn't want to do anything to mess up my redemption.* I worried constantly (worry is a tool of Satan).

In an attempt to find peace, I vigorously studied the Scriptures regarding the topic of fellowship with Jesus. Here is just one of my discoveries.

> *When we were utterly helpless, Christ came at just the right time and died for us sinners. Now, most people would not be willing to die for an upright person, though someone might perhaps be willing to die for a person who is especially good. But God showed his great love for us by sending Christ to die for us while we were still sinners. And since we have been made right in God's sight by the blood of Christ, he will certainly save us from God's condemnation.* **For since our friendship with God was restored by the death of his Son** *while we were still his enemies, we will certainly be saved through the life of his Son.* **So now we can rejoice in our wonderful new relationship with God because our Lord Jesus Christ has made us friends of God.**
> Romans 5:6-11

This passage opened my eyes and set me free — free, I tell you — free! Christ died so we could be in a continual fellowship with him. Our fellowship with Jesus is based completely on Jesus' work — not ours.

> *So now there is no condemnation for those who belong to Christ Jesus.*
> Romans 8:1

No condemnation, no condemnation, no condemnation, no condemnation!

Of course, our fellowship with Jesus should be a great reason to live moral lives as directed by the Holy Spirit. Right believing is the seed for right living.

> *But the Holy Spirit produces this kind of fruit in our lives: love, joy, peace, patience, kindness, goodness, faithfulness, gentleness, and self-control. There is no law against these things!*

> *Those who belong to Christ Jesus have nailed the passions and desires of their sinful nature to his cross and crucified them there. Since we are living by the Spirit, let us follow the Spirit's leading in every part of our lives.* Galatians 5:22-25

God no longer sees our sins

> *"I—yes, I alone—will blot out your sins for my own sake and will never think of them again."* Isaiah 43:25

"And I will forgive their wickedness,
*   and I will never again remember their sins."* Hebrews 8:12

Then he says,

"I will never again remember
*   their sins and lawless deeds."* Hebrews 10:17

Christians are made saints

Christians are both sinners and saints. All humans are sinners by birth because of the sin of Adam, but only Christians have the joyous distinction of being saints. In the New Testament, the Greek word *hagios* is translated into English as *saint*, which means *set apart by and for God as holy/sacred.*

> *To the church (assembly) of God which is in Corinth, to those consecrated and purified and made holy in Christ Jesus, [who are] selected and called to be **saints (God's people)**, together with all those who in any place call upon and give honor to the name of our Lord Jesus Christ, both their Lord and ours:*
>
> *Grace (favor and spiritual blessing) be to you and [heart] peace from God our Father and the Lord Jesus Christ.* 1 Corinthians 1:2-3 (AMP)
>
> *To the **saints (the consecrated people of God)** and believing and faithful brethren in Christ who are at Colossae: Grace (spiritual favor and blessing) to you and [heart] peace from God our Father.* Colossians 1:2 (AMP)

I emphasized the phrases that use the term *saint* in the passages above.

Depending on the Bible translation, the term *believer(s)* is used approximately 150 times, *saints* 50 times, but *Christians* only three times. Believers, saints, and Christians are God's people, but the term *Christian* has become popularized so I use it to describe a believer.

The New Testament is devoted to instructing humans how to be saved, plus how to live after being saved — as saints. A saint is not someone who has done astonishing things, nor is it someone who has been titled a saint by a church or organization. *Saint* is a synonym for a Christian, a true believer whose sins have been washed by the Blood of Jesus Christ.

Sinners become saints by being *born again*. Jesus Christ (God) has freely offered the only process for regenerating a sinner into a saint. He or she is washed in the Blood of the Lamb.

> *God saved you by his grace when you believed. And you can't take credit for this; it is a gift from God. Salvation is not a reward for the good things we have done, so none of us can boast about it.* Ephesians 2:8-9

> But—"*When God our Savior revealed his kindness and love, he saved us, not because of the righteous things we had done, but because of his mercy. He washed away our sins, giving us a new birth and new life through the Holy Spirit. He generously poured out the Spirit upon us through Jesus Christ our Savior. Because of his grace he declared us righteous and gave us confidence that we will inherit eternal life.*" Titus 3:4-7

All believers are made holy by their faith in Jesus Christ.

> *I am writing to God's church in Corinth, to you who have been called by God to be his own holy people. He made you holy by means of Christ Jesus, just as he did for all people everywhere who call on the name of our Lord Jesus Christ, their Lord and ours.* 1 Corinthians 1:2

Christians are in constant fellowship with Jesus whether they like it or not

Mr. or Mrs. Legalist, I ask you: How could a Christian fall out of fellowship with Jesus if he or she is made a saint when born again?

The righteousness of a Christian is imputed. Imputed righteousness is not conditional or temporary. It is free, complete, all-inclusive, magnificent, and permanent. You think about that.

> *And we know that the Son of God has come, and he has given us understanding so that we can know the true God. And now we live in fellowship with the true God because we live in fellowship with his Son, Jesus Christ. He is the only true God, and he is eternal life.* 1 John 5:20

> *You say, "I am allowed to do anything"—but not everything is good for you. And even though "I am allowed to do anything," I must not become a slave to anything.* 1 Corinthians 6:12

<u>Conclusion</u>

Jesus loves us in spite of ourselves, so *there is no such thing as falling out of fellowship with him*. Jesus is not an instiller of guilt, but a purveyor of forgiveness. He is stable in his attitude and his mood is not affected by our transgressions. He may not agree with inconsistent behavior, but unlike our fellow humans, he is always a friend and confidant. THANK YOU, JESUS!

<u>**Notes:**</u>

Chapter 35

Beware of Christian Police

My purpose is not to attack those who mean well (OK, maybe a little), but to warn new Christians of the pitfalls of following mentors who are not qualified, and to caution that there are some spiteful Christians who will attempt to put fellow Christians into religious bondage by maliciously looking for other's faults while not recognizing their own.

> *"And why worry about a speck in your friend's eye when you have a log in your own?"* Matthew 7:3, Jesus' words

This witch hunt is a major problem in Christendom.

Christians put me in a deep dark hole

I accepted Jesus Christ as my Savior in 1980. Knowing very little about the Christian faith, I desperately wanted to become a worthy follower of Christ. I began to attend church, various Bible studies, Christian men's groups, and other activities that were labeled Christian. Aware there were denominational differences, *I was unaware there was so much judgment and bigotry*.

Much of what I learned was false teachings and manmade taboos disguised to appear as biblical truths. Some came from well-meaning people, but even more came from overbearing Christian policemen, whom I refer to as *modern-day Pharisees*.

My quest to be a good Christian, coupled with my lack of Bible knowledge, made me extremely vulnerable. I was criticized for almost everything, from the translation of my study Bible to the food I ate. I was even censured for wearing "worldly" aftershave. I assumed that because my critics were Christians, their opinions were biblically correct. Ha!

In my attempt to become pure, I began to modify my personality dramatically. Acutely aware of my entire behavior, I made every effort not to do anything to offend

God. *I was on a journey to perfection, but I did not realize my voyage would end up in a deep dark hole.*

Increasingly, because of the non-biblical criticisms by my brothers and sisters in Christ, I realized how imperfect and immoral I was. Not only did I acknowledge my flaws, I considered myself despicable — so despicable I thought it impossible for God to love me. Although not suicidal, I was anxious, depressed, and immobile. My Christian brethren had contributed to my fear by assuring me that many of my day-to-day behaviors were offensive to God. I had learned I was washed clean by the Blood of Jesus Christ, and I did not want to do anything to tarnish me again, so I crawled into the hole so graciously dug for me.

This once happy-go-lucky, life-loving 34-year-old man checked into the psychiatric ward of Riverside Hospital in Columbus, OH. I was relieved to be there, because I did not have to face my holier-than-thou Christian brethren. At the facility, I did not have to hear how badly I was doing, plus there were limited opportunities for me to get caught in worldly endeavors. I was safe from the world, although I felt guilty for looking appreciatively at a few of the cute female nurses.

Fortunately, I was not given any treatments because the docs could not find anything seriously wrong. Sitting around most of the time so as to not do anything immoral, I did make some beautiful leather belts and key chains, which I worked on daily in the therapy room. It was kind of fun, although I had developed the stigma of being both a disappointment to God, and mentally ill. So embarrassed, I could not admit to being in a psychiatric ward for many years. I had always prided myself for being strong minded, but was humbled.

There is a happy ending to this story, thanks to the Holy Spirit. Following two weeks of hiatus, God spoke to me through the Holy Spirit. *He told me he alone is my counselor and judge.* The greatest thing he affirmed was he loved me just the way I was created. I departed the hospital that day with a new attitude about myself and God — and skepticism regarding demanding Christians.

> *Dear brothers and sisters, when troubles come your way, consider it an opportunity for great joy. For you know that when your faith is tested, your endurance has a chance to grow. So let it grow, for when your endurance is fully developed, you will be perfect and complete, needing nothing.*
>
> *If you need wisdom, ask our generous God, and he will give it to you. He will not rebuke you for asking. But when you ask him, be sure that your faith is in*

God alone. Do not waver, for a person with divided loyalty is as unsettled as a wave of the sea that is blown and tossed by the wind. James 1:2-6

God allowed me to see the dark side of religion, which is created by men and women. He enlightened me through the Holy Spirit to the fact that he did not come to Earth in the form of a man to die on the Cross so others could condemn me.

> *So now there is no condemnation for those who belong to Christ Jesus.* **Romans 8:1**

Those two weeks were truly a gift. They allowed me to comprehend the purpose of Christ's life, death, and resurrection. It is impossible to live a life bound by laws.

<u>**I am free! I am free! I am free!**</u>

> *For no one can ever be made right with God by doing what the law commands. The law simply shows us how sinful we are.*
>
> *But now God has shown us a way to be made right with him **without keeping the requirements of the law,** as was promised in the writings of Moses and the prophets long ago. **We are made right with God by placing our faith in Jesus Christ.** And this is true for everyone who believes, no matter who we are.* Romans 3:20-22 (Emphasis added by me.)

The passage you just read is why I am a Christian — Halleluiah!

CAUTION! Modern-day Pharisees

Pharisees were a prominent, devout sect of Jews reputed to be experts in Jewish law and tradition. They were the policemen of the Jewish faith.

The Christian police are those I refer to as *modern-day Pharisees.* They roam around Christendom stalking those who do not adhere to what they consider legal. They load their guns with their favorite Bible passages and fire at those who do not believe or behave as they do — bang, bang, bang! They love to shoot their wounded. They appear to walk the walk and talk the talk — and they insist that other Christians walk their same walk and talk their same talk. Tragically, to the novice Christian, they seem to make sense.

Many may mean well, but others are just plain mean. Undoubtedly, they have scared millions of would-be Christians from the loving Jesus by their overbearing demeanor. These legalistic promoters are quick to share every **shall not** and **must do** they can fabricate. They convolute the *Good News* into bad news by attempting to add man-made Christian laws to the old Jewish laws, creating a very unforgiving environment.

Christians should not be purveyors of guilt

> *For the Kingdom of God is not a matter of what we eat or drink, but of living a life of goodness and peace and joy in the Holy Spirit. If you serve Christ with this attitude, you will please God, and others will approve of you, too. So then, let us aim for harmony in the church and try to build each other up.* Romans 14:17-19

I am not suggesting you stop listening to the teachings of other Christians, but that you use discernment. Seek a Bible-believing church that does not have a guilt-provoking pastor. Study the New Testament Bible with the assistance of the Holy Spirit. Read the New Testament before delving into the Old Testament, and only as you mature as a Christian should you begin to study the Old Testament.

When you begin to read the New Testament, first read the Book of Galatians, which is the Magna Charta of Christianity.

Many of the TV and radio pastors are knowledgeable, thus were helpful in my learning. Discernment must be exercised when viewing TV preachers.

WARNING: Do not allow legalists to place you in a *Procrustean bed*.

A Procrustean bed

In Greek mythology, Procrustes (*the stretcher*) was a bandit from Attica. He had his stronghold in the hills outside Eleusis, where he had an iron bed into which he invited every passerby to rest. If the guest proved too tall, he would amputate the excess length; if the victim was too short, he was stretched on the rack until he fit.

Nobody ever fit in the bed because it was secretly adjustable, and Procrustes would stretch or shrink it upon sizing his victims from afar. Procrustes continued his reign of terror until he was captured by Theseus, who "fitted" Procrustes to his own bed and cut off his head and feet. Because Theseus was a stout fellow, the bed had been set on the short position. A *Procrustean bed* is an arbitrary standard to which exact conformity is forced.

Procrustes is a myth because his method was ludicrous. Unfortunately, those who utilize his methods are not astute enough to realize it divides the body of Christ. It also is in direct opposition to Christ's synergistic method — referred to in the Scriptures as *love* — which unites Christ's body.

A great percentage of self-righteous Christians foolishly attempt to use their flawed nature as the supreme model for all. Unfortunately, many of those who subscribe to the Procrustean method believe they are living the perfect Christian life. Their judgment of whether you fit into their family of Christians is determined by your fitting into their mold, which has been cast from their own nature. Those who are more lenient will allow some wiggle room, but unless you fit perfectly, you are not of their caliber.

Mahatma Gandhi

Mahatma Gandhi (1869-1948) is one of the most respected leaders of modern history. Although a Hindu, Gandhi admired Jesus and often quoted from the *Sermon on the Mount*. Once when the missionary E. Stanley Jones met with Gandhi he asked, "Mr. Gandhi, though you quote the words of Christ often, why is it that you appear to so adamantly reject becoming his follower?"

Gandhi replied, "Oh, I don't reject your Christ. I love your Christ. It's just that so many of you Christians are so unlike your Christ."

Apparently, Gandhi's rejection of Christianity grew out of an incident that happened when he was a young man practicing law in South Africa. He had become attracted to the Christian faith, had studied the Bible and the teachings of Jesus, and was seriously exploring becoming a Christian. He decided to attend a church service, but as he went up the steps of the large church to enter, a white South African elder barred his way at the door. "Where do you think you're going, *kaffir* (a disparaging term for a black person)?" the man asked Gandhi in a challenging manner.

Gandhi replied, "I'd like to attend worship here."

The church elder barked at him, "There's no room for *kaffirs* in this church. Leave here or I'll have my assistants throw you down the steps."

From that moment, Gandhi said he decided to adopt what good he found in Christianity, but would never again consider becoming a Christian if it meant being part of a church.

God permits non-conformity

<u>It is ridiculous to demand we Christians must all think and act alike.</u> Not only do we each have the Holy Scriptures to guide us, but we also are given the Holy Spirit as our personal and individual counselor.

> *"And I will ask the Father, and he will give you another Advocate, who will never leave you. <u>He is the Holy Spirit, who leads into all truth.</u> The world cannot receive him, because it isn't looking for him and doesn't recognize him. But you know him, because he lives with you now and later will be in you."* John 14:16-17, Jesus' words

> *But you have received the Holy Spirit, and he lives within you, <u>so you don't need anyone to teach you what is true.</u> For the Spirit teaches you everything you need to know, and what he teaches is true—it is not a lie. So just as he has taught you, remain in fellowship with Christ.* 1 John 2:27

> *"But when the Father sends the Advocate as my representative—that is, the Holy Spirit—<u>he will teach you everything and will remind you of everything I have told you.</u>*

> *I am leaving you with a gift—peace of mind and heart. And the peace I give is a gift the world cannot give. So don't be troubled or afraid."* John 14:26-27, Jesus' words

The underlined sections of the above passages are to emphasize it is the Holy Spirit who teaches us truth, thus leading us to peace. Although we can learn from others, please listen intently to the Spirit, who is gentle and peaceful.

> *But the Holy Spirit produces this kind of fruit in our lives: love, joy, peace, patience, kindness, goodness, faithfulness, gentleness, and self-control. There is no law against these things!* Galatians 5:22-23

Our personalities, just as our physical characteristics, differ. As created by God, no two of us have identical abilities, capabilities, or responsibilities. Because of our uniqueness, ***the Holy Spirit works differently and personally in each Christian.***

Our differences make Christ's body of believers synergetic. God chose many individual personalities to further his Kingdom, from Adam to you, with many in between and many to follow. Jesus gave us the perfect example of a synergistic effect, evidenced by the growth of Christianity from a dozen mavericks to more than a billion people worldwide, including new mavericks like you and me.

No more bondage

The term *religion* comes from the Latin word *religare*, meaning "to tie or bind." I will never again allow religious people to put me in bondage. I found freedom, balance, and guidance in the Holy Spirit. You do the same.

In Romans 14, Paul emphasizes several matters where believers have disagreements. In this time of history, the disagreements were mostly concerning Jewish law versus the new freedom found in Christ. Today, we encounter the same types of disagreements over similar issues. However we could add things like drinking alcoholic beverages, watching TV, going to movies, playing loud music, tattoos, dress codes or the lack-thereof, etc.

Some of our modern-day endeavors can result in sinful behavior, but on the flip-side legalism can destroy the fellowship that Jesus desires within his family of believers. **Legalism can become a false idol.**

> *Accept other believers who are weak in faith, and don't argue with them about what they think is right or wrong. For instance, one person believes it's all right to eat anything. But another believer with a sensitive conscience will eat only vegetables. Those who feel free to eat anything must not look down on those who don't. And those who don't eat certain foods must not condemn those who do, for God has accepted them. Who are you to condemn someone else's servants? Their own master will judge whether they stand or fall. And with the Lord's help, they will stand and receive his approval.*
>
> *In the same way, some think one day is more holy than another day, while others think every day is alike. You should each be fully convinced that whichever day you choose is acceptable. Those who worship the Lord on a special day do it to honor him. Those who eat any kind of food do so to honor the Lord, since they give thanks to God before eating. And those who refuse to eat certain foods also want to please the Lord and give thanks to God. For we don't live for ourselves or die for ourselves. If we live, it's to honor the Lord. And if we die, it's to honor the Lord. So whether we live or die, we belong to the Lord. Christ died and rose again for this very purpose—to be Lord both of the living and of the dead.*

So why do you condemn another believer? Why do you look down on another believer? Remember, we will all stand before the judgment seat of God. For the Scriptures say,

> *"'As surely as I live,' says the Lord,*
> *'every knee will bend to me,*
> *and every tongue will confess and give praise to God.'"*

Yes, each of us will give a personal account to God. So let's stop condemning each other. Decide instead to live in such a way that you will not cause another believer to stumble and fall.

I know and am convinced on the authority of the Lord Jesus that no food, in and of itself, is wrong to eat. But if someone believes it is wrong, then for that person it is wrong. And if another believer is distressed by what you eat, you are not acting in love if you eat it. Don't let your eating ruin someone for whom Christ died. Then you will not be criticized for doing something you believe is good. For the Kingdom of God is not a matter of what we eat or drink, but of living a life of goodness and peace and joy in the Holy Spirit. If you serve Christ with this attitude, you will please God, and others will approve of you, too. So then, let us aim for harmony in the church and try to build each other up.

Don't tear apart the work of God over what you eat. Remember, all foods are acceptable, but it is wrong to eat something if it makes another person stumble. It is better not to eat meat or drink wine or do anything else if it might cause another believer to stumble. You may believe there's nothing wrong with what you are doing, but keep it between yourself and God. Blessed are those who don't feel guilty for doing something they have decided is right. But if you have doubts about whether or not you should eat something, you are sinning if you go ahead and do it. For you are not following your convictions. If you do anything you believe is not right, you are sinning. Romans 14:1-23

Great advice, Paul. Thanks!

Chapter 36

You make the Decision — not God

You make the decision as to where you will spend eternity. God made eternal life with him very simple by initiating the New Covenant, which is salvation by grace through faith. It is a gift given by Jesus Christ, but you must accept it.

> *God saved you by his grace when you believed. And you can't take credit for this; it is a gift from God. Salvation is not a reward for the good things we have done, so none of us can boast about it.* Ephesians 2:8-9

The New Covenant is God's agreement that replaces the Old Covenant. It is not only for the Jews, but also for all mankind. Those who accept the New Covenant are referred to as Christians.

When one accepts Jesus as Savior, righteousness is imputed. We know we are righteous because of our faith in Jesus finished work — not based on our works. Our days are filled with so many actions that are contrary to righteousness that we must trust in what Jesus did to make us righteous. We are made righteous in him and by him. This is called *imputed righteousness*.

Jesus' finished work not only includes Jesus' death, which resulted in forgiveness for all sin, but also his resurrection that gives Christians eternal life. Many people believe salvation is just the forgiveness of one's sins, but it is more. Salvation is being made alive in Christ as the result of one's Spiritual birth.

> *"For God loved the world so much that he gave his one and only Son, so that everyone who believes in him will not perish but have eternal life. God sent his Son into the world not to judge the world, but to save the world through him.*
>
> *There is no judgment against anyone who believes in him. But anyone who does not believe in him has already been judged for not believing in God's one and only Son."* John 3:16-18, Jesus' words

"I tell you the truth, those who listen to my message and believe in God who sent me have eternal life. They will never be condemned for their sins, but they have already passed from death into life." John 5:24, Jesus' words

We are made right with God by placing our faith in Jesus Christ. And this is true for everyone who believes, no matter who we are. Romans 3:22

All major world faiths except Christianity involve good behavior to receive God's favor for eternal life. Christianity is a way immoral people (we are all immoral) can spend eternity in Heaven with the Creator God, clothed in the righteousness of Jesus Christ. Christianity demands nothing more than faith. Good behavior is desirable, but not mandatory for salvation.

And if by grace, then is it no more of works: otherwise grace is no more grace. But if it be of works, then it is no more grace: otherwise work is no more work. Romans 11:6 (KJV)

God established the tenet, but the decision is yours. See you in glory that awaits us in the next life.

Chapter 37

Could Satan go to Heaven?

Throughout this book I have emphasized the biblical fact that we are saved by *super, abundant, radical, undeserved, amazing, grace.*

> *God saved you by his grace when you believed. And you can't take credit for this; it is a gift from God. Salvation is not a reward for the good things we have done, so none of us can boast about it.* Ephesians 2:8-9

I have been evangelizing salvation by faith for three decades successfully, but my mission has not lacked criticism and questions from those who have not completed an in-depth study of soteriology (the study of the Doctrine of Salvation).

One of the first statements made by students when I teach salvation by belief (faith) is: "Satan believes in Jesus, so will he go to Heaven?" Following are my replies.

1. Jesus died for humanity, not angels.

2. *"When the thousand years come to an end, Satan will be let out of his prison. He will go out to deceive the nations—called Gog and Magog—in every corner of the earth. He will gather them together for battle—a mighty army, as numberless as sand along the seashore. And I saw them as they went up on the broad plain of the earth and surrounded God's people and the beloved city. But fire from heaven came down on the attacking armies and consumed them.*

> *Then the devil, who had deceived them, was thrown into the fiery lake of burning sulfur, joining the beast and the false prophet. There they will be tormented day and night forever and ever."* Revelation 20:7-10

This makes it very clear that Satan, an angelic being, will not spend eternity on the New Earth (the New Jerusalem). He and his armies will be cast into the fiery lake of burning sulfur forever and ever.

Notes:

INDEX

Notes:

SELECTED SCRIPTURE INDEX